Visionary Voices

WOMEN ON POWER

Conversations with shamans, activists, teachers, artists and healers

Interviews by
Penny Rosenwasser

aunt lute books
SAN FRANCISCO

First Edition

10-9-8-7-6-5-4-3-2-1

Aunt Lute Books
P.O. Box 410687
San Francisco, CA 94141

Cover and Text Design: Pamela Wilson Design Studio

Cover Art: Wilson Design Studio

Typesetting: Debra DeBondt

Production: Joan Pinkvoss   Kathleen Wilkinson
            Jayna Brown   Michelle Davis
            Jennifer Tseng   Eileen Anderson

Photocredits: Front cover—top to bottom: Rachel Bagby by Irene Young; Winona LaDuke by John Ratzloff; Hi-ah Park by Darryl Clegg; Naomi Newman by Valerie Haimowitz.
Back cover—top to bottom: Suha Hindiyeh by Susan Dorfman; Lakota Harden by Happy Hyder; Barbara Smith by Judith McDaniel; Ying Lee-Kelley by Happy Hyder.

"Eagle Poem" reprinted from *In Mad Love and War* © 1990 by Joy Harjo. Wesleyan University Press, by permission of University Press of New England

Interviews with Suha Hindiyeh and Veronika Cohen reprinted with permission from: Curbstone Press
            321 Jackson Street
            Willimatic, CT 06226

Printed in U.S.A on acid-free paper

Library of Congress Cataloging-in-Publication Data

Visionary Voices : Women on Power : conversations with shamans,
    activists, teachers, artists and healers / edited by Penny
    Rosenwasser. — 1st ed.
        p.   cm.
    ISBN 1-879960-22-2 (lib.bdg. : acid-free paper) : $19.95. — ISBN
1-879960-20-6 (pbk. : acid-free paper) : $9.95
    1. Feminists—United States—Interviews.   2. Women political
activists—United States—Interviews.   3. Minority women—United States
—Interviews.   4. Power (Social sciences) I. Rosenwasser, Penny, 1949-
HQ1426.V57   1992
305.4' 092'2—dc20   92-5113
                                                                    CIP

for my mom and dad, Dutch & Artie,
who taught me
the power of
unconditional love

ACKNOWLEDGEMENTS

If there is power in these pages, I have simply been the conduit. Many voices, hands and hearts helped bring me to this work and this work to fruition. A lively and loving circle of women (plus my Dad) enthusiastically lent their support, enabling me to complete this project. I thank them for believing in me:

Linda Allen, Ana Amour, Lucia August, Lisa Beamer, Gail Benvenuta, Rokie Bernstein, Chela Blitt, Leslie Bonett, Barbara Borden, Gail Bourque, Kristin Buckner, Barbara Burdick, Louise Dobbs, Penelope Douglas, Susan Floethe, Lynn Halpern, Diana Hamid, Barbara Hazard, Mooh Hood, Valerie Kay, Ariah Keller, Colleen Kelley, Janet Kranzberg, Rosemary LePage, Catherine McCann, Janet McEwan, Naomi Newman, Fran Peavey, Nathalie Prettyman, Dutch & Artie Rosenwasser, Susan Runyan, Cornelia Schulz, Gayle Scott, Mae Stadler, Regina Sumner, Celia Thompson Taupin, Vivienne Verdon-Roe and Patricia Waters.

For contributing invaluable logistical assistance, I am greatly appreciative to Curbstone Press, Patrice Wynn, Joan Marler, Gail Benvenuta, Jean Caiani, Jeanne Park, Minn Chung, the wonderful librarians in the Berkeley Public Library Reference Room (main branch), Moli Steinert, Donna Canali, Krissy Keefer, Cindy Cleary, Melissa Austin, Kayla Kirsch, Christy Lubin, Khara Whitney-Marsh, Chaya Gusfield, John Morin and Paul Rauber. And without my computer teachers: Jun Capulong, Judi Clarke, Jorge Emmanuel, Robert Fabic and Howard Levine, this work feels unimaginable.

When my graduate school application was rejected, astrologer and wise woman Demetra George guided me towards my communication and networking skills: "Think big," she advised. Vivienne Verdon-Roe gave up her interview program on KPFA community radio in Berkeley, California, and KPFA Women's Department Director Asata Iman offered me the opportunity to begin my "Women of Power" interviews in that slot. Immeasurable thanks to all of them, and to my exquisitely gifted and supportive radio engineers: Gwen Jones, Noelle Hanrahan and Fiona Reed, as well as to the KPFA family and listeners.

A special thanks to all the photographers whose talents adorn these pages. For their writing and inspiration, I joyfully thank Marge Piercy, Joy Harjo, Ruth Gendler, May Sarton, Audre Lorde and Starhawk—along with my Muse and HP.

Making it through would be impossible without my rich family of friends, including Poco, Elizabeth Fides, Lisa Vogel, Laurie Mattioli, Barbara Higbie and many more: you know who you are. Thank you...

Joan Pinkvoss felt the breadth and power of this work as soon as I 'put it out there.' I thank her deeply for that validation and her ongoing enthusiasm. I also am grateful to the other women of Aunt Lute who brought so much joy and care to this project: Fabienne McPhail Grant, Lisa Hall, Melissa Levin and especially Jayna Brown and Jennifer Tseng who spent many hours polishing this manuscript. If the great gift of Robin Candace had not magically entered my life, to transcribe and painstakingly retype the vast majority of these interviews, this book would've taken several years to emerge.

Women's Alliance Solstice Camp changed my life, opening me to so much of what is in these pages. My gratitude goes to my soul sister Gayle Scott who insisted (in her Scorpio "8" way) that I come to camp, and who provided me that opportunity; she continues to teach me about women's spirituality. I deeply thank Women's Alliance Director Charlotte Kelly for her tremendous vision in organizing camp, and her tenacity in keeping it alive, as well as her consistent support for my work. To all the women who make camp what it is, and all the spirits and creatures who allow us the use of that sacred space each summer solstice season, thank you.

All the women interviewed in these pages have been my teachers; many have become dear friends as well. To each of them I give my love and respect, and my great appreciation for the gifts they share here. Other teachers also led me to this work: Lynne Gelzer taught me more than I can say; as well as the Sister Sparks of Sisterfire 1987; Wendy Palmer provided insights through aikido and intuition training; and Suann Hecht, Livvy Mellan, Sue Hopkins, Susan Bradford, Jeanne Mackey and Maria Barron have taught me invaluable lessons about healthy uses of power and love. I continue that work with Claudia Cranston whose guidance, skill and support have unalterably changed my life. Cris Williamson "put wings on my earth shoes" and along with Flor Fernandez, urged me towards the work inside of me, along with my work on the "outside." And Flor led me to my Dancing Bear, and has taught me in the deepest place about quiet power, and especially, the power of humility.

A special thanks to perhaps my main mentor on this project, Fran Peavey, who pushed me to follow my creativity, and to ask for help—who nurtured, advised, teased, fundraised and assisted me every step of the way—and most of all, when the strain was greatest, who kept me from feeling all alone.

My love and appreciation to you all.

Introduction

*Whirling across the floor in the aikido
'two-step,' I stumble, then glance around
to see if anyone has noticed. "There's nothing wrong with losing your balance," my
teacher grins. "The point is in learning
to recover."*

These conversations—with women healers and activists, shamans, artists and teachers—are about life-affirming uses of power. That power,
I'm increasingly convinced, flows from how well we maintain
balance—with the universe, with each other, within ourselves.

As we begin a new decade, and soon a new century, how can we
integrate our creative, spiritual and political paths to lead the world into
an era that values Mother earth, cooperation and peace with justice,
over warfare, material comfort and 'power over'? How do we teach
without domination, organize without intimidation, disagree without
degradation, relate without manipulation, and practice compassion
without losing our focus or strength? In other words, as women—how
do we learn and teach each other to do it differently?

The impetus behind these interviews sprang from the belief that as
women, our society's conditioning does not teach us self-esteem and
empowerment. Instead it dictates forms that contradict intuitive modes
of power and leadership—modes which are truer to our inner beings
and to fulfilling the healthy needs of each other and the planet. What
leadership models—and which uses of power—can best serve this
earth and ourselves, in all our diversity and potential? What hasn't
worked, and why? Who are our truly valued foremothers and heroines
and what have we learned from them? What are our priority struggles
of today and tomorrow, and how can these best be addressed, keeping
in mind the needs of the next seven generations?

How can we allow ourselves to really *feel* the alarming situation
around us, and yet not operate out of panicky crisis mentality that only

serves to perpetuate the problems? How do we serve others and stay true to ourselves? What have we learned about power and control, about confronting our racism, classism and anti-semitism, about being accountable and moving forward, not just ahead?

These are the questions. And here are the voices and the visions of women like Lakota and Colleen, Maudelle and Ying, Papusa, Vivienne, Suha and Naomi. Visionary voices describing healthy uses of power—guidelines possibly—for exploring more deeply how to live and develop, flourish and grow, and create positive change in balance with each other, with our planet, with ourselves. Guidelines requesting our willingness to not know, to be open to learning something new…

This book is about empowerment. It's not one view, one approach, one answer. "The answer is that I have no answers," Lakota Harden reminds us. "That you have your own answer." I present this material hoping that it becomes, as Naomi Newman suggests, "the question that guides you…because the answers are the end of something, and the questions are the beginning of a process."

Who are these women? They are "first generation lesbian" and former military wife; high school dropout and Doctor of Transformational Psychology; Orthodox Jew and practicing Buddhist; Academy-award winner, aikido black belt, mayoral candidate and draft counselor. These women are grandmothers and poets, lawyers and bodyworkers, actresses, publishers, comedians and dancers. They're the children of immigrants; their grandparents were slaves; their homes are on reservations. They've walked out of poverty in China; they've grown up in Cleveland and Cuba, Mexico and Philadelphia, Arkansas and Korea, Palestine and Oregon and Great Britain and Idaho. Ranging in age from their 30's into their 80's, they've changed laws, battled chronic illness, won recognition as human rights champions, recovered from addiction, endured family suicide and worked for their national liberation.

Some of their voices are motivated by anger. Many are moved by "an enormous unbearable love for the planet." Others are working to empower their people by reclaiming identity and rebuilding community. Again, in Lakota's words: "If we're comfortable in who we are, then we are not…threatened by somebody else."

My own story spans coming of age in the counter-culture days of the early '70s in Washington, D.C., when the second wave of the women's cultural and political movement in this country was rising, along with an explosive growth of decentralized community-controlled institutions. Living and working collectively, I saw huge windows of potential and promise opened up in my vision—an exuberant feeling that anything was possible. It was a blessed period of discovery and self-discovery.

I played my kazoo on the White House lawn at Nixon's tumultuous departure; paraded jubilantly down Pennyslvania Avenue for women's and lesbian rights; absorbed the intricacies of consensus decision-making; researched, wrote and produced community organizing manuals with my collective members; learned car repair, organic farming and newspaper layout—as well as how to produce an event, interview a therapist, and organize against a neighborhood rapist. I temporarily bonded with political dogmatism, and opened to a new level of intimacy in relationship. I revelled in community.

Life was full and challenging and often rewarding. But over the years, the burdens of addiction issues, trying to take too much care of too many people, 'saving the world', and operating a business with integrity and mutual respect, which would also support myself and others, took its toll. Eventually life swerved out of control and I stumbled into rooms of 12-step recovery programs, meditation retreats, and soon, women's spirituality.

Learning to accept change, let go of control, take responsibility for my choices—and above all, build self-esteem—were enormous tasks and lessons. The fog was starting to clear, in terms of how to proceed. But I knew the process of changing my life, of learning a new way to function and thrive was just beginning. Being rejected from graduate school in social work soon after my fortieth birthday was a humiliating blow; but it redirected me through another door. It gave me a new opportunity to delve more deeply into what I was learning, to pursue a quest that had been persistently beckoning. Within weeks, my series of monthly "Women of Power" radio interviews were born and I began actively seeking women's guidance on 'how to do it differently'.

Where did these women come from? Something in each of them called out and pulled me in. I sensed that they had something to teach me and something valuable to share—not just what they were doing, but how they were doing it.

And what were the scenarios for these conversations? We spoke in a canoe on summer solstice; after a major earthquake; at a kitchen table with children clambering onto our laps; live on the radio just after a war; in an elementary school; on occupied land—and one interview was completed long-distance on my answering machine.

Balance emerged as an unanticipated theme throughout these stories. Although empowerment is the goal, perhaps the process of finding and maintaining balance is the form. Framing it succinctly, Winona LaDuke says that "trying to change this society is very consuming...you have to always balance internal and external...My ability to face the big external challenges is totally affected by my ability to retain my own spiritual relationship to the earth...as well as my own integrity."

Flor Fernandez relates her grandmother's message: "She taught me ...that we are all in this world to learn from each other...that anytime we step outside that concept and become inflated, feeling we are better or more powerful than others, we break that balance and cause ourselves...and other people pain." Fran Peavey and Barbara Smith remind us that changing an attitude or opening a mind will not by itself create change—there must be an integrity of organizing as well. Suha Hindiyeh adds, "I don't believe in one hero, because you learn from the people more than you learn from one person...collective work brings success more than one person's work."

As these women describe the power of our community connection, they also emphasize allowing our power to unfold from the wellspring within each one of us; of staying open without giving our power away and of taking responsibility for making choices.

From Papusa Molina's perspective: "We run around trying to avoid conflict, being very fearful of saying 'I made a mistake'. We don't realize that sometimes honest acceptance of our mistakes...is where we gain power." And Maudelle Shirek remembers, "My father always said, 'Show me a person that hasn't made a mistake, and I'll show you someone that has never done a damn thing.'"

The sister of balance is integration, so aptly described by Naomi Newman: "I often think of pulling a multicolored thread, and as you pull the thread, it keeps changing colors. And I think that's what our life is like. It's all one thing, and the colors keep changing, so for one moment we'll be doing this and for the next moment we'll be doing that—but our central essence, our central truth, is moving through it." Along this theme, Rachel Bagby suggests we surrender to our intellect and our intuition in turn, allowing their teamwork to create magic. And Bernice Lee's 'no strings attached' self-acceptance is a continual source of inspiration, reminding us that without this inner foundation, our words and actions cannot ring true.

Expanding the focus, Deena Metzger and Winona LaDuke both describe how we are only one part of an eco-system so much larger than ourselves. That when we use more than our share of resources, and we poison so much of the land and water, it spins the entire system out of balance, greatly imperiling our future existence. Various voices express how the balance within ourselves and with each other is intimately connected to preserving our balance with the very life source that sustains us—and the absolute necessity of our finally learning to cooperate with the rhythms of this system, rather than trying to dominate it. As Deena articulates: "If women want to be empowered, we must be ruthless and rigorous in our affiliation with the life force."

These are also stories of victories. "Surviving as a Black woman has been a victory—with sanity intact," Barbara Smith relates. "If I don't have the faith that my work matters, and matters a great deal," Ying Lee-Kelley confides, "then I can't get up in the morning." Vivienne Verdon-Roe reveals, "When you're able to let...that very controlling edge...go, and allow things to manifest, so often things happen that you never dreamt of." And when people ask Israeli peace activist Veronika Cohen, "Are you optimistic or pessimistic?", she replies, "I'm neither, I'm working. Because if I meet somebody or something that I don't like, I think maybe I can change it."

And lest we forget—these are *women's* stories. Hi-ah Park views the twenty-first century as a time for women to awaken and "accept who we are, as we are...We have to touch that inner energy life force that is the real empowerment." Another side of that? If we aren't "vigilant about our rights and about justice for women...we'll lose everything," insists Barbara Lubin. Rachel Bagby has found "the company of other women who are in their power...the absolute acceptance and love of other women...is incredibly nourishing." Spelling out her vision of women's personal process in reclaiming our power, Vicki Noble explains: "It's not adversarial—it's *I am*. It's very creative, and so it's like fire. It's not... a fight, it's not war, it's not polarization. It's not irreconcilable conflict...It's just, 'this is how it is, because I'm experiencing it from inside my own reality'...and that carries weight." Lifting it to the next level, Colleen Kelley tells us: "I have such a sense of women being able to somehow turn the tide, step in, pick up their vision, have the faith to do it and do it....it's really time for that to happen."

So this book is about taking action—and taking no action at all. About allowing time to hear the inner voice and finding your own way. As Flor Fernandez suggests, about "going deep into yourself to find your own powers, so then you can help others"—and about doing whatever we do, whether cleaning a house or teaching a class, "with a sense of connection." With love and courage, joy and commitment. With an open heart. About feeling the resonance, humming the tune, following where it leads—singing the song together in imperfect but full-bodied harmonies. About dissonance, and not only allowing for but embracing that dissonance. Knowing that it makes for a richer deeper song, with far-reaching appeal. About a process more than an outcome. And as Atomic Comic Fran Peavey insists, about "car[ing] for life at every turn" and having fun doing it…

"The…challenge," posits Deena Metzger, "is to render this. To be available to bring the beauty…or…awareness through….To feel compassion on a regular basis. To strip myself down to wherever I have to go. To suffer whatever it is that I have to suffer, in order to know what I have to know. Not to be afraid of that, even though it hurts a lot. Or to be afraid and not let being afraid stop me…To find friends who support…[me] and understand what…[I'm] doing…And to hold onto love as a great passion. If you keep your eye on what you love, it's like a mantra; if you keep your eye on what's precious, the fear goes away."

These women's voices let me know deep inside that integrity prevails. Our tender, resilient and empassioned love blended with right action—a willingness to listen to each other, to share the power and control—can melt the fear, the ignorance, the greed. It will take time, courage and connection to spirit. For though we can't control the outcome, between us we have endless energy to do the footwork for creating change—in balance, from our own power. From our own visions.

Visionary Voices

Eagle Poem

To pray you open your whole self
To sky, to earth, to sun, to moon
To one whole voice that is you.
And know there is more
That you can't see, can't hear,
Can't know except in moments
Steadily growing, and in languages
That aren't always sound but other
Circles of motion.
Like eagle that Sunday morning
Over Salt River. Circled in Blue sky
In wind, swept our hearts clean
With sacred wings.
We see you, see ourselves and know
That we must take the utmost care
And kindness in all things.
Breathe in, knowing we are made of
All this, and breathe, knowing
We are truly blessed because we
Were born, and die soon within a
True circle of motion,
Like eagle rounding out the morning
Inside us.
We pray that it will be done
In beauty.
In beauty.

—Joy Harjo

TABLE OF CONTENTS

Visionary Voices

Photos by Marilyn Humphries

Papusa Molina

JULY 1990

"We run around trying to avoid conflict, being very fearful of saying, 'I made a mistake…' [We] don't realize that sometimes honest acceptance of our mistakes…is where we gain power."

A fiery energy, mixed with a fine blend of love, surrounds this Mexicana organizer. Even when relaxing late at night after a full day's work, Papusa Molina conveys a sense of being constantly in motion. Whether mediating a dispute, teaching a workshop or leading a conference, she perceives and communicates nuance. To be around Papusa is not only to be seen, heard, acknowledged—it is to feel actively engaged in living.

PENNY: *Papusa, I know that you're a founding member of Women Against Racism in Iowa City. You're also the director of the Women's Center at the University of Iowa as well as an organizer, a teacher and a poet. I know you primarily from your workshop: Naming and Celebrating Our Differences. How did you come to this work?*

PAPUSA: It was first from an intellectual understanding, but definitely from personal experience. I always tell the story how I grew up in a very intellectual, liberal family in Mexico. My father gave me Karl Marx books to read—existentialism, Simone de Beauvoir, and those kinds of things. But I think his expectations were always that I would understand things from a liberal-intellectual point of view; he never expected me to be an activist, to really practice what I was reading. He thought intelligent, educated people needed to know these things.

I grew up in this upper-middle class family, with all the privileges that middle class white people have in this country. When I came to this country to go to school in 1981, I suddenly became a 'woman of color.' Everything that I knew at the intellectual level hit me in the gut. Suddenly I was a second-class citizen. The ability to speak several languages, English among them, was not an asset anymore—because I have a strong accent, because my grammar was not one hundred percent correct.

It was an eye-opener for me. Oppression stopped being an intellectual exercise and started being very real. It was the way I was living my life everyday.

PENNY: *What really made me want to speak with you was how I've seen you work in conflict situations, in stressful situations. You have the ability to be calm, to be clear, to be very loving, to go to the heart of what's going on without attacking. You move with integrity, and you're very much in the moment. It's an amazing and positive use of power, and I'm wondering how you learned how to do that?*

PAPUSA: I think I learned it almost through the opposite extreme. I'm a person who's very emotional. I'm a person who, when something hits me, I scream and yell and cry and shout and tell you horrible things.

But through nine years of work with Women Against Racism, and this collective process in Iowa City, I realized that it was important for me to let out my emotions, but also that it was very important to see the other person as participating in the same dynamic that I was participating in—to see the other person, not just as an oppressor, or not just as the person who was attacking me, but also as participating in a system that makes a victim of that person.

And realizing that ninety percent of our communication is not really with each other, but is with what we represent to each other, with the representations of who we really are. The understanding of that has helped me deal in difficult situations with calmness and clarity about what the issues are.

I think that when you provide a space where people can express their emotions, their feelings, their ideas—and you provide that space respecting those differences, and trying to raise the question that will take you to the central issue—things can get resolved. And if not resolved to everybody's satisfaction, at least you can get to a space where you can establish a real dialogue.

And that's what I have proposed, not just for myself in my personal life, but also that's the work that I'm committed to do—to facilitate these types of interactions among people. To really get to that understanding of difference that comes out of a commitment—where people from different genders and races and classes and sexualities and religious and cultural backgrounds and ages and abilities can come together and create this space that is safe, not because of preconceived ideas of safety, but because it's respected; it is safe because differences are accepted.

That's what I've come to, but I came through a lot of pain to that space, because I was the type of person who reacted very emotionally, and I still do, sometimes...

PENNY: *Well that's what I wanted to ask you. That seems like quite a leap. I would like to know a little more about what that process was like, of all of a sudden realizing you were a woman of color and getting to work through the pain to a larger consciousness.*

PAPUSA: I cannot say that it was one thing that happened, I think it was a set of circumstances. One is definitely my work with Women Against Racism. The work I do doesn't come from Papusa being in a corner meditating, getting enlightened. I feel that is important, but I need to make it clear *that* doesn't come out of *that*. I feel liberation work comes out of a collectivity, comes out of a community. So that's the first thing for me; that I learn to see each other by struggling with other women, by confronting other women, by other women confronting me in a loving, caring way. And Women Against Racism gave me that.

The other part comes out of a political commitment to change at the individual level and at the institutional level. I believe that we need to change the institutions that we participate in, and we need to change ourselves. In that constant transformation of the self, the other and the institution, we start creating those spaces where differences become an asset instead of a hindrance.

PENNY: *Is there any time that this process hasn't worked?*

PAPUSA: Oh yes. And I think that sometimes the process doesn't work because people's levels of commitment are different. Sometimes it's ignorance—people really don't know what else to do and don't want to know. Sometimes it comes from a lot of fear and pain. It's not that people are awful, it's just that maybe they are not there yet.

I have had a couple of experiences at the national level with different groups where we were trying to work together—white women and women of color, lesbians and straights, Jews and Gentiles, working class and middle class women—and we couldn't. We couldn't create that space. When I go back and look at those experiences, I realize that there was a lot of fear, an inability to understand power and an inability to let go.

And when I talk about power, I'm talking about that power that is structural power—the inability to understand that the position that you play in the structure creates a power relationship among the individuals within that structure or organization. And if you are not willing to acknowledge that structural power, and you want to deal with everybody outside this context, things do not work.

For example, if you pay me, if you are 'the Boss,' we're never going to be equals unless you are capable of recognizing that you have some power over me. Because in the moment that I argue with you, I am afraid that you have the power to stop my paycheck. Unless you acknowledge that you have the power to stop my paycheck, I will never feel comfortable to argue with you or to disagree with you or to raise a question with you.

That's the context I'm talking about. I think that sometimes as women, as feminists, as activists, we forget that institutions are real and they exist, and the structures within institutions and organizations create certain power relationships that we need to acknowledge. In a situation where we are working or organizing together, and the worker, the colleague, the ally, does not have a space where this person can respond at the same level, everything is very difficult from the beginning.

PENNY: *But then how do you deal with a situation where someone controls your paycheck?*

PAPUSA: It all depends whether or not that person wants to be your ally. Because not everybody's committed to working in an alliance. If you work with a person who controls your paycheck and this person is not interested in being your ally, there's nothing you can do about it. Stop trying to be an ally to this person, because you will never change the power relationship. This person needs to be committed to being your ally, and this person needs to be committed to acknowledging the power that s/he has over you.

PENNY: *I know that you do this work not only with feminists and lesbians, but you also work in corporations and in universities. How do they respond to this kind of work?*

PAPUSA: It's very interesting. I have had very few experiences with corporations, but I have had a large experience with colleges and universities, given my context at the University of Iowa.

What I have discovered is that especially some white men, who have a certain level of consciousness, are really afraid. They feel very guilty and paralyzed, like there's nothing that they can do. And they want to let go of the power that they have.

I remember once I was giving a workshop in the Napa Valley in California with a group of professors and administrators from Berkeley. I made a kind of parentheses in my talk, and I said I want to talk for a moment to *you*, to the white middle class professional Christian men—and I want to talk to you about the power that you have. They couldn't believe that I was asking them to take their power seriously. The majority were very liberal, well-intended men, and they were terrified of people always accusing them of all the power they had. And I said, 'You cannot let go of that power, you need to use the power that you have to transform the institution.'

And I think that that is very seldom acknowledged, because as middle class women, as white women, as straight women, as Christian women, as able-bodied women—as women who have a certain amount of power—many times we feel so guilty that we want to let go of that power. We don't want to take control of the power that we have, and we want to almost divest of that power. That's why we cannot do anything effective.

I think that part of the privilege is accepting and recognizing the power that you have because of your privileges and using that power precisely to transform the institution that provides power and privilege to you. In other words, white women are the ones who need to do most of the anti-racism work. Women of color need to be involved, and we need to do our own work, but unless white women take control and decide seriously to do anti-racism work, racism in the women's movement and in the feminist movement will continue.

Unless straight women decide to do anti-homophobia (anti-heterosexism) work, homophobia will be rampant in the women's community. In other words, unless the people who have the privilege decide to fight the system that provides them with privilege, the system will stay in place. Because these people, willingly or not, are supporting the system that provides them with privilege. So every day, every moment, every instant that they don't challenge that system, nothing will change.

But from my experience, the trick in doing that in a multiracial context is in learning how to share the power—give up some of my power and control—with the people of color with me. There's part of me that wants to either give it up or take it all.

Because we see the situation as an either/or situation. You don't need to give up anything; you need to share it. And that's a different concept. You need to let go of a totalitarian type of power and be willing to share that power within the structure with women of color. What I'm saying is white women need to step back. Precisely because you have the power, you have the power to place yourself outside of the power position. It seems complicated, but that's really how it works.

In other words, the women of color shouldn't have to fight you for a position of power within the organization. Let's assume that you and I work together in an organization. You, Penny, should say, 'I will take the power to remove myself from this position so you Papusa can have it,' and not wait until Papusa fights with you, organizes a rally, calls you racist every day, for you to get out of the way.

The power needs to be used to subvert, to really reshape the organizations in which we work. And those who have the power within the organizations have to take the first step, have to move and start changing those organizations. At least, that's what I believe. I always like to say that what I say is not truth and is not the only way; it's just the way I have learned through my experience.

That's important because many people then start quoting you as the absolute thing, and I don't think that that works. I talk about my experience, my perspective, which is also a privileged perspective because I didn't grow up here. I didn't grow up as an oppressed person; I grew up as an oppressor. I became an oppressed person at the age of thirty and I think that that provides me with an insider/outsider point of view. And that's a position of privilege. Maybe I'm capable of saying the things I say because I've been on both sides of the fence.

PENNY: *What you're saying right now leads into what a colleague of yours told me about you—that one of your great marks of leadership is your ability to take responsibility for your mistakes. In North American culture, that's a rare trait. How did you come by that?*

PAPUSA: It's nothing sophisticated. I learned since I was a kid that the most important thing in life was to be honest and to be responsible. When I translated that into political terms, I need to be responsible for the situations I contribute to creating. Sometimes I put my foot in my mouth and I have to chew a lot of food [sic] and admit that I did it. Because the more I resist or try to avoid my responsibility for the part I played in that oppressive dynamic, the more that this dynamic is going to become a mess.

That is what's happened to us in the feminist movement many times. We are terrified to say, 'I did it wrong; I made a mistake,' instead of saying, 'Okay, I made a mistake—what can we do? Is there something now that can be fixed, or at least, what can we learn so in the future this doesn't happen again?'

But instead, we run around trying to avoid conflict, being very fearful of saying 'I made a mistake.' We think everybody's going to attack us and don't realize that sometimes honest acceptance of our mistakes—our miscalculations, miscommunications, misunderstandings—is where we gain power.

I become powerful in the moment that I'm not trying to run away from myself. Because in the moment that I'm not capable of admitting the part I played that contributed to a misunderstanding or an argument, I'm taking away my own power. I'm not fooling me. Because I always said we are not perfect. If we were really Goddess in the complete sense of the word, totally and absolutely perfect, why in the hell are we here? Why are we doing workshops and trying to educate ourselves and others about issues of oppression? We could sell the formula and become millionaires...I always said, I can sell the formula, retire to a small island in the Caribbean and write for the rest of my life!

PENNY: *It's hard to imagine you making that choice, Papusa.*

PAPUSA: Well who knows, it's very attractive...

PENNY: *Of course it is. I think it's healthy that we find that attractive... You've talked around this, but I wanted to focus in on it. This past weekend at the National Conference of Women's Centers, of which you were one of the organizers, you introduced Luisah Teish[1] as the person who really put you in touch with your own spirituality. You said she helped you to see how your spirituality fed your politics, and your politics fed your spirituality. I was wondering how that integration is working for you?*

PAPUSA: As I said earlier, I grew up in the stereotype of the Mexican family: Catholic, Christian, going to church. I was later involved with a very progressive group that was doing liberation theology[2] in Mexico, because I realized that the roots of liberation theology were very important. I think a lot of the work I do today has its roots in the understanding of liberation theology. But the church itself as a structure was very oppressive, and I needed to dismantle that church that oppressed me and oppressed others. It became a contradiction to be working within liberation theology groups in the context of a church that was so oppressive.

So I let go totally of the Catholic church, and I became a good atheist—here they call it more like a Pagan. But it was not really Pagan; I was not into anything. I was not into crystals, I was not into any type of spirituality—until I met Teish four years ago, in the context of another group. What Teish gave me back, for the first time, was the practicality of spirituality.

Spiritual beliefs are rooted in the welfare of the community. Teish helped me realize that my political work was spiritual work. By liberating people, by liberating myself, I was liberating my spirit, and the spirit of the people. And the more I understand that, I realize again that spirituality cannot be an individual thing.

And this goes against everything they teach us. They teach us spiritual beliefs are very personal, very individual, and I have realized, at least for me, that's bullshit.

If we look at the roots of spirituality, it's a community celebration, it's an act of transformation. Look at whatever tradition you want to: the Pagan tradition, the Judaic tradition, you can look even in the Christian tradition with all its oppression. You can look at the Moslem tradition, the Buddhist tradition. Look at any spiritual belief tradition, and you will see that the root of that tradition is the community, the collectivity. And we forget that.

And that's what Teish gave me back—the knowledge that every concrete act of my life that's directed toward my liberation and the liberation of the people really translates as a spiritual act. That politics are spiritual is really what I have come to understand.

PENNY: *Can you give an example in your community of that connection?*

PAPUSA: It's everything I do, even doing this interview is a political act. I believe that individual acts are political acts. Maybe somebody who hears/reads this, something will click in their life and they will say 'Oh, I had a spiritual experience with this!' I think that happens when we do workshops, when we see people going through their catharses, going through a healing process with themselves around oppression.

It happens every time we work with women who have been victims of sexual abuse or incest. In the moment that it clicks for them and they can start their healing process—that's a spiritual experience. And we can call it spiritual work or we can call it political work; it doesn't make a difference.

It's what priests and priestesses did in the past; that was their job—to heal people and to start that healing process. But what happened is we made a division between the priestess and priest, and the activist. And I believe we are both. Activists are spiritual leaders and spiritual leaders are activists, and political work is spiritual work and spiritual work is political work. It sounds kind of funny, but it's what I believe.

PENNY: *Do you have anything else that you want to say about women and power?*

PAPUSA: Maybe the only thing that I always want to remind myself and other people is that we cannot do it alone. The act of transforming ourselves and transforming our society, the act of working in liberation processes, has to be rooted in the collective. We need to go back to forming communities, to strengthen our work and the work of other people.

N O T E S :

1. Born and raised in New Orleans, Luisah Teish is an initiated priestess of Oshun, the African Yoruba tradition's goddess of love, art and sensuality. Teish is also an author, dancer and storyteller who performs ancient African and African-American tales with an emphasis on reclaiming their significance for contemporary women.

2. Liberation theology is a twentieth century Christian theology emphasizing the biblical and doctrinal theme of liberation from oppression, whether racial, sexual, economic or political.

Photo by Valerie Haimowitz

MAKING THE MOMENT LIVE

Naomi Newman

NOVEMBER 1989

"For me, if I can live by a truth inside of me—that's my source of power. Just what is really important to me? What am I thinking? What am I feeling? Where do I feel like my body, my mind and my heart have come together in a unity and I'm not split off?"

Naomi Newman's small but elegant frame exudes warmth, humor and personal dignity. Darting about onstage through various characters' incarnations or drinking a cup of tea after her performance, Newman has a focused and gentle intensity. Sprinkling us with wisdom gleaned from Hebrew sages, Buddha, aikido and motherhood, she leads us through a garden of pathos and delight.

PENNY: *Naomi Newman: Co-founder of The Travelling Jewish Theatre, actress, musician, writer, director, psychotherapist. A friend who once stayed in your house said, 'Here is a woman who's always willing to learn. She asks big questions and tells big truths.' I wondered what some of those questions are, what some of those truths are?*

NAOMI: I wonder who the friend is…What kind of big questions do I ask? It's probably harder to ask the questions than to come up with the answers. I know that at the end of our plays, people ask us what we're trying to say. My real conviction is that we're not trying to give answers to anything; we're trying to present the material that becomes the question that guides you. I think there are certain questions that guide us in our living, and never the answers—because the answers are the end of something, and the questions are the beginning of a process.

I think a really important question I ask of somebody who's staying in my house is 'How are you feeling today?' How we are feeling today is a wonderful guide about who we should be and what we should do and where we should go and what kind of energy we should put out into the world.

PENNY: *We spoke on the phone soon after the earthquake,[1] and you talked about the positive responses that could come from that experience. What did you mean?*

NAOMI: I think one of the positive responses we do is that we begin to feel, with awareness and attention, the gratitude for every moment that the ground is there, that the sun comes up, that the sky is there—grateful we can breathe and feel and touch somebody—and we start reshuffling our priorities. We start facing our fears.

I think those repressed fears motivate us into this fantasy of control and into a lot of armoring that cuts us off from really being able to live our lives in an empathetic and pulsing way. You know we get stiff, we get hard, we get protective, we get removed, we get...unalive. We deaden ourselves in the hope that we can control life, and we make the moments dead. I think what we have to start to do is make the moments more alive.

PENNY: *You clearly know a lot about healing, and from what I know of your life, that's definitely a thread that's run through your life a lot. Your psychotherapy work has been focused on the psychospiritual aspects of life-threatening illnesses?*

NAOMI: That was in Los Angeles. For about seven years I worked at The Center for the Healing Arts, and we did one of the pioneer programs in working with people who had life-threatening illness, using visualization, psychotherapy, journal work, body work, meditation, theater games, group therapy, one-to-one therapy and artwork. That was an enormously important teaching time in my life, working with people as they were facing those life and death issues. So often we learned from the people we were working with as they began to say 'Now I begin to treasure life, to feel alive, to know what's important. Now I will finally pay attention to the things I've been wanting to do and waiting to do until I had everything resolved.'

Somehow we live our lives imagining that there's some point at which we're going to do...what is it we think we're going to *do*? Get something completed? Make ourselves perfect? I don't what it is we're waiting for. And then we're going to do all those other things that are meaningful to us.

PENNY: *So did that motivate you to stop living life as a dress rehearsal and get into whatever it was you really wanted to do?*

NAOMI: It helped…and I struggle with that every day. Every single day. Every day I try to set up a process by which I do the most important things in the morning, like walking, my meditation, trying to do some soul-writing and singing. But I can become very driven, I'm a quasi-workaholic and there's the signs that go on in my head, 'Do that business first. Get to that to-do list.' You know, I think we divide life between to-do and to-be…maybe that's what Hamlet was talking about!

PENNY: *How have you learned to give to others without abandoning yourself?*

NAOMI: On the way over here I was thinking about our telephone conversation and some of the issues we talked about. And I thought about 'what is power…what is women's power?' I don't identify my being powerful by thinking that I have power over anybody else. For me, if I can live by a truth inside of me—that's my source of power. Just what is really important to me? What am I thinking? What am I feeling? Where do I feel like my body, my mind and my heart have come together in a unity and I'm not split off?

My body is a great barometer to me because I have a tendency to tense up my body like I'm mobilized for some kind of an attack. If I'm in that mode, something is wrong—I'm not in alignment. I'm functioning from a place of trying to prove something, trying to get something, trying to defend myself. And then there are moments where it's like things go into an alignment, and I realize that my strength, and my sense of myself, and my clarity about what is right for me is not going to impress you. And I've got to trust that you are going to take care of yourself.

I've done a lot of, 'I've got to do it for everybody else.' So that's a real constant question in my mind: Am I doing this in a clean and clear way? Am I doing this for someone else because I want a pay-back, because I want them to think I'm wonderful? Am I going to be resentful if I don't get the appreciation I want? When I'm off, I can't think right. I don't know if you remember, but in *Snaketalk*,[2] when the Hag is talking to the audience and she says 'Think!' she points to her head and her heart at the same time. It's like the two have got to work together.

PENNY: *Related to that, as women, how can we be in touch in a feeling way with the pain and suffering that's around us, really be aware, and not get caught up in a panicky, crisis mentality?*

NAOMI: I think one of the keys is to know how powerless we are and not expect ourselves to have power *over* the situation. But that we can be compassionate and respond with our heart open—not be afraid to feel the suffering and be there, with the person or the situation—to the best of our capacity.

Sometimes we can't. Sometimes we can be there, bring our bodies there, but our hearts aren't really open. And I think our hearts being open is acceptance in a way—not resigned to the suffering of the world so that we don't try to improve it, but accepting that there is suffering, and that you can't magically make it go away.

One of the thoughts I had coming over here was, when did I do my biggest leaps in my learning process? And the truth was when I was down on the mat, when I was faced with situations where I wanted more than anything in the world to have power over that situation. And I didn't. Like with one of my daughters who was using drugs and alcohol, and I didn't know if she would live through it. And at a certain level, I had absolutely no power; I could not control her life. But I could let her know that I loved her, and I was there for her, and at the same time that she couldn't abuse me. That was a really hard one for me.

PENNY: *That must've required a lot of detachment.*

NAOMI: And it required a lot of times when I couldn't be detached, and forgive myself. And forgive her. I heard at a talk the other night that whatever happens, even though you may need to put someone out of your life, you never need to put them out of your heart. And that's a real question to carry around with you: 'Have I put this person out of my heart? Have I put *myself* out of my heart?' That's probably the toughest one.

PENNY: *We've been speaking to this somewhat, so let's just follow it up, because you've been referring to some recovery issues. In* Snaketalk, *your one-woman show about the various stages that a woman goes through in her life, there's a scene where you talk about going through the first step and going through the second step and the third step. Things are going very smoothly, and then all of a sudden, you get to the fourth step—kaboom!*

NAOMI: It's the Jewish mother of the piece, and she speaks with a Yiddish accent. She's talking about The Path, how you go your own way and make your own Path; it's really my recipe for the spiritual path. And then she says:

You take one little step, you take two little steps, you take three little steps, you take f——watch out! Watch out! You're about to fall into the puddle of anti-manifestation! Here on the fourth step you are meant to fall down—not once, not twice, not occasionally, but on every fourth step.

The ground opens up, the wind blows, a branch hits you on the head, you trip on the stones, you twist your ankle, your heart breaks, and you got to fold all the laundry—and they have closed the two left lanes! All of the forces gather together to stop you.

And some people, when it happens, they fall down. And they lie there for the rest of their lives.

Ah, but some people, some people learn how to fall-down-get-up! That is one move: fall-down-get-up!

And in there I talk about how you've got to get lost. And if you don't get lost, you're really not on the right path. Because if you think you know where you're going, you're going to end up where you came from. And another place [in the show] people really are so grateful for is when I talk about after you get lost, you have to sit and wait.

PENNY: *I hated that part.*

NAOMI: And you have to wait and wait and do nothing, until it's clear what you're supposed to do.

PENNY: *It makes my skin crawl just hearing that.*

NAOMI: We don't like waiting; we don't like the void. None of us. We're supposed to know.

PENNY: *Or go out and do!*

NAOMI: Yeah, just do something.

PENNY: *I can tell you're a woman who's not afraid of paradoxes.*

NAOMI: I really am not. And I think that was my most important 'aha!' in my growth: when I learned that that's what I think of as feminine consciousness. Feminine consciousness does not force one to look at anything dualistically. You can see the light and the dark, the right and the left, the doing and the being—that all sides exist together. And they may seem like they're conflictual or paradoxical, but both sides are necessary to make the whole.

A friend was talking to me the other day about something that she really thought so highly of, a training she was having. And I said have you seen any of the shadow side of that training yet? And she said no, not yet. I said well, don't be surprised and don't be upset. And only worry if you don't see it. Because if the shadow isn't revealed, then they're doing a lot to hide it. Because there isn't an organization, there isn't a group of people, there isn't an individual, there isn't *anything* that doesn't have its shadow side. I mean, how are we going to know what's light if we don't have…the dark?

I think our culture particularly denies the shadow, and then it really sabotages us. Then we can't go any further because we're disappointed. We have to understand that disappointment is an organic part of the path in order to keep going on—that's what it's all about.

PENNY: *So we're just supposed to accept that shadow side?*

NAOMI: First of all in ourselves. If we're not afraid of it in ourselves, then it doesn't blow us away when we see it in others. Now I don't want to sound like I don't suffer from these things. You know, I get hurt, I get disappointed, I feel betrayed, I do everything that everybody else does. But I think the difference is that maybe you do it for a shorter period of time, you pay less of a price, you're more forgiving of yourself and the others, and you get over it faster.

PENNY: *You're moving into the realm of relationship, which is something I wanted to also talk about. You and Barbara Meyerhoff and Deena Metzger shared a very powerful friendship, and I know you and Deena still do. I believe you all wrote each other letters on a very consistent basis and shared creative projects together. What does that kind of relationship require, and what did it teach you about women and power?*

NAOMI: Well, I was very fortunate in that Deena and Barbara, who had a long-standing relationship from their early twenties, allowed me to enter into that relationship and make it a triad. They were my biggest teachers about how to respect and honor and pay attention to women's friendship. They had the correspondence. They made sure that in spite of husbands and work and children, they saw each other every single week for a sacred period of time where they were really just with each other. I learned so much from them.

We did work together. Barbara came into the Center for the Healing Arts. She was an anthropologist and we did healing ceremonies together. For her that was so exciting because she had always only written about them, watching others, and then we created them together. I sang at the end of her film *Number Our Days*, and I went down to sing for the community of elderly Jews in Venice, Los Angeles.

Deena and I did workshops together on women and power—
Deena's a poet and a writer and a teacher—and then we would get
together along with two other women, Nancy Bacall and Jane Stewart.
We called ourselves The Faeries. We would meet, usually once a month
for a whole day, just to be with each other. And we would talk about
our concerns—what was troubling us, what was inspiring us—and then
we would all respond to each other. I attribute so much of my development and my growth to those women's relationships.

PENNY: *What did you learn from that, Naomi?*

NAOMI: My God, I learned about life. I learned about ceremonies. I
learned about having fun. I learned a lot more about appreciating
myself, my particular kind of intelligence, my creativity. I learned about
our differences. I learned about how to fight with each other—that's
still a hard one for me, to fight with somebody I love and not be afraid
it's all going to come crumbling down.

Deena and Barbara would scrap all the time. It was so funny! I
remember even when Barbara was dying of cancer how we would still
scrap with each other about things we believed in and things we
disagreed about. At the final place, our relationship was always the
most important thing. But that relationship was large enough to make
room for a lot of disagreement and a lot of differences. And they would
surface. They weren't easy relationships.

PENNY: *But they sound very intimate.*

NAOMI: They were. And very inspiring. Each in our own way, inspiring
each other, forcing each other, encouraging each other to go the whole
nine yards, not to stop. If I said to Barbara 'I really want to write,' she'd
say 'well, get up at 6:00 AM—get up at 6:00 AM if you want to write!
Do it first!'

PENNY: *Another trio relationship I'm aware that you had was with
Corey Fisher and Albert Greenberg…*

NAOMI: These two men and I have been working together now for
eleven years.

PENNY: *I just wondered about that dynamic and what you learned
about women and power from that. I don't know anything about it, but
it didn't sound like it would be easy—and I wondered how you made it
work for you.*

NAOMI: The main thing I learned in the creating of *Berlin, Jerusalem
and the Moon*, and especially in *Snaketalk*, is that I needed to stand by

my work regardless of what anybody said. And if I was waiting for a gentle acquiescence, acceptance, encouragement, it wasn't going to happen. I wanted the process to be gentler than it was. I don't think giving birth is a gentle process.

And I thought golly, Corey and Albert are so impossible to work with and they're so difficult. But since then I've worked with other people—we're all difficult to work with! You know, we all become prima donnas, and we all have our temper tantrums, and we all get threatened, and we all get cruel. And we are learning to be gentler.

I don't mean that one has to accept the unkindnesses or the abusive treatment. One should do what you can to change it. But don't let it stop you.

PENNY: *I know you've practiced Vispassana Buddhism for over ten years. I'm thinking that practice probably helped you in what you were just describing. And I'm wondering how you integrate that with being a Jew—how those two things relate to your relationship with power in the world today.*

NAOMI: Being in a Buddhist practice is a constant everyday teaching about acceptance. And I have to constantly differentiate between resignation and acceptance. Resignation is [when] you feel powerless and you say, 'I can't do anything about something, so I'm going to grin and bear it—grit my teeth and hate it, but put up with it.'

Acceptance is looking at reality and opening your heart to it, not hating it, but flowing with the dynamic of it, like the way you do in aikido—not trying to push it away, not trying to deny it. My practice also teaches that everything changes. Don't get too knocked out of shape—tomorrow it's going to be different. Don't completely identify with all those thoughts going on in your head, because they're just thoughts, and we have about as much control over our thoughts as we have about the earth underneath our feet. We run these tapes over and over and over again, and lots of times these tapes send very poisonous and disturbing messages. We think that we're listening to the word of God as we're listening to our thoughts, and especially the negative thoughts, especially the thoughts that tell us bad things about ourselves.

The first long Vispassana retreat I did—Vispassana meaning Insight Meditation—the first big insight I had was that I had a batch of repetitive tapes in my head. So I said, 'My God, what goes on in my head!' I understood that I had no control over my thoughts, my worries. They were just popping up like mental burps. I didn't have to pay that much attention!

So I think that that practice has given me a lot of openness, a lot of responsiveness, fluidity, to move with my life and to go with it, and to know that I'm going to fall down, but to know that when I fall down that I'm also going to get up.

My Jewishness? That's like asking me what did I get from my mother and father, my DNA and the rhythms in my ears! It's my passionateness, my juiciness, my relatedness. I think that it is part of my Jewishness to see divineness in my relationships, and that that's part of my Judaism—to really want to be deeply connected and to feel like I'm in a non-exploitative relationship. To care about others feels like part of my Jewishness. To give it a rest…the Sabbath is a very deep, wonderful concept. You know if the whole world took a Sabbath, I think that would be the end of war. Just one Sabbath, if everybody stopped and tuned in on their soul all at one time, can you imagine the energy shift in the world? It would be incredible.

Or if on Yom Kippur everybody took stock in their own way, in their own religions, of the ways in which they had not lived up to their intentions—if they tried to make right with their fellow human beings and then forgave themselves, started over again.

PENNY: *You've been talking around this a lot, but I just wanted to ask it specifically. I think you're a shining example of a woman who is fulfilling so many different parts of herself, who teaches and who remains open. I really want to know how to integrate my creativity, my spirituality, my politics, so that I am giving my best back to the world, providing the best leadership I can—so that I can do my unique part to help move the planet to a healthier place.*

NAOMI: I think that question comes from believing that they're not integrated. You know in *Snaketalk*, when people ask me to describe the piece, I often think of pulling a multicolored thread, and as you pull the thread, it keeps changing colors. And I think that's what our life is like. It's all *one thing*, and the colors keep changing, so for one moment we'll be doing this and for the next moment we'll be doing that—but our central essence, our central truth, is moving through it.

There are periods of your life where you do more of one thing than the other. But that's when we keep the delusion that life is linear, and I don't think it is. In the period of one day, it looks like we're doing one thing after another, but there is a central core, or the essence of ourselves. I think the integrative place is staying in touch with that essence. If we truly honor our own life and accept it in all its dimensions, I don't think we can go on to endanger any other life on the planet.

NOTES:

1. This major earthquake rocked Northern California on October 17, 1989.

2. *Snaketalk* is Newman's one-woman play about the three stages of a woman's life: Maiden, Mother and Crone.

Photo by Valerie Haimowitz

Maudelle Shirek

"If you don't have something you really believe in, life isn't worth living. I can't get anything out of life if I'm not standing up for worthwhile principles."

Peering out the window at the intersection below, I spot Maudelle Shirek's distinct, neatly shaped crown of white and silver hair, accented today by a bright serape around her shoulders. Stepping slowly and with steady purpose, Maudelle embodies community, fully alert to those around her. She is a beacon of dignity and humility, a fighter who will not be silenced: speaking out publicly against police brutality, in protection of the homeless, or for a peaceful settlement to international conflict. In private conversation she shapes her words with care, as if she savors each one's full meaning. Maudelle Shirek's very being defines the word integrity.

PENNY: *Maudelle, you're seventy-nine years old, you walk three miles a day and you spend tremendous amounts of time each week cooking and delivering meals for senior citizens who can't leave their homes. You're a consistently strong voice on the Berkeley City Council. You came to nearly every rally against the Gulf War, and you were arrested last fall at Highland Hospital in Oakland to protest the closing of the AIDS Ward there. How do you do it? How do you keep going?*

MAUDELLE: Well, you *have* to keep going. The struggle continues. I was taught this as a child by my father and mother, grandmother and great-grandmother. You have to continue as long as you can. I was always taught that you do what you can *while* you can, because there comes a time when your activities will be quite limited.

PENNY: *You grew up in Arkansas. Could you tell me a little bit more about what that was like? I'm assuming you grew up with a lot of racism, and I wonder how that affected the choices that you've made. I'd also be interested in hearing more about what you were taught as a child.*

MAUDELLE: I was born in Jefferson, Arkansas, June 18, 1911. I was brought up there on a farm where my grandfather homesteaded, he and my grandmother Annie, after they were freed as slaves from the state of Mississippi. They came to Arkansas and homesteaded 160 acres of land there, which at one time had belonged to the Algonquin Indians. I don't see much difference though between the separation of races then and racism now. In fact I think I was more clear as a child than some of our children are today.

PENNY: *What do you mean?*

MAUDELLE: Well, we had separate schools. In fact, our churches in most cases were used as classrooms. And in Jefferson, Arkansas, we didn't have a high school even, we only went through the eighth grade. And it was a one-room school. But the white neighbors had a high school and also a [separate] building for the grade school; it was a three-room building and they had three teachers for the first through the eighth grades. So it was quite clear how the inequities were. We only had five or six months of school per year, while they had eight or nine months of school per year. Also, the Board of Directors of that school district were all white. There were no African-Americans representing you on that school board.

My father had had an opportunity to go to Williams Industrial College there in Little Rock, and he was a schoolteacher, so I went to my father. He taught in one of the churches, until later on when the Rosenwald Fund built a school. They were building schools in the South for African-Americans at that time. We didn't call them African-Americans then, we called them colored people.

I learned quite early that in your community you needed to cooperate with each other in order to exist well. We farmed, we raised all kind of food crops. It was what you call 'hill land,' where it wasn't strong enough to raise cotton and corn. But we grew a lot of vegetables like potatoes, black-eyed peas and whippoorwill peas. We also raised chickens and ducks, geese, guineas, turkeys and pigs. So we were self-sufficient in a way with food stuff.

Now my grandfather on my mother's side of the family was Caucasian. He came into that little town of Jefferson when he was twelve or thirteen years old, from Georgia. When my grandfather came in there, just a kid, why the whites in the town wouldn't take him in. My great-grandmother took him in, and he slept at the barn. Later on he grew up with my great-grandmother's family and he married her oldest daughter Lula.

Of course this was a little sawmill town, and they would cut over the timber. He worked around that sawmill for probably twenty-five cents a day; he'd gotten no farther than the fourth grade. But he was thrifty and saved his money, and he could go into Pine Bluff, which was the county seat. As these mills cut over the timber, they would sell off the land, but the only ones could buy it would be whites. By my grandfather being white, he was able to buy up over a thousand acres of that old cut-over timberland that was in the hills. Then later he was able to buy some of the river-bottom land.

So I came up knowing the real inequities in our society. My grandfather was actually able to go into business; he bought up this land, and he had sharecroppers and renters, and he also had a little commissary. He would bring in from Pine Bluff barrels of flour and sugar and salt and furnish some of his renters and sharecroppers with things out of the commissary. I knew a lot of the neighbors that lived in Jefferson or down on the river didn't have equal opportunities to what I had, because my grandfather was white and because my father had had the opportunity to go to college and to teach. So it has always been very clear to me about the inequities in our society.

PENNY: *But where did you get the motivation to try to change them?*

MAUDELLE: My grandmother Annie talked with me a little bit about slavery. She didn't talk too much about it. I was the one that taught her how to even write her name, so I knew she didn't ever have a chance to go to school to learn anything. She would tell me about the beatings that were given to slaves and all, so that stuck with me.

My father and mother and all the family were trying to make a better life for all people. They taught us that although some of the people that lived in your neighborhood maybe were a little less well-off than you were, you didn't look down upon them—you looked to help them. We all worked in the fields together and my father always taught us to take care of the land and the farm animals. We had an NAACP [National Association for the Advancement of Colored People] too, and I remember the case of the Scottsboro Boys[1] and how the people in that community worked to bring them justice. So we were brought up knowing that it was a social world and that people must look out after each other.

PENNY: *I'm just curious how you ended up here from Arkansas?*

MAUDELLE: Well, I came out here during the War [World War II]. And had not intended to stay [laughs]. Course my father never wanted any of us to come out here—you know I'm the oldest of ten children. He said cities were jungles. I didn't understand what he meant then, but I've learned to understand it now; because at least when you're on the farm you do have a way of helping to make your food. It wasn't easy. But in a way, compared to what people have in the cities, nothing but the concrete, it was a much easier life.

There were other farmers in the area that would work cooperatively with each other in breaking up the ground for planting and also at the time of harvesting. One of my uncles was a shoemaker, so he kept our shoes always in repair. Another uncle took care of the plows, keeping them sharp, and he also put shoes on the horses. And they would swap services with each other.

PENNY: *I remember reading in an interview with Ron Dellums that you were the person who really pushed him to run for Berkeley City Council.[2] This was the turning point for him, from social worker to politician. Thank heaven we have him...my friend Vicki Noble told me you were the one who literally took her in when she was having a hard time; you helped her change her diet and heal her sickness. It seems you have a gift of being a catalyst, of helping provide conditions for people with great leadership potential to come into their power. How have you done that?*

MAUDELLE: Well, you know, none of us are equipped with everything. I learned very early that people, a number and variety of them, can help solve many of your problems. You can't just depend on yourself. A long time ago I decided I would try to get other people in here who could help us in this struggle that we go through.

I remember the first time I ever saw Ron Dellums, in a meeting over at Franklin School. It was during the time of the Black Power movement. It was the first time since I'd been in California, really, that I had seen that many young Black people together and talking about some serious things. That was very interesting to me. Matt Crawford and I got together right after that Sunday night meeting and decided we must contact these young people right away because, as Matt said, 'Maudelle, we have something here.'

We immediately arranged for Ron Dellums and two other young men to come over to my house. We asked them what were they planning to do and how were they planning to get their message out.

They talked about going on campuses and whatnot. I remember Matt explicitly asked, 'But man, when you going to get out here with the *folks?*'

I said, 'You know, right now we are looking for a second Black person to put on the City Council in Berkeley. I've heard there's been some meetings already with a few people, but they're trying to keep it closed. I'm going to ask them to open it up.' I immediately called Councilman Jim Sweeney and told him I'd heard about the meetings at his house and was I invited? Because I had some people I wanted to bring there also. And he said, 'Why sure, Maudelle.' So that's how we really got Ron Dellums involved in being elected to the City Council in Berkeley.

PENNY: *Maudelle, when I called you to do this interview, you said this was one of the most difficult periods of your life, and that you had thought it was going to get better when you got older. Could you talk a little bit more about that?*

MAUDELLE: Well, when you see very clearly how so many people were maneuvered into accepting this war [in the Gulf], that's very hard for me to accept. Many of them just haven't figured out that our priorities in this country are really against humanity. To know about the thousands of Iraqis who have actually been killed and how that country has been just destroyed—and we can call it 'sorties' and 'collateral damage'—I'm almost in tears any time I think about it.

I know that tears doesn't help, you must keep trying to educate and help people to understand the humanity of the Iraqi people.

PENNY: *Where should we go from here—what should our priorities be?*

MAUDELLE: We must continue to teach. And I don't like to say teach so much, it makes you feel that you're trying to be superior. But [we must] reach the humanity of people for them to understand that each life is sacred. And each life can be beautiful. It doesn't have to be like this. We don't have to have people homeless, or people without health care. No matter what colleges you go to, that doesn't make you a good human being. All those generals and all those presidents that we've had—they've been to good schools, haven't they? What makes them think that you've just got to go killin people? We can solve problems without that.

In fact, war has never solved any problems. It's made more problems than it has solved. Not only the number of people that's been killed, but the people that have been maimed and left here to suffer now: the Palestinians, the South Africans, Nicaragua, Panama, El Salvador, Chile, Puerto Rico...and we have been the first to drop an atomic bomb on Nagasaki and Hiroshima. It is just unthinkable in a way that a human can be so *inhuman* as to think in these terms, much less carry out those kinds of things.

PENNY: *But what can we do about it?*

MAUDELLE: We can't let it discourage us. I'm with a group now, African-Americans Against—what I call—Bush's Wars. And it really was much more than a war, it was a real massacre. You think back on all these wars, all our energy and money going to destroy. Why can't it be used for building? There's so much research that should be done to cure AIDS, cancer, leukemia. That's where our energy and our technology should be going. I just lost a dear friend, Richard Naives, from leukemia. He was the director of our only high school Black Studies Department in this country. If we had been putting our money into research, we wouldn't have had to lose Richard like that. And I know if people ever get the glimpse, the idea, of really making this a better world—that it *can* happen—then it *will* happen. That's what I put my faith in and my hope in and my work in.

We've got to find some way to reach our young people. I heard a young man speak last night and he gave a very good quote from Malcolm X.[3] But then he came on later and said, 'to bless our troops that have gone to save this country.' That poor young man, he didn't know. So I'm going to have an audience with him and help him understand that this war was fought for the rich. For the oil barons. For the multinationals. It wasn't fought to save this country. And the young people have to see that. Because we're not taught real history. If we were ever taught real history we'd understand, and that's one thing that I understood, that even though my grandparents on my father's side were freed from slavery, that economically they *were not freed*. This country was not built on peace and justice and loving for all. It was built off the slavery of my foreparents, of many foreparents of ours, and off cheap labor, and all kinds of inhumane things. You know, we were considered only three-fifths of a human being.[4] In the Constitution! This is the history our young people must learn.

PENNY: *Who are your heroes, or your heroines?*

MAUDELLE: I have many. W.E.B. Dubois. Paul Robeson. Fannie Lou Hamer.[5] She stayed at my house when she came out here. My grandmother. My great-grandmother. My mother. My father. A lot of friends and relatives that I have back in Arkansas even now.

PENNY: *If you had to pick two or three lessons to pass on from your experiences, what are some of the first ones that come to mind?*

MAUDELLE: Be curious. And understand that you'll make some mistakes. But that can't stop you from doing what you should do. My father always said, 'Show me a person that hasn't made a mistake, and I'll show you someone that has never done a damn thing' [laughs].

PENNY: *Maudelle, you were on the first North American delegation to the Occupied Territories after the intifada started,[6] and you helped found the U.S.-Grenada Friendship Association. You spend your days helping people that are less able than you are. I know you've been under attack for your views, yet you seem to be doing what all of us want to do: living your values and integrating your beliefs in a day-to-day way. How do you manage that?*

MAUDELLE: If you don't have something you really believe in, you know, life isn't worth living. I can't get anything out of life if I'm not standing up for worthwhile principles. And if I get attacked for that, so be it. I can't cringe and run away just because I get attacked. You have to really believe in what you are doing.

N O T E S :

1. In the 1930's, nine young African-American men in Scottsboro, Alabama were accused of raping two white women. Although the U.S. Supreme Court overturned the convictions, Alabama refused to drop the case, despite the fact that one woman not only retracted her charge of rape, but also joined in the growing movement to free the Scottsboro boys. Five of the defendants served long prison terms. The case represented the mass-murder by lynching of thousands of innocent black men during this period, as well as the day-to-day oppression experienced by African-Americans in the South. It also ignited political protest organization at that time.

2. Congressman Ron Dellums [1935–] has been representing Oakland and Berkeley, California in the House of Representatives since 1970 and consistently advocates peace and rights for the poor, women and people of color.

3. Malcolm X (Al Hajj Malik Shabazz) [1925–1965] a leading African-American revolutionary of the twentieth century, was assassinated while speaking in Harlem. He received the 'X' when he became a member of the Nation of Islam. It replaced his given name, Little, the name imposed on his family by the slave master. The X represents the unknown, the mystery; i.e. the African names, languages and culture stolen from African-Americans. An intelligent and powerful speaker and "man of the people," he advocated self-help, self-defense and education for his people. He was a follower of Elijah Muhammed before founding The Organization of Afro-American Unity.

4. Maudelle is referring to the 'three-fifths compromise' devised by the Constitutional Convention of 1787. The number of Congressional representatives apportioned to each state was to be determined by the size of its population. Since slaves were not considered citizens, the Convention decided that three-fifths of the state's slave population could be counted as part of its population—or one slave was counted as only three-fifths of a human being.

5. W.E.B. Dubois [1868–1963] was an African-American intellectual: educator, writer and speaker. He argued against the views of Booker T. Washington, instead demanding immediate and unsegregated equality. He joined the NAACP [National Association for the Advancement of Colored People] and became one of its most important members. He received the Lenin Peace Prize in 1959 and emigrated to Ghana in 1961, where he died. He edited the *Encyclopedia Africana*, and wrote numerous books, including *Suppression of the African Slave Trade* and *The Souls of Black Folk.* *(Encyclopedia Americana International Edition, vol 9. Danbury, CT: Grolier Inc, 1985.)*

Paul Robeson [1898–1976] the son of an ex-slave, was an athlete and a scholar, as well as an actor and a singer, known for his interpretations of the spirituals as well as his roles in *Porgy and Bess* and *Othello*. Robeson was politically active and outspoken in his support of racial equality. Publicly sympathizing with communist ideas, he was brought down by McCarthyism in the 1950's. *(Martin Bauml Duberman,* Paul Robeson *NY: Knopf, 1988.)*

Fanny Lou Hamer [1918–1977] the granddaughter of a slave and the youngest of twenty children, was a leader in the Civil Rights movement. Thrown off the plantation where she had sharecropped for eighteen years, she was inspired to political activity after she tried to register to vote. She was repeatedly jailed, beaten and shot at. She was a source of great spiritual strength and a brilliant movement strategist. In 1964 she co-founded the Mississippi Freedom Democratic Party, which challenged the all-white Mississippi delegation to the National Democratic Convention, and finally won all of Mississippi's delegates' seats in 1972.

6. The intifada is the organized Palestinian uprising against the Israeli government's occupation of the West Bank and Gaza; the intifada began on December 9, 1987.

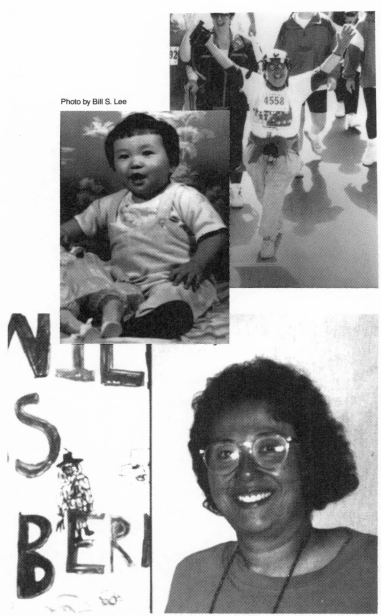

Bernice Lee

JUNE 1990

"I'm not all Chinese and I'm not all American, but…I'm 100 percent lesbian …It's part of my nature, it's part of the freckles on my face, it's part of the flab around my belly, it's part of the dirt in my fingernails…And how you respond to me says a lot more about you than it does about me."

Genuine, creative, in the moment
A strong sense of fair play
Accessible
Warm
Respectful
Community leader
Sensitive
Solid
Loving
Bernice Soohoo Lee.

I spoke with Bernice during her lunch break at the Yuk Yau Child Development Center in Oakland's Chinatown, as the children squirmed restlessly on their mats in the adjoining room.

PENNY: *Bernice, why did you decide to become a teacher? And what do you focus on in doing this work?*

BERNICE: I'm a 'born-again teacher.' When I graduated from college in Vermont, I was heading toward a career in theater. I loved being on stage and pretending to be all the things I'm not and also pretending to be all the things that I am. I came to San Francisco, got involved with filmmaking and fell into a part-time job working at a daycare center in the Western Addition [neighborhood]. I loved being with the kids and being in touch with what it was like to be a child again. I became an assistant teacher, then a teacher, and eventually became Program Director for the Child Care Information and Referral Agency in San Francisco.

That brought me to law school; I thought I would become a *true* advocate for children and families by having a legal background. Well, that wasn't the case. Law school was a rude awakening, because it wasn't very empowering to me at all. Growing up in New York City on the trains and buses of Manhattan, I didn't get a sense of how classism or racism permeates our society. Because when I was growing up, everyone in New York rode the trains and buses. There were people in minks and poor people all traveling the same way, coexisting together. Survival in a big city like that was part of my life—it was normal. It wasn't until I left there and went to law school that I realized just how institutionalized life in America was. And I was very disappointed.

So I returned to the field of education and decided I didn't want to be a director. It's very lonely to be on top, plus I am a raving codependent[1]—so I decided *this* is it. I love kids, it's touching a part of me, and what I do well is to empower children; I guess somewhere along the way I had a teacher like me. I just want kids to be a lot more empowered so they can grow up to be leaders—mindful, loving, serene adults.

PENNY: *So how do you empower them? Especially the girls?*

BERNICE: That's a toughie. You know I have dear friends with a daughter, and they're very progressive. Two women. And I just don't understand—their daughter's favorite color is *pink*. It makes me realize that no matter how hard we try, we just have to accept on a day-to-day basis that this is the best we can do. And hope that somewhere along the line, on issues more critical than the color pink, the girls will be and feel as empowered as the boys.

It's very clear with the children that I work with, especially the Asian children, that girls are a lot less verbal, a lot less visible than the boys. Because the mothers are a lot less visible, even though they're the major caretakers around the kids.

What I try to do in my classroom is create an environment where kids can take risks, where they can take chances, where they're not going to feel humiliated, put-down or embarrassed. And if they do, maybe it's only going to happen once or twice, and they'll realize from first-hand experience that the person sitting next to them is just as terrified. And that I'm just as terrified. Yet we learn, a day at a time, a little bit at a time; the fear gets chipped away and we become empowered.

I do a lot of work with kids in conflict resolution[2] which I guess is my reaction to the legal system, rather than to become the kind of advocate that takes power away from people. I would rather empower those who have say-so in their lives in the first place. The kids really learn to say, 'Hey, I don't like it when you go into my locker and take my things!' And rather than say it to me, they say it to the other kids, and the other kids acknowledge, 'Well I guess I wouldn't want my locker being tampered with either.' It becomes more empowering because they're using their words, their language. It's *their* experience.

And it's a skill that goes with them for the rest of their lives—rather than the teacher interfering and rescuing a situation. Of course, if it comes to health and safety, I need to step in. Yet it's really important to look at the day-to-day issues and use them as learning tools, so that the kids can be immersed in this kind of recovery program.

I try to practice that in my own life. I realize that I'm still unlearning a lot of things I didn't have the opportunity to learn in the more appropriate way as a child. For me, it's very important to take my job seriously, to have fun doing it and to know that I'm not just a teacher—that I am an influence in a little being's life who is going to affect the world.

PENNY: *Are there examples that you can give them of healthy uses of power in the world around them?*

BERNICE: One of the things that I love to do is to exercise what I've learned from my mentors in life, and one of them was Ricky Sherover-Marcuse.[3] She helped me be in touch with my racism. We all have it—what can I say? The kids have it too. They learn it from their parents, they learn it at school, they learn it from each other. What I like to do, and what I see really productive with the kids, is to show them how they can use their power, by saying, 'Hey, wait a minute. The kid in the schoolyard didn't push you down because he spoke Spanish; he pushed you down because he pushed you down. Not because the kid was a Latino.' You know? 'That teacher over there didn't give you a lot of homework because that teacher, as you call that teacher, is a Black teacher. That teacher's a person. You don't like that teacher because that teacher gave you a lot of homework! Not because that teacher is Black. Color has nothing to do with it.'

When I use myself as a role model and try to interrupt it [racism] in a loving and caring way, and at the same time earn their trust and respect, then they learn to do what I do, right? Kids *mimic.* I am a role model.

PENNY: *So how do they respond when you give that example of the Black teacher or the Latino kid?*

BERNICE: Well, they stop and look at me, and they don't quite get it. I can't push it. I mean, I can't do mind control and say, 'You will eliminate racism from your thinking, you will eliminate racism from your little spirits.' I let it go. Yet I follow it up with other activities, with stories, with writing letters to friends. We have a pen-pal program. And, lo and behold, someday in the schoolyard, I'll hear one kid saying to another child, 'Wait a minute! He didn't push you down because he's from Vietnam. He just pushed you down because he didn't like you.' And you know, that's okay. I let them know that we don't have to like everybody. But we can respect them for who they are.

If I went around preaching 'Peace and Love and Woodstock'[4] I'm the biggest fool around here. It's not the way life is. The world is full of pain and suffering. And we can minimize it to a certain extent. So when I hear one child interrupt another child, I know that I've done a good job, because they learn from each other. They can get an idea, they can get a hint from me—yet they empower *themselves.* And there's nothing like going around saying, 'Hey, I did it all by myself.'

PENNY: *They get a sense of power connected to responsibility.*

BERNICE: That's right. And not just in terms of racism but in terms of their likes, their dislikes, who they are as a brother or sister, a daughter, a son, a niece, a grandchild, a classmate, a student. Because we have all these different roles which put us in the position of either responding in the moment to certain situations or reacting to things that have nothing to do with what's going on in the moment.

PENNY: *You told me over the phone, Bernice, that you were not Chinese, you were not American, you were Chinese-American. And right after that, you said you were a 'first-generation lesbian.'*

BERNICE: Right.

PENNY: *I think the fact that you are out as a lesbian is a very powerful stance. Where did you find the courage to do that for yourself?*

BERNICE: I came out when I was two years old. I was dangling out the second-floor window of my apartment in New York, calling 'Connie, Connie!' to this really good friend of mine. I was so into it, I fell out the window and onto the awning. What I do for love! Well, that's who I am. It's part of my name, it's part of my nature, it's part of the freckles on my face, it's part of the flab around my belly, it's part of the dirt under my fingernails. For me to be a teacher, to be a community leader, to be a Chinese woman, a Chinese child of two people who've had a very hard life in two countries—it's important for me to sing my song.

Being a first generation Chinese-American, I am really NOT an American. I don't look American; my roots aren't from Western Europe. And I'm not Chinese. I haven't been able to go back to China yet, or to Hong Kong. I know that every day I'm not all Chinese or I'm not all American, but I do know in my heart that I'm a hundred percent lesbian. It's important for me to pound my chest like King Kong and say, 'Here, this is what I am!' You don't have to like it, you don't have to take it. And how you respond to me says a lot more about you than it does about me.

And I know there are repercussions. I know there are people who would probably feel 'guilt by association.' I can't take care of them. I wish I could. And I can't. Because if I was taking care of them, I wouldn't be taking care of me. I've learned in the last ten years that having secrets is something that chips away from my soul and from my spirit. So, it's take it or leave it.

PENNY: *You've brought up recovery issues a couple times now, and over the phone you mentioned that 12-step programs have been the 'Triple-A Triptik'* [5] *to getting you where you are today.*

BERNICE: They certainly have been. There are many different ways to get where you want to go, and the twelve steps of recovery have been my spiritual path. They saved my life. With my recovery as an adult child of an alcoholic I've learned to really forgive myself.

My father committed suicide when I was twenty-four years old, about eighteen years ago. He was addicted to prescription drugs and kept alcohol locked in the cabinet. Back then, there wasn't a Betty Ford Treatment Center. His own doc was the guy writing the prescriptions. After my father died, I talked with my mother, who finally told me that he went cold turkey a month before he jumped from the roof of his business.

And that said a lot to me, because it says that he died in recovery— he tried to stop something that he didn't quite know how to stop. He knew that drugs were making him a maniac, and he may not have found a best solution for him. But he tried. And for all the things he did to me, and all of the things he didn't do to me, I found that I can forgive him. The [12-step] program has really helped me deal with my issues as a daughter, as a child, as a niece, so that I can share my recovery in different ways with different people.

I don't tell the kids that I work with, 'We're going to have a moment of silence now, followed by the Serenity Prayer.' We have *centering*. And they're quiet, they breathe deeply, they check into their hearts, and they create an 'energy star.' For me, it's very much the same as what I do in 12-step meetings. I walk out [of each meeting] with a pearl of wisdom, and if I choose to string it to my strand of pearls, fine. If I don't, that's fine too. Who says there has to be 108 beads? There could be 1008 beads. There could be eight. It's all relative to who we are.

PENNY: *I also know you're struggling right now with Chronic Fatigue Syndrome. What are you learning from that process?*

BERNICE: I was diagnosed with Chronic Fatigue in October 1989. About six months before that I was just not doing well. I thought maybe I was slipping in my recovery or that something was going on. I became very tired, and I thought maybe because my lover and I had decided to join households that I was 'resisting'—you know how they say in those therapy terms. It seemed reasonable that I was feeling this way. But I started to get a sore throat, and I couldn't sleep, and I became really grumpy. Through my forty-one years I've had a lot of issues with my health: I was dependent on steroids for asthma, and I was shooting insulin for about three-and-a-half years of my life. I've learned to read my body, and I knew something was not right.

I went to my doc, a wonderful person, and she kept saying, 'it's nothing, it's nothing, all the tests are coming out negative.' Well if you rule out something that isn't there to be ruled in [because you weren't looking for it] it's not going to be there. Finally I called some friends of mine who are health care providers but who have a different kind of perspective. I asked, 'What does this test mean, what does that test mean?' And I told them my symptoms. They said, 'You better come into the office. We have a feeling this is Chronic Fatigue.'

And I was just not ready. Many of my friends have been diagnosed. I've watched them slowly withdraw from the community because of the *unableness* to sit up. To pay attention. I was walking into walls; I thought I was having the preliminary signs of MS [multiple sclerosis]. I was scared. When I was told that it was Chronic Fatigue, in some ways I was relieved, and in other ways I was angry that this is a product of taking all these antibiotics all these years. It's like a disease of the progress of the medical profession. I took six or seven years of the Pill when I was pretending to be a straight woman. Then the steroids. So it was very difficult.

And it stopped my activity. I stopped going to my meetings. I resigned from the Boards of Directors where I was doing my civic service. And I was very much into them. I was a Co-Chair for the National Center for Lesbian Rights, a legal firm that really represents the interests of lesbians and gay men. I was on the Board of the Bay Area Women's Philharmonic—the arts. That was a nice way for me to balance my service. But I knew now that I had to say no. Because somehow this illness was an opportunity for me to zoom in on myself, to really take care of me. My parents didn't take care of me, and this was a chance for me to *re-parent* myself. If I could find a spiritual way to look at this disease, that would be the way. A way for me to see what I'm eating that triggers things, to see how many hours I'm sleeping, to really look at my relationships.

I've lost a lot of friends from being sick. People look at me and say, 'You're not sick, you look terrific!' Yet I don't hear from them, they don't call. And it hurts me. But I also know that this is a time when I can weed and harvest things that are important. It's becoming very clear that there are definite constellations forming in my universe that I'm going to die with. I really care about the people I have in my life now—whether I see them once a week, twice a week or two days a month—and the relationships are unconditional. So I'm very grateful for this opportunity.

And I'm very grateful to the women and some of the men who have been dealing with Chronic Fatigue, because they paved the path for me. I was diagnosed at a very early stage, and I have more energy today than I did six months ago. If I can just keep moving along at the same clip, I think I have a good chance of getting some of my energy back. But it's been an opportunity to sit, to be quiet, to be mindful, and to let go of taking care of other people in a real tangible way.

PENNY: *On my way over here, Bernice, I was struck by the reality that today is June 4th. Last year at this time I remember you were very sparked by what was happening in Tienanmen Square. In fact you were contemplating a trip to China…Does that bring anything up for you today?*

BERNICE: That's a big one for me. I spent so many years of my life being ashamed of being Chinese. It wasn't until college, when I did my own research, that I realized there was so much more to my culture and my history. My parents didn't want to talk about it, because they were in great pain about the Chinese change in government and the Cultural Revolution. Plus they wanted to assimilate me in ways that I realize now are sort of shocking. But I can understand what they wanted to do, as immigrants.

Last year I was planning a trip, and right after I had gotten my first set of shots, the massacre occurred. I was more than ever determined to go. My lover said, 'I can't stop you,' but that she would be very frightened. My travel agent put an end to that. She just wouldn't issue the ticket. So that was that. I didn't go.

But I really felt my culture. I felt the students as being a part of me, and it's just so interesting because here I am, living in the United States, and I bitch and moan about this country in many different ways. In the guise of democracy we have so many issues that are not fair, you know. It is racist, it is classist. We are so homophobic, we're ageist, we're fat-phobic. We have so many *safe* prejudices. And I realized that these kids in China, when they talk about democracy, it is beyond their wildest dreams what I have here. I'm very sad today about the first year anniversary for Tienanmen Square, because I feel that last year at this time the Chinese students were the ones who brought democracy to a standstill, in terms of world events: the kid [climbing up on the tank, trying to stop it] and everybody just holding their breath [watching][6].

And now the Berlin Wall has come down. Everyone has been on this democracy movement and I feel a great deal of sorrow that it's not happening in China. I don't want it to happen in a way that's not going to work for the people there. But just thinking about the families who are still unable to practice the Four Freedoms[7] that we have here makes me realize how much work I have to do. It's a matter of setting priorities and making plans and moving on. And who knows? Dreams do come true.

PENNY: *Tell me one of those dreams.*

BERNICE: I want to go around the world and empower people. The seeds are already there; I just want to be the water to sprinkle on the seeds so they can germinate. I can help start daycare centers throughout the world. I can help kids deal with issues of conflict resolution and help them stay in the moment. I want to spark the interest and let people know they're not powerless. I'd like to be a consultant that way;

then I'd want to move on. We can all feel empowered if we're just a little bit less afraid.

N O T E S :

1. Bernice is using the term 'codependent' to describe a series of behaviors, as outlined by certain current therapeutic schools of thought concerned with the common effects of alcoholism and addiction on the families of the alcoholic or addict. Codependent behavior can be, among other tendencies, when the person "knowingly and habitually gives up personal power in a situation." As Bernice says, "When we can't use NO as a complete sentence."

2. For Bernice, conflict resolution involves solving a conflict where the parties directly involved are empowered to talk about the conflict and work out a solution that is mutually acceptable. It is creating a balance, where all parties retain their personal dignity and the integrity of their views.

3. Ricky Sherover-Marcuse [1938–1988] was a Jewish woman activist, thinker and visionary who did groundbreaking multicultural work through her workshops on unlearning racism and anti-semitism and on internalized oppressions. Much of this work she did through the organization New Bridges.

4. Bernice is referring to the music festival held in 1969 in Woodstock, New York at the height of the 'Hippie' era, an era which promoted these values.

5. A 'Triple-A Triptik' is a linear map to a particular destination, using a route suggested by the American Automobile Association or AAA. 12-step programs are several different anonymous organizations, based on the structure and principles first developed in Alcoholics Anonymous. These programs were designed by the members themselves to help others like them recover from alcoholism, addictions and other related behaviors.

6. The most famous media image from the Tienanman Square uprising [the organized protest by Chinese students and their massacre by the Chinese military on June 4, 1989] was of a Chinese student climbing onto a moving tank, in protest of the military's repressive and violent tactics.

7. Bernice is referring to the Four Freedoms that President Franklin D. Roosevelt, in 1941, declared all people were entitled to: freedom of speech, freedom to worship, freedom from want and freedom from fear.

Photo by Irene Young

BACK TO THE INSTINCTS

Vicki Noble

DECEMBER 1990

"When women speak from that place of silent knowing, it carries authority...If you start raising your voice, people are going to get upset. But if you raise your power, if you amp up your power, they're going to hear you in a different way."

Earlier in the day we had waved to each other across the throngs of nearly 200,000 people, marching to stop the U.S. massacre in the Persian Gulf. It was January 26, 1991. Vicki had her young son, Aaron Eagle, by the hand; together they were walking for peace.

That night in a concert setting, Vicki again appeared, her white hair flowing majestically around her animated face. Still wearing my clothes from the march, I squeezed into the front row, filled with grief, I felt in desperate need of sustenance. "Think of the world as your body," Vicki told us. "It's made up of healthy cells and unhealthy cells. The unhealthy cells are a cancer, and are multiplying each other wildly...Now think of yourself as a healthy cell in this sick body. We can work to stay healthy and multiply, and together heal this body, the earth." As we all clasped hands, chanted and sang together, I repeated the affirmation Vicki had given us:

> I am a healthy cell
> I am a healer
> I want to live in peace.

I felt the blocked energy break free and surge through me. As the tears of relief came, so did the sense of renewal, the ability to carry on.

PENNY: *Vicki, among other things you're co-creator, with Karen Vogel, of the MotherPeace Tarot Deck and you direct the MotherPeace Institute in Berkeley, which focuses on women and healing. I also happen to know you have a history of activism around women's health issues and you have three children.*

I'd like to explore some of the innovative ideas around women's power and healing practices that you've been developing. In your book, Shakti Woman—Feeling Our Fire, Healing Our World: The New Female Shamanism, *you say: 'Women are choosing to heal ourselves from the world illness of patriarchy. We're having a collective near-death experience, and the blinding light of it is showing us how to transform our lives.' Can you elaborate on that a bit?*

VICKI: This sums up my present view of things. Like so many other people, I feel that we're in a state of ecological crisis and global war. But I'm viewing what's happening as an emergence of healing energy. As a healer, I see that when the body is sick, it has the capacity through some sort of miraculous transformation to recharge itself and to open to healing that Western medicine can't explain. I see this all the time as a healer. So do other healers. Bodies just miraculously get well; even people with serious cancer and immune system problems just 'get well.' Sometimes there's a high fever that precedes what they call a 'spontaneous remission.' Through a certain kind of catalyst or stimulation, the body knows how to throw out this power, this energy that heals itself.

I know the earth is a body, and I believe we're cells in her body. We're the cells that need to get well, in the way that the cells in our body need to get well for cancer to go away. I really believe there's a global emergence of power happening, almost as if from her belly the earth is throwing up this amazing power—this fire, this heat—that is like a throwing-off of toxins. It would be like if we had a fever. It's also a little bit like a miracle, an ecstatic healing, a faith healing. My work these days, and my whole view of things, is about getting as many people together as I can and raising as much energy as we can together to create this kind of faith healing. I believe that the cells vibrate all together when you put your hands on a body and heal it; I think if we, as cells in the earth's body, all get together and drum and sing and chant and celebrate and raise our vibration, raise our energy, then it actually heals *her.*

PENNY: *You had your own healing crisis a few years back?*

VICKI: That was really what opened me to my shamanic work. This was in 1976. I had had terrible headaches for ten years and I had become addicted to Western medicine, to prescription drugs. But I still had headaches, and there was no relief. The pills were getting bigger and bigger, and I was getting more and more numb as a human being with all of these drugs in my small body. I gave up on Western medicine and said NO—to the doctors, to the medicine, to the concepts—without knowing what lay ahead.

As soon as I did that, I began to have spontaneous amazing experiences, psychic experiences, energetic experiences and ways of healing that I had never even heard of. I just began to transform as a human being. It came from my body, and as that happened, of course I felt better and better. For example, one night I was in the bathtub. I used to cry and cry in the bathtub and didn't know why. I was touching my stomach because it hurt—I had begun to develop an ulcer—and I was touching my stomach in circles. At a certain point it was as if my hand went inside my stomach and it released something like an orgasm, but in my stomach. After that I didn't have an ulcer any more. And I had heat in my hands for healing. So it's energy that comes unbidden in a way and from where I don't know; it just healed me. And as it healed me, of course it made me want to heal other people, and it's been a circle like that now for fifteen years.

PENNY: *You're leading right into some other areas I wanted to talk about. Recently I heard you say: 'The source of our power as women is way down deep in the biological taproot, and we have to come back to our instincts...Learning to act from our bellies will make us women of power, the knowing and the acting from the same place.' This came from your experience with your own stomach?*

VICKI: Right. All my work comes out of my own experiences. It's almost like coming in the back door. I have the experience, and *then* I discover what it means. Or I have the experience, and then I read about it or I learn that it's yoga, it's shamanism, it's psychic healing, it's something that exists in a tradition. And then I teach it. So when I say working from the belly or working from the instincts, I mean it literally. Our consciousness has become fixated in the head and we have to get it to drop down with gravity, with our breathing, with our relaxation techniques, down into the belly where we can begin to feel our power center. That *is* the power center for women, the biological womb, the place from which we source.

I have maintained for a long time, from my own experience and from watching my students, that women's intuition actually hasn't been killed by patriarchal culture. We *know* things, but we're not allowed to *live* from what we know, to *move* on the information we get through our instincts or intuition. It's just…the body *knows*. And that's what I'm really wanting women to come back to. Our biological birthright is very instinctual—from having menstrual periods, from having a uterus, from being potentially mothers. I think it must be a survival mechanism. But we don't use it. We become victimized, we are afraid to take a stand, we're afraid to say, 'No, that's not alright. Don't touch me. Don't hurt me.' We're afraid to act on what we know to be true. I'm trying to help women connect up those two things: to validate the intuitive way of knowing, and also to strengthen our ability to take a stand—to really *know* where we stand and to clearly establish our limits and boundaries. And also to take action. To have courage. To move forward *against* things when it is necessary.

PENNY: *You've recently begun ritual healing circles with groups of women, which incorporate the laying on of hands. Do these connect to this whole instinctual, intuitive process?*

VICKI: Completely. In fact, when I first started the work, I had to tell my students over and over again that what we're doing is not psychological. I told them they could never try to figure out what caused a client's illness or what was wrong with her relationship with her mom and her dad. We don't do any of that, because the healing work isn't happening from the mind, *at all*. It takes awhile to catch on to that, if you've learned any systems of creative visualization or sending blue light for this and red light for that. I'm not working that way.

I'm working from this emergence of energy in the body and also from learning to become empty. Through the shamanic practices you learn to be clear and to empty yourself of your thoughts. Also energetically, through the practices that raise the vibration, which are often Buddhist or Yogic practices—I think this is what happens—the molecules move apart. There's more space and fluidity between them. The physical body and the energy body are not so separate, and there's not such a strong boundary around the physical body. One can move more easily out of the physical body into the energy body or merge with the group energy. To somebody who hasn't had the experience or hasn't done the practices, that might sound a little zany, but it's really just a natural outcome of the Yogic or shamanic practices. And truly, every time you do something that allows you to bring high voltage energy through the body, the molecules do respond by moving farther apart. So there's more and more freedom for the individual; there's more of a feeling of emptiness in the body, the feeling of being a vessel.

When we get together in the healing circles, we begin to drum, we begin to chant, we begin to pray I suppose you'd say, asking the healing power to be with us. And it immediately begins to come forth through the body. Any bodyworker who runs energy knows this, but when you do it in a circle it's a hundred times as strong. Sometimes my tailbone will begin to tingle and literally I'll feel the Kundalini[1] move. Other times it's as if the top of my head opens and tremendous energy comes through and rivets me to the ground. It's very grounding, very supporting; it's very empowering, and it's hot. It's literally hot. I sweat, I get very warm all over, sometimes in specific places. If I'm chanting, it'll often be in my throat; if I've got my hands on someone it will be in my hands. And the heat moves from our hands, so the body of the person we're working on gets very hot.

We did that for a long time without having any particular philosophy about it. It's just what happens. Sometimes the room would get like a sauna. But I read at some point that western science has now come to the conclusion that you can cure cancer by raising the body heat, raising the body temperature. There was someone in the South who actually created a machine to recycle the blood out of a person's body into the machine, and the blood would be heated up in the passage through this machine and put back into the body. That was to help people with AIDS. It was very controversial, but it runs on this same premise—only we're doing it without taking the blood out of the body. It's very basic. And I've now found more research to support that: that if you can raise the temperature of the body and keep it raised for an hour, then you're very likely to create the same kind of conditions that a fever creates, which often leads to a spontaneous remission. So it's *very* exciting work.

We didn't know any of this. We're just doing the healing, praying and putting our hands on, and asking, 'Please heal this person.' We're also of course telling people we can't cure them, because we haven't any power to do that. I feel like we're simply rewiring some new circuitry or something like that. The energy is electric and it seems as if we're just catalyzing, 'jump-starting' a person.

PENNY: *And they're getting better?*

VICKI: We haven't been working long enough to say that with any kind of legitimacy. So far all of our clients feel immediate relief, and they love the nourishment of being held by the circle. They all say that it's very exciting. Sometimes the miraculousness of the physical phenomena—feeling your own body get really hot through someone singing and drumming and putting their hands on you—that's amazing in North America. I think our clients go away very changed. So that's very helpful.

People who work with cancer and other life-threatening diseases say that an experience of religious ecstasy of some kind is often the cure. Again, they don't understand why or how. They just write it down; it's statistical.

So we're doing certain things that are physical, and we're doing certain things that are something beyond the physical, something in the nature of spirituality. And all of that is happening at the same time. I would say that the clients we've been working with the longest, who are the most seriously ill, are doing great; but it's been a very short time really, six months, that we've been practicing this work on a weekly basis.

PENNY: *Vicki, these healing circles are a group ritual, and my understanding is that most of the work you do is in groups. I'm assuming that's purposeful—what do you feel the connection is between working in groups and women accessing their power?*

VICKI: That's a wonderful question. I began to feel years ago when I was doing bodywork one-on-one with people, women mostly, that they were coming in with the same problem. Everybody that lay on my table in a given day would basically tell me the same story over and over. The only thing that disturbed me about that was that each woman seemed to feel she was the 'only one' or that it was somehow *her* problem. I thought,'we have to do this work in groups, because we share these issues, and it's very important that we understand that.'

It's almost as if there aren't any personal problems anymore. There aren't any personal issues. It's all global. We really are cells in the larger body, and the larger body really is ill. There's a healing crisis happening, and we're just part of it; it's not personal. That's been very compelling for me.

And the specific energy work I'm doing is enhanced by more bodies. The more people come together, the more high voltage the work—and the high voltage is what heals. Ten people can do much much more than one person, and a hundred people can do much more than those ten. I literally have visions of thousands of us doing this work, Pentecostal visions of the Goddess religion at work through the hands and the bodies of all of us.

PENNY: *Conversely, how can an individual woman access her power in her day-to-day life, without that group energy?*

VICKI: I think the best way is always through ritual and prayer, asking and then surrendering. Lighting a candle, taking a little time, making some kind of altar where she does some form of worship to whatever way the universe looks to her. For me, it's the Goddess, the Mother. I especially work with images of the Dark Goddess. I feel that the Dark Goddess is the healing Goddess—she comes to us from the night, from the unknown and from the deep—and it's that part of the Goddess especially that's been demonized and rejected. We have trouble accessing the Dark Goddess, because we raise up the demon of our culture when we do.

PENNY: *Something else that I read of yours caught my attention. I wasn't sure that I agreed with it, but it made me think: 'After twenty years of active feminism, many women have almost no idea how to actually take back the authority that has been systematically stolen from us and projected onto men, who in every situation are assumed to be the experts.' I thought, 'Well, I think we've done better than that! I think we're more empowered than that.' Now in other articles I read, you seemed to answer that—and you've spoken to this somewhat—saying that female shamanic work is 'being geared to helping women make a stand, not as an argument or a fight, but on their own behalf and on behalf of the planet.' Can you elaborate on both sides of that concept a little more? As well as what you were saying about going out into the world—because I'm very interested in how we access our power and then use it for our personal healing and the healing of the world.*

VICKI: Yes, I am too. I think the first statement about dealing with men has really to do with authority. My sense is that all of us women have been socialized, from such an early age and from such a deep level, to believe that the authority is male and that it is outside of us. And *that* socialization is structural. Much of the work that I do is focused on the psychic structure, the energy body; I'm really going back before psychology in a way. In looking at that, it looks to me like we've actually been taken out of our own body, and that when any question comes up, there's a certain way we have this conditioned knee-jerk reflex; we don't think we know. And we feminist women, of course, want to take that back—so there's a period, or even a lifetime, in my experience in watching other women, where we take that back in an adversarial way: 'Oh yes, I do *too* know. Oh yes, I will *too* do it my way.' That's all right, that's wonderful, that's the beginning of our rebellion and our attempt to gather ourselves back into ourselves.

But I think the work that has to be done is metaphysical. We have to change the structure through meditation or bodywork, something that literally reaches those places where the material is embedded and releases it structurally—from the body, from the muscles, from the places that hold the very early experiences that may be what we got in the womb. Most of our mothers were certainly not empowered, and they saw authority on the outside. So this is more than a psychological thing that I'm talking about.

The work I think, in a nutshell, is to bring the standpoint back to the belly. This is what we started out talking about. Get yourself grounded in your own belly—not in your head, because that's conditioned. Men have told you what to think there. Given that, even when we're trying to make changes, it has to be more than intentional. If you're going to only use the intention, then you need to ritualize it, because ritual strikes at the invisible structural level. It's fundamental. So if you want to work from intention, then light a candle and do it in a sacred way, and it might work.

Or you can literally get into the body and start releasing those things that are obstacles. And finally, you find yourself in the body, and it's a feeling. It's a place you haven't been. It's a place they don't allow little girls to be in; certainly if you masturbate, they're going to stop you from that. If you have any kind of wild, reckless physical drives like little boys, you're likely to be stopped because you might get hurt, and little girls aren't supposed to get hurt.

When all of that gets released, there is some way that we actually come back home. We begin to take what I think are political stands really, but it can be one woman in relation to her husband, or her father or her brother. And it's not adversarial—it's *'I am.'* It's really different from 'I am *not.*' It's very creative, and so it's like fire. It's not like a fight, it's not war, it's not polarization. It's not irreconcilable conflict, which is what men and women generally experience when they begin to talk about feminism. It's just '*I am*—this is how it is, because I'm experiencing it from inside of my own reality.'

And when that happens, I think you begin to create a female-centered reality, which is female authority. It comes from inside of me. I source from the deep Feminine. Not from out there. I don't need anyone's approval. 'I am.' And that transmits authority, it carries weight. And men and women will be moved by that.

When women become healers, they gain this sense of being in the body and being in their own space. If there's any kind of emergency, everybody gravitates toward them because they're grounded— they're present and ready to respond. And we all need to be present and ready to respond, because we're in crisis.

PENNY: *How do we access that energy and use that power in a group—if we're activists, if we're leaders, if we're trying to work in the world beyond a one-to-one level?*

VICKI: I tease my students and myself that being in a one-to-one relationship with a man is like being on the front lines—it's where you get to practice the art. You can just take that a step further when you're in a group. It could be a woman who's taking leadership in her community; maybe she's at a community meeting where people are going to make some decisions about how the community functions.

We need to learn as women to just get very quiet inside of ourselves and drop down. When we do that, we get information. The next step is to practice speaking up from that place of information, which has been a primary trauma for women, because when we do that, we're often trivialized or ignored. Instead of becoming more argumentative or adversarial—which then raises up the whole 'spectre of feminism' for everyone in the room, immediately causing the opposite of what you're trying to achieve—a woman needs to get *more* quiet inside of herself. Like an animal. Deeper in the belly, more alert. She has to wait for the voice within her to make itself known.

If we can learn to do that…I know that this works; because when you speak from that place of silent knowing, it carries authority and people listen in a new way. If you start raising your voice, people are going to get upset. But if you raise your power, if you amp up your power, they're going to hear you in a different way.

To do that, you have to take yourself seriously. To take yourself seriously, you have to be inside of yourself. So it's very complex, and it takes time. It takes practice. We ought to practice this every opportunity we get, and just keep practicing, and then we'll have larger and larger opportunities. I really believe that the Goddess makes available more opportunities, as we grow into the ability to speak in larger groups, in more serious situations.

PENNY: *There's just one question I really wanted to ask you before we end. Who are your heroines?*

VICKI: When you ask that, immediately I see Marija Gimbutas.[2] Isn't that great? I love her. Her work is so profound, the way that she has done archeology and has continued to dig up and tell the truth about what she finds—no matter how much the boys make fun of her, no matter how much criticism is heaped on her for supposedly having fantasies about the ancient Goddess religion. She's found her standpoint, and her life is as much of a role model as her work. That's why I appreciate her so much. She's just the genuine article, and I love to look at older women who are so integrated.

NOTES:

1. Kundalini is the tantric image of latent personal power, coiled like a snake at the bottom of the spine, the lowest chakra of the human body. When she is awakened, she raises her head and by doing so opens the other chakras of the body (*Barbara Walker, The Women's Encyclopedia of Myths and Secrets. San Francisco: Harper and Row Publishers, 1983*).

2. Marija Gimbutas is an archeologist, an expert on the European Bronze Age, who created the interdisciplinary field of 'archeomythology.' In researching the era before Indo-Europeans, what she uncovered revealed a continuity of images pointing to a world view which was ecological, considered the natural world divine and saw the female body as the primary metaphor of the sacred universe. Two of her important books are *The Civilization of the Goddess* and *The Language of the Goddess*.

Photo by John Ratzloff

Winona LaDuke

NOVEMBER 1991

"I think it is essential that people use their power in a way that influences their government, influences change and supports our rights—not because they feel sorry for Indians, but because they understand that everybody's survival is linked to the survival of other people."

In between sips of tea to coax away laryngitis, Winona LaDuke talks about her people's struggle to reclaim the resources which are rightfully theirs. Her approach is genuine, compelling, to the point. Moving with an easy grace, Winona is clearly someone who gets things done— often several things at once—in a way that is both attentive and steady, like breast-feeding her son on stage as she speaks. Winona's lessons to us are not only of right action, but of integration: of relationship between individual and community, between survival and spirit.

PENNY: *I've heard about you for years now, Winona, but I had no idea of the broad scope of your activities. I know you grew up in Oregon and you're from the Bear Clan of the Mississippi band of the Anishinabeg [meaning 'people'] known to non-Indians as Chippewas—and now you move a lot between Moose Factory, Ontario and White Earth, Minnesota.*

You're President of the Indigenous Women's Network, which is an international network of Pacific and Native women, and much of the work you're focusing on is trying to stop the exploitation of energy resources in indigenous communities. You've won the Reebok Award, among numerous others, which is considered the Nobel Peace Prize of people under thirty. You have two children, a Master's Degree in Rural Development, and you lecture at places like Harvard, Smith and Dartmouth as well as in Europe. You're also a writer, and I'm sure this only scratches the surface. I'm very interested to know, growing up as a Native woman in this culture, what drew you to activism?

WINONA: I never had a sense that things were right in this society. As a person who was raised between two cultures—I'm half-Indian and half non-Indian—I didn't feel comfortable with the way things were.

I guess what you do first is take it personally, and it's you who is the problem; I think that's the automatic reaction. Some people never get over that, I suppose. Then you try to figure out if there's something wrong with the bigger picture, which is what I came to from my perspective—that there's something wrong with the construct of society. So I decided to try to do some work on it.

Coming from where I came from, the government process of trying to deny Native people our own identity is such a horrible process that it means most people are faced with a lot of extra problems. That process of trying to reclaim identity and rebuild community—because in reclaiming identity one also has to heal your community, where you're from—has really engaged me in the process of social activism.

PENNY: *You also work with the Ikwe Marketing Collective of indigenous women on the White Earth reservation [Ikwe means 'woman' in the Anishinabeg language] and that sustains twenty craftswomen and fifty wild rice growers. I was reading in the magazine* Indigenous Woman, *where Julie Moss' article says: 'As long as we continue to be passive about economics, we will continue to be powerless.' Is your marketing collective part of a large-scale economic strategy to empower indigenous women?*

WINONA: In the context of our community, there's a picture that needs to be painted. Statistics indicate that for Native people at White Earth there's an 85% unemployment rate, but this is unemployment in the wage economy. The reality is that 75% of the people hunt deer and take more than one deer a year. Over 50% harvest wild rice, over 50% produce crafts for their own use and for sale, and about the same number harvest berries and medicinal plants in the woods. So you have a whole traditional economy which has always existed and that continues to exist to this day. That economy is in many ways much more on our own terms, and women have a more equal part in it than in a wage economy or a hierarchical system, such as the dominant economy. Our work is to revitalize that economy as a part of rebuilding culture, and to recognize [that] women are an integral part of that.

The intent of Ikwe is to rebuild the economy and through that process figure out ways to capture the fair price for our resources. Instead of Indian women getting paid three or four dollars for earrings that are selling for fifteen to twenty dollars, we decided that we should try to get that money ourselves—that that was the fair way to do things. That meant if we have to live in a cash economy, we should be paid with respect for our time.

And similarly with the wild rice which we harvest. We don't grow it; it grows on the lakes, and we go out in a canoe with two sticks and knock it into our canoe, because that's the way it always was. Instead of getting paid fifty cents a pound for rice that's selling for five to ten dollars a pound on the market, we thought that we should get that money. So it's this bigger picture—it's community empowerment, of which women are a central part.

PENNY: *Are there other projects like this in indigenous communities around the country? Is that something new that's happening?*

WINONA: I think increasingly, indigenous people are trying to capture the value for our resources, and it's a whole process of regaining control over community, regaining control over economy. The reality is that Indian communities have a lot of wealth, but most of the wealth is either expropriated or systemically drained—whether it is by harvesting timber on our lands or taking our other resources or money that comes into an Indian economy.

On White Earth, for example, we did a study of our economy. We found out that ninety-five cents of every dollar is spent within a few days in an off-reservation border town. For the most part, any money that is actually generated [in our community] is drained off immediately, generating jobs in other communities and not in ours. So this model is something that a lot of communities are looking at now, to recapture and control our economies, whether through the traditional or cash economy.

PENNY: *Winona, you've also written and spoken about the situation of battered women in indigenous society. A fairly recent study [1989] done by the Ontario Native Women's Association said, 'eight of every ten Aboriginal women have been abused or assaulted, or can expect to be abused or assaulted.' What is being done about this?*

WINONA: There's a growing number of shelters for Native women and there's a growing number of people involved in the whole issue. In my sense, there's a couple of reasons for this. The reality is that colonialism destroys people and it destroys communities, and the consequence is that there's a pecking order. In that pecking order, women and children are towards the bottom. In our own communities, we're recognized as more important and more respected—but when colonialism strikes, that's how it strikes; it re-orders the community.

I guess I'm trying to point to the larger problem, which is not just that men hit women. The problem is that our communities are abused, and that abuse is translated to women and children. A lot of us work in this bigger context, trying to rebuild and strengthen community as the basis for healing that whole piece.

At the same time, we work a lot with empowering and encouraging women to do work, because that is at the center of it, that whole process of women being able to feel decent about themselves and to rebuild their own lives with their children and their families. A lot of the work of the Indigenous Women's Network is trying to encourage women's participation in different political processes—whether it's testifying at local hearings or getting involved at the reservation level in activities like a women's marketing collective, or issues around childcare or natural resources. We try to encourage women to become involved, because that process of consciensado—

PENNY: *Consciousness-raising?*

WINONA: Yes. [That process] is one where you begin to see the problem is not yourself; the problem is a larger piece, and you have a part in changing that.

The other piece though is that, in the discussion of colonialism, I find it so striking to look at the whole impact in recent years of militarization in the Native community. We have a tradition of respect for ogitchida, or warriors—people who protect or defend their village. That's a long-term respect that's always been in our community. How that is translated today is that there is a really high rate of enlistment by Native men, for a couple reasons. One is because of this cultural respect, which is not accorded to Native men generally by [non-indigenous] society. The other piece is the whole economic reality of why men of color and poor men are more represented in the armed forces.

For example, in the Vietnam era there were the most Native men per capita of anybody. In the Persian Gulf war it was very similar. I was reading a story about the Lakota Nation, and they estimated that there were 500 Lakota people [serving] in the Gulf.

I guess what I want to say is that militarization affects the community when people return. A lot of the men who came out of the Vietnam conflict suffer from Post Traumatic Stress. When they returned to reservation communities or communities where they were essentially forced into powerless situations, living in HUD [the U.S. government's Housing and Urban Development Department] housing projects with a lot of social problems forced by the society, an increase in domestic violence occurred. It's something that we don't really address that much, but it is beginning to be looked at, and we need to heal that.

PENNY: *When you spoke in the Bay Area in March [1991] at the Women's Voices in Troubling Times Conference, you said that the people who weren't invested in getting a piece of this society's pie would be the ones most likely to create change. And you thought that the women's movement had the potential and numbers to do that. How do you see that happening? Do you think women have some qualities that men don't— that make us more likely to create those changes?*

WINONA: I think that the women's movement has less of a vested interest in society because there's the whole marginalization and lack of access that women have been subjected to, which means that they are in a better position to resist and a better position to look at society critically. So I'm committed to that idea.

And I think women have an understanding or a direct involvement with birth and rebirth and cyclical cycles. I think we're more in touch with the earth than men, and because of that women are in a good position to understand the need to protect and honor the earth. We all need to regain that relationship, but I think women are a little bit closer by their nature, and so it's not such a big step.

PENNY: *One of the major tenets of the second wave of the women's movement in this country was 'the personal is political,' focusing on the process of how things get done. Again, when I was reading* Indigenous Woman, *there was an article by Luz Guerra describing the First Continental Meeting of Indigenous Peoples. Something that she said really struck me: 'What really mattered was that the process we went through was as equals, as partners. At first it was a struggle, but by the end of the day we didn't want to leave each other.' In the indigenous groups you work with, is there a particular kind of process that is used and is that something you would see as a model for what the rest of us could be working towards?*

WINONA: Most groups that I work with operate on consensus,[1] which is something that a lot of social change movements and other groups try to do as well. And I think it's a good process. However, indigenous people are in a little bit better position because we're more homogenous. We have more shared common history and shared common culture and oppression—so converging is a little bit easier sometimes for Native groups, whether it's a reservation-based group or an urban-based group. The consensus process I've seen in other groups as very arduous, is arduous in our groups too, but it is a little easier sometimes.

When you're talking about consensus, I think that speaks to the need to address the long-term issue of community. You cannot always take a model from someplace else and put it in a different context, if that context is not capable of acting exactly the same way. It's a model that's applicable and I think more people are looking at the consensus model, but there is this structural problem that is faced.

In our community traditionally, there is also a representation model. Obviously the whole concept of democracy was taken from Native communities, but it was pretty much screwed up in the process of applying it. We have extended family representatives or clan representatives; it's a decentralized system of bosses or chiefs—headspeople—in our community. They would come to consensus, and so it was not everybody that participated in the consensus process, but it was their representatives. So there's a combination of representation and consensus that I think traditionally has occurred. In community organizing we still do that—we have heads of families or representatives of families that are a part of the process.

PENNY: *You also work with non-Indigenous groups; for example you're on the Board of Greenpeace.[2] In the alliance-building work that you do, what are some guidelines that you find useful—specifically from your perspective as an indigenous woman to non-indigenous people like me who believe in working in these alliances?*

WINONA: First of all, the nature of this society is that a lot of us are different parts of different things, and so we're in a good position to figure out how to work in alliance with other people, because we are that. That's my personal experience, coming from two cultures, so I have always tried to resolve things in a way that I could live with both of them.

As another piece of looking at that, we know that the environmental movement is essentially dominated by the white middle class and all the things that go along with that. That is the history as well as the present status of the environmental movement. Now that is not a bad thing. The reality is that those people have a lot of power in this society, and I think it's really good that they try to utilize their power in ways that honor and protect the earth. I think, however, that there are shortcomings inherent in coming from that class and that place—and it is essential, if we are going to save the earth and survive, that the environmental movement broadens its perspective to a deeper understanding of relationship to the earth.

For example, the origins of the environmental movement in this country are around basic concepts of 'wilderness'. The whole idea of wilderness implies that it is wild and it needs to be tamed. Or that it is wild and that nobody lives there. It's a totally non-indigenous way of looking at the land, without seeing that humans are a part of that way of living there, that we have a certain role to play and a certain relationship to the earth. Humans are parts of ecosystems, and we need to figure out how we can live here within ecosystems. In not having that piece of understanding, one is in a strange objectifying relationship with the earth, which I think is a basic tenet of the problem.

PENNY: *When I heard you speak before, you talked about indigenous culture being a dynamic culture that changes over time, and that what was important was to control the terms of the change. Can you articulate more what those terms are?*

WINONA: That indigenous peoples and indigenous cultures are dynamic changing cultures is a really important concept for people to understand at the outset, because the tendency is to view Native people as an image out of Hollywood. The consequence of that is we are not allowed to be alive, and we are not allowed to change or do whatever we need to do to live—which is the essence of what we've always done.

In a process where we control change, my sense is that we pick and choose technologies and concepts that suit us and that make sense to our communities, so that we still retain a way of life that is based on a good life. An essential value in Ojibwe culture is bimasiwin, which means 'good life.' It also means 'continuous rebirth,' and in order to acquire that, there is a whole set of relationships and behaviors and codes that go along with it—like that you take only what you need, and you leave the rest. You understand that what you do now is going to affect you in the future. You understand yourself as a part of a cyclical continuum—that you are related to people who were before and people who are coming. And so one chooses things that support those concepts.

PENNY: *You just referred to choosing different technologies. And last March you said that, 'industrial societies have declared war on land-based societies.' In terms of a future vision, do you think these two societies are mutually exclusive? Where's the place for any kind of industrialization in the future, if we want to change this society to become more land-based, more earth-centered?*

WINONA: I think that industrial society is out of order, and that is the essence of the problem. Because the basic value in capitalism, and I think it's true in other industrial societies as well, is that you take labor and capital and resources and you put them together for the purpose of accumulation. But the essence of accumulation is that you take more than you need—so you cannot have a good relationship with the land, because you are, by the construct, being greedy. And that's not really ethical.

In an earth-centered era, we have to rearrange the values of the society so that when we take something, we give something back—this value permeates indigenous cultures all around the world. Just like equal terms of exchange with people, there has to be equal terms of exchange with the earth—because we're totally dependent on the earth.

So to start with, we have to change the nature of the relationship and that implies a whole set of changes in industrial society. I have to say that I think a lot of technology is in itself bad. In a new time, we will have a lot of things that we have in this time, but it will have to be different; we have to critically analyze tools and technology to see what is appropriate. It's very difficult to convince North Americans in particular, the people who consume the most, that they are going to give up everything. But the ecological crisis is going to precipitate economic and social change, and I think the question is how we decide to relate to that, and if we decide to begin dealing with it now. If we wait until we have an ecological collapse of many of the ecosystems, that may make it close to impossible for us to live in them. I think that's really the issue.

PENNY: *What would you say is one of your biggest challenges?*

WINONA: Aside from raising children? I think that balancing it all is a big personal challenge. I find that trying to change this society is very consuming. And you have to always balance internal and external, so you have to work at doing that consciously. My ability to face the big external challenges is totally affected by my ability to retain my own spiritual relationship to the earth, as well as my own integrity. That kind of balance is a difficult piece.

On the other side, I think that we are looking at giant corporations: Hydro-Quebec, American Express, the New York Power Authority, the German government—that's who we're fighting about a series of dams in Quebec and Ontario and Manitoba. They are very big and very greedy, and they have no concept of what is at stake. All they have is their vision of a society, which is a vision that I am absolutely sure will make it impossible not only for indigenous people to survive, but for everyone else to survive. The big challenge is taking on these people, because we have no choice; if we let them do what they want to do, then we will not be able to live there.

I have two children who are Cree, from James Bay [Ontario], and if the corporations succeed in putting in all the dams, my children will not have inherited a part of an ecosystem in which to live. They will not be able to do things or say those words—those words will be of places that no longer exist. And I find that concept totally unethical. That is why I engage in doing things, because of this whole relationship of internal to external. It's not an intellectual process—it's a process of understanding your relationship to the land, or your relationship to place.

It's not only a challenge to take on these companies—I expect them to act like that, because that's how they are, that's why they are what they are. But we really need to undo colonialism and undo how North Americans think. We need to re-evaluate the values we are taught in this society, but to get people to do that is very hard. Not to judge them poorly, but I feel sorry for them—because a lot of people live at a superficial level in which continuous consumption of things, and buying, and TV, is their spiritual basis. That is what we've been taught—that if we consume a lot, it will make us feel okay. And the problem is that it's addictive—so we are electrical junkies and consumer junkies at this certain level.

But from what I can figure out, how one feels good about oneself is about your relationship to the earth, your relationship to other people, and being able to have integrity—which I think one is stripped of in this society. If you have some integrity, then you don't have a need for all those other things. I guess what I'm talking about is at that personal level, changing how people think. When people get a grasp of it or see something, many times they will change—but getting to that point is the very hard thing.

PENNY: *So what sustains you? What keeps you going?*

WINONA: My relationship to the earth I suppose is the central part of that.

Other parts which sustain me are just experience—for example, seeing that Innu women in Labrador [northeast of Quebec] successfully fought a North Atlantic Treaty Organization military base [from expanding onto their land] and defeated it. That there were supposed to be 1000 nuclear power plants in the United States by now and there are only 120. That we have suspended indefinitely a series of dams in Ontario that were proposed for James Bay. People engaged in struggle are able to change things, and when we know these stories we are sustained by other people's courage. That is a real big thing which sustains me.

The other piece is that I am uncomfortable in this society. And because I am not comfortable, I think that all humans have a need to be comfortable. To make it comfortable requires that I engage in change. And as I said, there are a lot of very good people who are involved in this whole struggle for change, and it is their courage and work that enables all of us to keep going.

PENNY: *You've been working so intensely. What are some of the lessons you've learned that you would want to pass on to others?*

WINONA: I think that in my experience, one always needs to balance the internal and the external—both of those healings are essential. This society teaches us to spend a lot of time on our internal, and the internal cannot be changed without changing the external. We need not to be narcissistic, or punishing, on either end.

I heard a medicine person once say that it is not necessarily fighting evil to make good, it is a balance between good and evil, and that that is what we need to strive towards. I found that to be less punishing and punitive, cause I'm not always good! [laughs]

Other people's victories and resistance is always exemplary to me. I was at an international women's conference on the environment a couple of weeks ago in Miami, Florida. There were remarkable women there from all over the world talking about work that they were doing. I always feel good hearing people talk about those things. Then I left the conference with some Indian women and we went to visit some Seminoles, who are Indians living in the Everglades.

They had traditional houses, a very little amount of electricity that they had chosen to have in there, and a phone. They cooked outside in a common house, they conducted their ceremonies—and they all talked Seminole. So about an hour and a half outside this obscenely over-developed city of Miami, there are these people living with such integrity, you know? I think that that kind of resistance is really striking—I get a lot of courage from the tenacity of people like that.

PENNY: *How can those of us who are non-indigenous best support you in your struggle?*

WINONA: I think that the Seminole case is a good example, because there is a tendency in the New Age movement and to an extent in the women's movement, to try to practice indigenous spirituality. Now I don't have a corner on religion, and I don't think that indigenous people have a corner on relationship to the earth. We have a corner on some relationship to the earth though; everybody needs to have that relationship. But people have to get right with the earth, without exploiting other people—and when people have this relationship, it is much easier for them to have compassion, for people and for the earth.

A second thing to understand is that it's not about 'saving Indians.' Because then we become endangered species and 'endangered Indians.' Look at the Seminoles or other people who practice some of these ceremonies—what they are doing is following their original instructions. Those instructions are what I am convinced enable us to continue to survive, because the majority of everybody else is totally out of order. And the Seminoles don't even have land. They are tenants on a farmer's land in between two big tomato fields, and they're there at the farmer's grace—they've been there for seven years. They had another place where they practiced some of their ceremonies, but a developer bought it, and they're no longer allowed to practice their ceremonies there. Non-Indians own land in their own minds in this country.

Now the Seminoles are talking to the Nature Conservancy about helping them acquire a piece that they can protect. I think people need to figure out how to support and sustain groups like the Seminoles, how to keep other people from walking on them. They don't want to own land, but they need to be able to continue their practice.

That is obviously the situation of the people of Big Mountain[3] and also of a lot of Native communities in Northern California who were affected by the Goroad Decision which gave the government the right to log in a sacred area.

During the Vietnam War, someone asked the Vietnamese how people could help them. And a Vietnamese person replied, 'Change the policies of your government.' To me, that's a lot of what this is about. I understand that non-Native people, essentially white middle class people in this society, are accorded much more respect than Native people are. They are recognized as having rights which Native people are not recognized as having. I think it is essential that people use their power in a way that influences their government, influences change and supports our rights—not because they feel sorry for Indians, but because they understand that everybody's survival is linked to the survival of other people.

The third thing is that it is critical to engage in a social and ecological change of relations in this society. This society consumes far more than its share of resources, and the consequence is that those resources have to be stolen from other people. As long as this society continues to consume this level of resources, then other people and other ecosystems are going to be devastated for the benefit of this society. I saw some graffiti the last time I was in San Francisco, during the Persian Gulf war, which said, 'How did our oil get under their soil?' I thought that that was really the essence of the problem: your right to destroy somebody else for something you perceive that you need.

PENNY: *What struck me the most when you spoke here in March was when you said, 'When Indian people are no longer essential to the practice of our own spiritual traditions, it's very dangerous.' In In*digenous Woman, *Andrea Smith was talking about Indian spiritual abuse and the silence of white feminists. About this, she particularly mentioned the prominent display of Lynn Andrews' books at the 1989 National Women's Studies Conference. She went on to say that the promotion of this material by white women ensures 'that our voices will never be heard...It seems profit always gets in the way of solidarity between white and Indian women...[But] our spirituality is not for sale.'*

I have become familiar with some land-based traditions that have resonated for me, and in my personal spiritual practice I struggle to understand if there is any way I can use those that is not exploitive and that's respectful? I don't know if you want to comment on this anymore or not...

WINONA: It's a hard call. I basically think it is possible; and in my own personal opinion I think that people who are residents in North America have to engage in a spiritual practice which in part resonates from this land. Because that is the nature of residency. But the question is the terms and how it is undertaken.

The other side of it is that I can't tell you how to pray; that's not my business. But you cannot replicate the practice of indigenous ceremony. There is something that is individual practice—and it is also essential to have a relationship to community when one practices that. That is the absence in white feminism—there is a belief that they are practicing something Indian, but the fact is that they have no relationship to Indians. Half of them have never even seen an Indian or talked to an Indian, and no Indians benefit from what they do. And that is an unequal term of a relationship.

That is what is wrong—Indian people have no rights to practice our religion, but somebody else perceives they are practicing our religion, and they have a right to do it because it is their 'religious freedom.' They miss the basic point of the practice, which is that when you take something, you give something back—you have to have a dynamic relationship of respect with those communities or that ecosystem. I think that the practice is quite possible but the relationship is what needs to be changed.

PENNY: *Who are your heroes, your heroines?*

WINONA: Katherine Smith and Roberta Black Goat from Big Mountain, women in their seventies who've been fighting relocation for many years…Meridel Le Sueur[4] who has always been a voice of people's resistance and talked about the legacy of people's struggle…my own mother…a lot of different women and men who continue to resist, who continue to be vital and loving—who engage in what they do out of love, and not out of anger or hatred…and a lot of my friends. I love my friends—they're my heroes too, and my heroines. They're very good in what they do, and they keep doing it.

N O T E S :

1. Simply put, the consensus process involves everyone in the group agreeing to a particular decision, no matter how long this process takes.

2. Greenpeace is an international environmental organization. It works to change government and industrial policies that threaten the world's resources. Greenpeace

calls attention to the dangers to the environment of such actions as offshore drilling, nuclear bomb testing and the dumping of radioactive wastes into oceans. It also opposes whaling...and the inhumane killing of animals. Members of Greenpeace use direct and nonviolent methods of protest. It was founded in 1969 by a group of Canadian environmentalists. *(World Book Encyclopedia, vol 8. Chicago: World Book Inc, 1989.)*

3. Big Mountain refers to the joint use area of northern Arizona, where traditional Dine (Navaho) elders, mainly women and their families, are resisting forced relocation from their sacred ancestral lands, to make way for coal, uranium and water extraction by Peabody Coal Company.

4. Meridel Le Sueur [1900-] is an award-winning writer, poet, labor reporter, actress and teacher whose writings focus on the people, history and traditions of her native midwest, especially the struggles of women. Hailed in the 1930's as a major writer, she was blacklisted in the 1950's because of her radical ideas, but her work has become increasingly popular since the resurgence of the women's movement in the 1970's. She uses writing "to express the lives and thoughts of people, that were unexpressed."

Photos by Irene Young

Rachel Bagby

JUNE 1990

"Now that those two, intuition and intellect, come together, that's where my power comes from—not denying any of those parts of myself. And having them surrender to each other is really what's working."

Banner flaring from high-flung arm...head arched above a dancer's frame...our own Olympic goddess of alacrity and grace. Rachel Bagby both transcends the present moment and is in it completely, with utter presence and intensity; her torchbearer's dance is spellbinding. And this is the magic of Rachel: whether sounding the heartbeat's drum, or mediating a community dispute, she calls us to absolute attention, to our own inner selves.

PENNY: *By way of introduction, I know you, Rachel, as a performance artist and teacher. You're also an attorney; you've been involved in eco-feminist and civil rights work, and I've seen you do some marvelous work in conflict resolution. You've released your own music cassette,* Across The Lines. *And you are currently performing with Bobby McFerrin's ensemble, Voicestra.*

I've experienced you holding power in a way that is very calm, sensitive and loving, but that's very riveting—that really allows the rest of us to cooperate with you and also allows us to fly with you. And I'm wondering what guides you in your own sense of personal power?

RACHEL: I don't know that I would use those words, 'personal power,' but in the conflict resolution you witnessed with the group of 200 women, I guess it was that. First of all, I ask permission to find out if there is a *willingness* [in the group]. If there is, and if I feel I can trust myself to be centered and unbiased, and I can trust the willingness is *honest*, then I surrender.

I surrender all thoughts of what should happen, what ought to be, how it ought to be, and what my role is. I then take my cues from what's going on moment to moment. So I trust both the intention of the women, in this case, who said 'Yes, you have our permission,' and I trust that my love of this community, in this particular situation—or my love of this planet, if it's something I'm doing in the ecology movement—or my love of whatever I'm involved in, will carry me through.

I just surrender to whatever is the highest good of the moment and trust whatever I bring to that will be what is needed. And whatever I hear and respond to from my heart, my intuition, my intellect, my body, will be right for the moment. It is a place of trust, and it is a place of serving life, and I trust life.

If it best serves that situation for me not to be up there, then I am able to let that go and call for help, which I did several times. When I felt like I was in this tangle of words and emotions, then I said, 'Does anyone have any other wisdom?' I don't have any investment in being 'the one' at all, and that gives me the power to say, 'I don't know what is going on.'

At the end, when I felt as though it started going like a broken record back over territory we had covered, I just fessed up and said, 'The process is not over, but I am through.' So, knowing when I've reached my limit, and being willing to say, 'I've given all I can, this is what I see, and I'd like to close it from where I sit. If there is more that needs to happen, blessings on working it out.' It really is trusting life to carry us through.

PENNY: *Have there ever been times when there were obstacles you weren't sure how to move through?*

RACHEL: There was one time where someone in the group had something very personal that they were working out with me. I represented something to them that brought up anger and rage and resentment. What I did in that instance was to say, 'It sounds to me like you need something from me personally, and it has nothing to do with this group process. I want us to have time to handle whatever is going on here between us, and I have no idea what that is, but let's make an appointment to do that,' so that dynamic does not then take the focus of the entire group. Being willing to be in that place of conflict where

I know there is a lot coming at me, setting aside a time for that and not letting that take over—that's one thing I can think about.

PENNY: *Where did you learn this?*

RACHEL: That would be harder to say. One thing that contributed to it is the role I played in my family of origin with my mom and dad. I was the one in the middle telling this one that they weren't listening, and that one to shut up. So I remember taking that on, early on.

I think that my training as a lawyer helps me look at the discrete aspects of a particular disagreement, as opposed to getting lost in the whole glob. In my mind I could say 'ABCDEF' as a possible way of approaching it, so that all the possible concerns have just been laid out and can be considered one by one.

Another part has been growing up Black in this culture, which has meant constantly being in an environment that did not much affirm me. I had to learn how to figure out what was going on, listen very well, and not internalize it so much so that I lost all sense of myself, but be there and figure out the language. Cause the language of what I was learning in school—the information, the history—had nothing to do with the people that lived around me and didn't reflect the reality I knew. I was able to be in a reality that was absolutely foreign to me, but that is somehow connected to me and has something to do with my survival—so I learned the ability to translate constantly.

And, referring back to the original example, that was something I saw that came out. When the women had various perspectives, I was then able to use a language that could be used by everyone. I think that skill really comes from those childhood experiences. I have studied conflict resolution just recently, because of personal conflicts. The ones with large groups have been something that has come relatively easy, but interpersonal conflicts have been harder. Studying that by going to a woman who specializes in that has been helpful.

PENNY: *Someone just told me that one of the very powerful things about working with you in a group is how you provide a platform for others' creativity and power to come through. I'm wondering how you both model the leadership I've seen you provide and also are so open to receiving from those you're working with.*

RACHEL: Well, yeah, I'm just greedy [laughter]. I want the goodies. Everybody has their place of just absolute brilliance and I *want* that. I want everybody to be in that place of self-knowledge and ecstasy, cause that means we're all free. From my own self-knowledge, I know that when I am centered in that place for myself, then I don't act out on other people. There's more room for me to encourage whomever to do whatever they need, to be in that place with me.

And if they are in that place with me, then they are less likely to act out all over me or to be jealous and envious. That has been where I have felt sabotaged, by people who were envious or jealous, feeling I had something they didn't have. By being in my power, and encouraging others to be in their power and not thinking they need mine or there isn't enough, by that we have a fuller world.

I think that also gets at the bottom of the greed that kills the planet. It's because we don't recognize what exquisite beings we are. We don't need to murder a thing at all. We don't need to *destroy* in order to *have*. We have so *much*, just *inside* of ourselves. To realize that, I think, gets at the root of what ultimately leads to trying to grab so much *outside*. That is part of my reverence for life.

PENNY: *What do you think are the major obstacles that keep so many of us as women from empowering ourselves, from finding that brilliance in ourselves?*

RACHEL: The major obstacles…one I think would be a real lack of self-knowledge. Through school I heard, early on, 'To thine own self be true.' But what I was *fed*, was somebody *else's* self. It would have been more honest for them to say, 'You be true to *me*.' So there wasn't the place for me to touch that place of power inside of *myself*. I think that's a major obstacle.

That's why I think places like Women's Alliance Camp are so essential, because it is a place where the intention is to provide room for women to experience that part of themselves and then to learn how to develop that.

PENNY: *That was the other thing I wanted to ask you: with all the different things that you do, how do you do it? How do you nurture yourself so that you can keep that energy going?*

RACHEL: One thing that I do—and this is new—I am learning to really have reverence for the breath; it is a miracle. The air pressure on this planet is just right for us to breathe. A little bit on one side or the other—a little bit less, a little bit more—we could not exist. That's a miracle for me. That's something I came to appreciate more after the fire [in our house], when I could not breathe. When the smoke was so thick and I was fighting to get out of the house so I could live, you can imagine that my sense of breath is incredible.

Walking, I broke an ankle once, and I saw how dependent I was on being able to walk. That's something that nourishes me, just knowing what magnificent gifts we have in our bodies. Another thing, is that I take time and do nothing. I just sit and do nothing. Not as much as I'd like to [laughter] but I do, I do, I stay with my own thoughts. Also, I keep a journal—I have since I can remember. My mother just sent me something that I wrote when I was seven years old. So I've kept a journal all my writing life.

And the company of other women—where there is not that sense of competition for men or that sense of competition for whatever the goodies are. The company of other women who are in their power, the love of other women—the absolute acceptance and love of other women—has been, and is, incredibly nourishing.

PENNY: *You mentioned the fire, which burned your house down, and you were also recently in an automobile accident. Those are pretty major events to go through. What opportunities did those provide for you?*

RACHEL: One thing is that I owe my survival and recovery from that fire to my community. It gave me a stronger sense of the strength of that community. Through a series of miscommunications, we didn't have insurance to cover the losses. The things that we have recovered have come as gifts from our community. I am really grateful for that. The clothes that I have on, everything except my necklace, was a gift from someone; I don't own anything that I purchased, very few things. And the things that were purchased, were purchased as a result of monetary gifts from others.

It also has given me back my relationship with my husband, Martin, in that we've seen ways that we miscommunicate. It's meant a closer and deeper appreciation of what home is and means. Now home is a priority, as opposed to before when our priority was work.

The accident has given me back my body, because I've needed to give particular attention to just doing basic things like sitting in a chair for an hour. I didn't realize the skeletal system is just incredible, it's just outrageous! You know, I learned anatomy through high school, but it wasn't, 'Look at this magnificent spine!' So, it's given me a lot of gifts; I think the greatest one is that of community.

PENNY: *Moving a little more globally…when you look around at your community, your world, the U.S.—do you see any examples of healthy uses of power?*

RACHEL: Healthy uses of power…One would be when the students protested in China. I think that was a very healthy use of their ability to have influence on what is going on in their lives, to have a voice. For me, power means using our abilities and our capabilities to be able to speak up—to walk, it can be that simple. It means using whatever resources we have at our command, with some consciousness, to reach some sort of goal.

I see Johnetta Cole, who is the President of Spelman College, use her position and the forum it gives her to speak out in a very clear way about the situations of women and people of color in this country. She does it in a way that neither points the finger at something else, nor focuses on blaming anyone, but rather focuses on 'This is the situation as we are now faced with it; these are steps that I think will return us to sanity.' She says, 'This is what we've inherited, now what?' I have a deep respect for that.

PENNY: *What do you think is the most empowering work that women can do right now for themselves and for the planet?*

RACHEL: I was really deeply moved by Deena Metzger's talk about getting in touch with that vision of what the world would look like if it were really something sustainable and then moving from that vision to saying what it is that we can do. I think, for instance, of how dependent I am on trees. I am a writer: the writing that I do, the correspondence, the toilet paper, what I blow my nose with, the napkins I bring the students to serve them meals, the paper bags, the pencils. Stanford [University] as an educational institution is also heavily dependent on trees. When I heard Deena speaking I made a commitment to do one thing a week to use less trees in my life. I still get paper bags from the supermarket; I'm going to get a canvas bag and carry my groceries in a canvas bag.

I think one of the most powerful things to do is to *move out* from that personal of 'how do I live my life' in ever-broadening circles. That's really salient for me, because so much of the time when I'm out speaking or doing that kind of work, I make excuses. I say, 'Oh well, if I think about the good that it's doing I don't have to think about how much oil this is using.'

What I am now doing is turning it around and making a commitment to learn about the cost to the earth of the various industries in which I am an active participant. For example, because I travel a lot, I'm asking what the airline industry uses up in resources and is there a way I can reduce that by organizing what I do differently? Maybe I can drive together with another woman who is also going out to speak at various places, carpool to various states, as opposed to traveling back and forth across the country. Just trying to figure out different ways, no matter what we do.

What is the cost of the industry that produces audiotapes? What is the technology of audiotapes—isn't that a petroleum product? I don't even know, and yet I participate in these forms of communication. It is my responsibility not to be ignorant about the price I am exacting from our natural resources to do the work that I think helps…It is my responsibility to be more conscious and make the way I *live* consistent with my *values*.

PENNY: *As we're talking about power, words that you've mentioned that are staying with me, are commitment, responsibility and earlier you talked about surrender.*

RACHEL: Yeah, I guess those are pretty much my key values. I think life is incredible. I think that it is a gift to be hanging out at this time. I really think that life is its own entity, so I surrender to it a lot, especially when my thinking mind stops working. I say, 'Okay, life, what's going on?' It kicks in, it kicks in. And those three words: surrender, responsibility and commitment—that's what shapes my relationship with life. Thank you for giving it back to me.

PENNY: *I'm realizing as you're talking that I left one out, and that is intuition. It seems like you really rely on your intuition for your sense of power.*

RACHEL: I do, I do. I rely on my intuition and intellect to be buddies. They really are buddies; they weren't for a long time.

PENNY: *Really? You…?*

RACHEL: No, no. When I was going through law school it was intellect, intellect, intellect. And I absolutely ignored intuitive messages that would have made that experience a lot easier. So then I said, 'Forget the intellect, I'm just going with intuition, intuition, intuition,' and told the part of me that could stand up in front of large groups and help mediate to just take a walk. But now that those two come together, that's where my power comes from—not denying any of those parts of myself. And having them surrender to each other is really what's working.

PENNY: *That's a lesson to me, because I see you work and you seem so integrated. I think, 'She must have been born that way,' as opposed to* *someone like me who operates so much from my head. I'm just learning how to focus from my whole body. So, I'm glad you gave that as an example.*

I just want to get back to racism for a minute, which you mentioned earlier, because that's such a clear instance of power imbalance in this country. How can your white sisters best support you as a woman of color?

RACHEL: When we spoke earlier about this, I said that one of the strongest ways that my white women friends can support me is to love themselves. If they love themselves with a profound and very deep and fully accepting love, then they are not coming to me from a need that says 'Take care of me,' where that would characterize the relationship. There have been white women who have come to me with that kind of need, and it feels as though I am objectified and seen as 'the Loving Black Woman' or 'the Strong Black Woman' or 'the X Black Woman.' That's not a relationship that is mutually nourishing and supportive.

True friendship with white women comes where there is some match of the degree of self-love that we have. Otherwise, things fall through the cracks that split open where that self-love is not present. The inheritance of an antagonism between Black people and white people in this country is formidable. If there is not that degree of self-love, and something comes up in the relationship—like tensions, differences, misunderstandings—it has been easy for me to slip into roles or stereotypes that are difficult to get out of. And I'm not just talking about 'hearts and flowers;' I'm talking about self-love that comes from a deep self-knowledge and self-acceptance.

The other thing is to simply *ask the question* of the Black women's organizations, such as the National Black Women's Health Project, that you are in contact with. Ask, 'How can I support you?' rather than assuming that you *know*. Ask the question and then be willing to listen and ask more questions about the answer.

We have many different cultures in this country and they're not just racially determined. They're determined by class, they're shaped by region, they're shaped by educational opportunity or lack thereof. They're shaped by different work experiences. I no longer assume that a word that someone uses means the same thing to them that it means to me, if I think about the many differences that may exist between us. I'm not usually afraid anymore of appearing stupid or of asking some-one to please explain what they mean. Sometimes, I still get a defensive answer or the person I'm talking to will wonder why I'm taking such pains. But usually my effort to listen really helps to create a bridge. And that's the kind of support I ask for from my white women friends, and that I receive—that support to really listen. To *really* listen, rather than in our desire to be helpful and sisterly with each other, to overlook the very real differences that exist between us.

Perhaps we can delight in and mutually benefit each other with those differences if we acknowledge them fully and explore them. Acknowledge their power and explore them with true caring. That's why I come back to that notion of self-love. If I am interested in entering into relationship with someone, it is based on a true caring, and I let that caring serve as my guide. What I give to the white women that I recognize as sisters is what I hope to receive and is the most important form of support: that quality of *attention*, without some preconceived notion of what will come back in response. I have my hopes of what will come back, but I'm learning not to expect it as my right.

That's another thing—often there's a sense of entitlement that I feel coming from white women who hope to be engaged with me. There's a sense that we're all the same. One of the ways that I make my way around in this world is to have certain filters, and I do have a filter for unknown entities with a certain pigment of skin. If I don't know or have any experience [with someone], there is a wariness there, as a result of some pretty horrendous experiences. My heart is precious. I don't let just anybody in. I don't. *Period.* So there may be some limits on the degree of intimacy that is possible. I'm not going to fake intimacy any longer. I've had white women come to me and act as though they expect me to treat them like the colored woman who raised them. And a lot of times I do fall into that role pretty easily. But Sisterhood is not an entitlement. Sisterhood is a gift. It's something that is developed, to be honored and respected.

PENNY: *Thank you Rachel, for that.*

I'd like to shift the focus a bit and ask you, who are your heroes, your heroines?

RACHEL: Well, I just found a new one—Fran Peavey. I really respect and honor her; she has taught me so much in the short time we have come to know each other...

Gandhi and his commitment to having his life of spirit translate into action and to create a world that would reflect that place of spirit he so believed in...

Martin Luther King, Jr.—he was able to live in a time and do work that amazes me. I'm amazed that he was able to do that and not hate...

My mama. She's an incredible human being, and at the age of seventy-four she's helping a community turn itself around. It's very inspiring the way she is helping a community raise itself, where all the other institutions and possible sources of that kind of support have absolutely abandoned this community. And I see young person after young person come out of there, with the influence of the group that she works with, and create lives for themselves and get over that hopelessness...My mama.

> I am a drummer's daughter
>
> daughter of pounding
> daughter of sound
> of dancing
>
> I am
> a child of music
> child of movement
>
> She
> who
> has
> learned
> to
> be
> quiet
>
> and still

excerpted from the poem "Bringings Up and Comings Round" ©1986 Rachel Bagby

Photo by Penny Rosenwasser

Veronika Cohen

JANUARY 1990

"When people ask me, 'Are you optimistic or pessimistic?' my answer is 'I'm neither; I'm working.' Because if I meet somebody or something that I don't like, I think maybe I can change it."

Veronika Cohen is an Halachicly Observant, or Orthodox Jew, who works in her spare time as a musicologist at Hebrew University in Jerusalem. Since mid-1988, she has spent most of her time organizing dialogue groups to bring Israelis and Palestinians together to try to understand each other's points of view. Originally, these meetings would alternate meetings between Israeli homes and Palestinian homes in the West Bank. Since the Gulf War, however, and the increased travel restrictions barring many Palestinians from crossing the Green Line into Israel, these meetings must now be held on the West Bank. While some groups are ongoing, others meet on a short-term basis. Participants average fifteen to thirty per group. At the time we spoke, over ten of the groups were meeting bi-monthly. How are people attracted to them? Essentially by word of mouth, Veronika says—in her own synagogue and in a circle of interested Palestinians.

Veronika's demeanor is gentle and alert—her round shoulders carry wisdom, kindness and hard work. From deep within her bubbles forth the humor of the ages.

I spoke with Veronika shortly after the December, 1989 international peace actions in Jerusalem.

VERONIKA: I became very active about a year before the intifada. I read a newspaper story about how we were treating Palestinian prisoners, and I had this unbearable feeling that I either had to leave the country or I had to work day and night to change the situation. I didn't see leaving the country as a solution. You can take the Israeli out of Israel, but you can't take Israel out of the Israeli.

PENNY: *What did you hope to accomplish by organizing the dialogue groups?*

VERONIKA: I thought that even those small-scale contacts between a number of Israelis and a number of Palestinians were crucially important.

PENNY: *Because?*

VERONIKA: I think it contributes to change, in both the minds of Israelis and the minds of Palestinians. To me, the long-term dialogue groups are the important ones because there you really have a chance to grow, to develop, to change. I feel deep within myself that I have changed, I have grown. And I see it among my friends, both Palestinians and Israelis. I think I still have the same political opinions or views that I had before, but I have completely different emotional reasons for having the same views.

PENNY: *Can you give me an example?*

VERONIKA: A lot of us in the peace camp felt, and still feel, that the Palestinians deserve to have a state of their own for both moral and security reasons. A lot of people feel that basically we would be more secure if they had their own state and we had our own state, and it would protect ourselves from within, not being intermingled as we are. Yet a lot of people feel that once they have their state, we really don't care what happens to the Palestinians. They would like to put up an iron curtain between us and them and say, 'All right, now you have your country, we have our country and now we don't need to have anything to do with each other anymore.'

Now that I've gotten to know Palestinian people, it seems to me both impossible and undesirable to have to try to separate our fates. Whatever the solution will be in terms of politics, I think it will have to include at least open borders or some kind of a confederation, in which we will continue to have very close contact with each other. You begin to realize that our fates are intertwined—that we need them and they need us. Whereas in the beginning, a lot of us felt that what we needed was separation.

A lot of it is simply personal. We feel that these people have become very close friends, so the idea that we wouldn't see each other anymore if there was peace is something that's really unthinkable. I think this kind of close personal contact is missing for a lot of Israelis who are very afraid of Palestinians. Who don't trust them. I think it's possible not to trust a sort of faceless mass of people, but it's something else to sit across from a friend at the table and say to him, 'I don't trust you.' And I think the kinds of things that happen in the dialogue are because we have an opportunity to say this to each other and then listen to the answer. And teach them why we don't trust them and let them teach us why we could trust them.

They give us very good, rational reasons why it is also in their interest to live with us in peace. Not because they are morally committed to peace, but because it is in their practical interest.

The topic that has come up in every group is the topic of fears. To Palestinians, at first it is shocking and unthinkable that Israelis are afraid. We have very good historical reasons for being afraid. And as time went on and they began to understand our fears, I think it really changed their relationship to us. So they learned about Jewish history. They learn about our traumas that we carry around with us. And we learn about their traumas. It's something very very different from reading it in a book.

PENNY: *Given what they experience in the Occupation, they are still willing to learn about Jewish history?*

VERONIKA: They are very well informed about Jewish history. I think they are much better informed, by and large, than we are. But together with that they are also willing, not only to learn, but to become engaged emotionally. Like they learned about the Holocaust from us. Not learning about history, but learning about our personal experiences, as each person in the group talked about their family, where they came from, how their family survived the Holocaust.

And so they become very very careful even in the language that they use. They were once trying to think of an expression, and they said, 'Well, this is a solution that we're looking for, but this is not the ultimate solution'—they were very careful not to say *final* solution, because they realized that that word is not a word that we can put up with.[1]

PENNY: *In terms of both the Israelis and the Palestinians in the groups, are the people that are involved from different classes and different educational backgrounds?*

VERONIKA: By and large, it's better-educated people in the long-term dialogue groups. But there have been a lot of shorter-term dialogues.

For example, in Dheisheh Refugee Camp we organized a press conference once for the people of Dheiseh to come and tell their message to the Israelis. Workers and very simple people came. There was a family whose thirteen-year-old daughter had been killed. And the girl's parents came to talk about the fact that they're still willing to live with us in peace. Or families whose houses had been blown up recently. And they came to talk about the fact that they're still willing to live with us in peace. In Jericho a lot of farmers came. But really everybody comes to the more open, one-time meetings.

PENNY: *Does it ever get really angry?*

VERONIKA: We try to keep a respectful tone. I think some of the unwritten rules are that every topic is acceptable, but everything has to be treated in a respectful tone. There have been very hot moments talking about violence, because a lot of Israelis look at the Palestinians as being the violent ones in this intifada. And so there are discussions about stones versus guns, and the Palestinians get very angry when Israelis talk about stone-throwing as a violent activity. They feel that basically their kids are facing Israeli soldiers with their bare hands. On the other hand, rocks can kill.

Maybe I'll tell you a story. One of my students once approached me and said that he would like to meet Palestinians. He told me that in the Reserves he held a very high position in the army. But he said that he basically considers himself a member of the peace camp, and he would like to meet Palestinians. I told him that there was a group meeting in a few days' time in one of the Palestinian villages and I would be delighted if he came. He said, 'Me, go there? You must be joking. I'm afraid to go there.' So I said, 'But you just told me that you came back from such and such a place and you were doing such and such, weren't you afraid then?' And he said, 'No, then I had my gun, I had my jeep, I had my soldiers. But to think that I would walk in there without my gun—I would never do it.'

So I think that that's something that maybe is difficult for you, when you're looking at the soldier blindly beating everybody in sight, to think that this person is terrified out of his mind.

PENNY: *Do people cry?*

VERONIKA: There have been times when I had a hard time not crying. I remember when one of our friends was telling us that the army had instituted a new practice of beating children in front of their parents.

Then I think of how I would feel if my children were severely beaten in front of me.

There was a dialogue I wasn't at, I was just told about it. One of the Israelis who came said that he was in favor of transfer. And I understand that one of my Palestinian friends dealt with it in a very sensitive way.

PENNY: *Can you just explain what transfer is?*

VERONIKA: Believing that the Palestinians should be forcibly removed from Israel to some other country. And apparently this Palestinian friend responded by saying that he finds it so hurtful to listen to that, that his first impulse was to get up and leave the room. But he realized that that doesn't solve the problem, and that in a way he's glad that he had the opportunity to meet somebody like that. To understand that even a person who believes in transfer is in fact a human being, a misguided human being, but a human being.

I think the other important thing that comes out of it is that once you become involved in a dialogue group, you feel a commitment to the people with whom you are dialoguing. So that if something happens to them it's very natural that you rush there and you try to help them. When friends are arrested, you start calling your member of Knesset[2] and the press, and the lawyer, and you try to appear at their trial as witness and do your best to get them out of jail.

We were called last year, the night before Passover. We got a phone call that the Israeli authorities were arresting our friends in Jabal Mukaber [a town on the West Bank]. The night before Passover is the night to stay home and clean your oven. But we just dropped everything and ran. And in fact it really helped. They had rounded up all these people, and they were sitting in a field with their hands behind their backs. And we just walked very close and started yelling over the fence, saying, 'We are here, and we hope that you are all right.' They said that the minute we appeared the Israelis stopped beating them.

When the massacre happened in Nahalin, they called us immediately and said that no ambulances were allowed through. So we started calling the Red Cross and the journalists and the embassies, and eventually the ambulances got through. And in Beit Sahour, where we have our closest ties, we really try to keep in touch with them, so whenever something happens we try to be a bridge between them and the outside world.

PENNY: *Are you ever able to get people out of jail or get charges dropped?*

VERONIKA: We've been able to have sentences reduced. By the way, I want to correct an impression. It's not a kind of charitable organization. We don't look at it as 'those poor Palestinians. Let's see if we can help them.' But it's the way you would behave towards your friends. If your friends are in trouble, you help. And unfortunately, in the present situation, they're more likely to be in trouble. But I think it's that kind of a feeling, that if there was a real situation in which I would need their help, they would rush to my aid.

PENNY: *Are there any risks for you in doing this work?*

VERONIKA: A group of five of us were nearly run over last summer. A settler [a member of a Jewish-Israeli settlement on the West Bank] tried to run us down with his truck. The case is still in the courts. So there is violence, there definitely is violence. A lot of people have been getting threats in the mail or by phone.

One of the larger events that we had planned in Beit Sahour was a Shabbat [Jewish Sabbath] that about twenty-five families, about seventy-five people all together, spent at Beit Sahour. Most of us were religious Orthodox Jews. We came with families and babies, we brought kosher foods from Jerusalem, and the people in Beit Sahour gave us an empty house to use as our synagogue.

Friday night we had dinner together for all the children. The Israeli and the Palestinian children ate together, and then they went out to play. They immediately became friends and somehow managed to communicate. Then the adults sat down to dinner together.

I think the very fact that Israeli parents could just let their kids go outside to play—they just disappeared into the evening somewhere in a Palestinian town, and nobody was particularly worried about what was happening to their child—was maybe one of the most important achievements. We were hoping that the Israeli public would understand that it's possible to go into a Palestinian town, it's possible to sleep there at night. Nobody will slit your throat in the middle of the night. Nobody will drink your baby's blood. You could go there alive and you could come home alive, and really, it felt like a taste of the world to come.

The army didn't know that we were there until the next morning when they heard it on the radio, and then they began to look for us. When they found us they immediately declared the area a 'closed military area.' Which, unfortunately, is one of the tools that the army uses against the peace camp to really keep Israelis from meeting Palestinians. The minute you appear somewhere, it becomes a 'closed military area.' But fortunately, a member of the Knesset who was with us argued with the commander and said, 'Most of these people are religious; they can't travel on Shabbat.' So they decreed that we could stay until the end of Shabbat. Really, the only disaster was that our hosts spoiled the children. Everything else was perfect.

PENNY: *Have you ever thought of doing the dialogue groups with young people?*

VERONIKA: Yes. We have three groups of young people meeting young people. It's much more difficult. I feel much less satisfied with these meetings. We have tried to let them run it without any interference from adults. And I'm not convinced that this was successful. The Palestinian teenagers were much more open, much more conciliatory, and it was very unpleasant for me to listen to the Israeli kids, who are extremely aggressive. They kept saying over and over, 'But why do you still throw stones at us?' And refused basically to listen to the answers.

PENNY: *Boys and girls?*

VERONIKA: Yes. I really feel that this has to be rethought. They have a lot of misconceptions. And somebody just really needs to fill in facts, at least historical facts. I was very disappointed that the Israeli kids, for example, just weren't really interested in hearing from the Palestinian kids about what their daily lives are like and what it is like to live under occupation.

They said, 'Well, I'm sure it's awful, but it doesn't matter. That's not what we're here for, you know.' They wanted to discuss politics and territorial settlements. And these are all kids who started out from a point of view believing that there should be a Palestinian state, but refused to let themselves become emotionally involved with the Palestinian kids.

I would say that my religious beliefs are basically behind my work. I see it as part of the ethical Jewish tradition. I see no contradiction between what I'm doing and what I believe. I find it heartbreaking that a lot of so-called religious Jews feel that land and power and strict observance of the letter of the law is of a higher priority than ethical behavior towards fellow human beings.

It also makes peace work a little more difficult. I have to rush home on Friday afternoon to be home for Shabbat. I can't participate in a lot of activities on Shabbat, although anything that's within walking distance, I can take part in.[3] Like last Saturday's Human Chain around the wall.[4]

I think the situation is changing. More and more peace groups are aware that there are enough religious people involved so that they have to make provisions for that. I know that a lot of groups that I'm involved in have now made adjustments because I'm involved, and [they] know that you can do things Friday morning as opposed to Friday afternoon.

PENNY: *Since we brought up the Human Chain event which happened last weekend, I'd love to know your reaction—if you think these actions will have any effect.*

VERONIKA: I think that what happened with the Human Chain and other similar events gave me a feeling of dejection, of sort of crying in the wilderness. Because you participate in an event, in a wonderful, beautiful event, and then you look at how it is reflected in the press, and you suffer cognitive dissonance. You don't understand; you think, 'What did the press see that was so different from what I saw?' Because what I saw was an incredibly uplifting, wonderful moment. Really a moment of such hope. And then you turn around and all you see are pictures of violence, which apparently was provoked more by the police than by anybody else.

So this kind of reporting makes you wonder, 'How do you reach the Israeli mind?' I think that is the most important task for the Israeli peace camp, to try to reach the average Israeli who is terrified of Palestinians. And what better medicine for their fear than to see them linking hands with Israelis and saying, 'We want peace.' But if you can't make your voice heard in the press, if the Israelis are somehow kept from hearing this message, then only the convinced are taking this medicine that might cure them of their fear.

Last Sunday, we participated in the event in Beit Sahour where Desmond Tutu came to the Shepherds' Field on Christmas Eve. Both myself and a friend of mine spoke as part of the event. My friend turned to the Palestinians and said, 'This is your chance to tell the Israeli people if you want peace.' And thousands of them yelled Yes! So we were wondering what kind of effect it would have on the Israelis. And it was simply not reported in a *single* Israeli paper. It was not on the radio. It was not on television. It's as if it didn't happen. So I wonder how the Israeli mind is going to be reached.

PENNY: *What do you think?*

VERONIKA: I have no idea. I really have no idea. The average Israeli is not going to go to the Palestinians to ask him, because he's afraid of him. The Palestinian is not allowed to come to the Israeli to tell him what he thinks. And the press does not report our meetings, which are crucial for the average Israeli to know about. So that when Teddy Kollek [the Mayor of Jerusalem] says, 'We are not like Romania [where thousands of protesters were shot by government troops] because we are a democratic country,' I wonder what he means by a democracy. Because in a democracy, it's not just a question of people voting for their leadership; it's also a question of having the information on which you can base a reasonable judgement. And I feel that the press, the government, is basically keeping the Israelis from hearing what they need to hear.

PENNY: *So what keeps you going?*

VERONIKA: Panic. I really have the sense of a unique moment in history. And if we miss it there could be decades, if not hundreds of years, of bloodshed, to pay for this missed opportunity to make peace. And I have this terrible feeling that the Palestinians are moving, and the Israelis are moving, and that we're moving towards each other. But the pace isn't right, and somehow we're going to miss each other and not meet. That by the time the Israelis are going to be ready to make peace, the Palestinians will have lost their patience, and they will be looking for a violent solution. So I am trying to push Israelis to not miss the moment.

PENNY: *Any message of hope?*

VERONIKA: A message of hope…I'm always hopeful. I think the spirit, the Palestinian desire for freedom is an inspiring desire. The same desire that we had in '48.

PENNY: *Do you have any message for the people in the United States? Anything else you would want to say to us, or ways that we can support you?*

VERONIKA: What's very important for us is balanced support from Americans. Americans who go overboard supporting Palestinians only make Israelis more frightened and more entrenched in their views. On the other hand, blind support of the Israeli government's position is probably the worst thing that can happen to us. So some kind of a balanced understanding of the complexity of the problem and gentle pressure to keep us moving towards some kind of political solution.

PENNY: *In this work you've been doing, what are the main things you feel like you've learned? Especially if you think there are lessons to be passed on from your experiences.*

VERONIKA: That's a difficult question. One of the things I'm very aware of is that I've been very fortunate in the way that I've been involved in peace work—I've been very aware of the humanity of everybody. Not only Palestinians but also the Israelis that I disagree with. And sometimes I feel that a Jew or an Israeli who feels as embittered about Israeli policy as I do really has to live here and has to have the daily contact with Israelis, so that you don't demonize your enemy.

You know, I'm aware of the fact that the same person who can break the arms of a Palestinian can turn around and be a very compassionate doctor or a very compassionate teacher. In other words, there is such complexity to the situation. There are no angels and no devils. The woman who works in the grocery store in our neighborhood is a very very lovely woman. She employs a Palestinian in her store and treats him like her own son. She's a kindergarten teacher. Once when I was ill she asked my daughter, 'Who is going to cook for you for Shabbat?' She was ready to close up her shop and come cook for me. Then when the intifada started, I heard her say to one of her kindergarten children who said her father was in the army, 'Well, you tell your father for me to break the arms and legs of every Palestinian.'

You have to realize that we're not dealing here with angels or devils. There's no black and white. Nothing is simple. And all the people who are involved in the situation are suffering. The Left and the Right and the Palestinians. I think maybe that's one of the most important things that I've learned. Because it's very very important to keep the perspective of the people who disagree with you, to keep that in mind as well.

Their perspective is that they're fighting for their survival. And that I'm pitting ethics against survival. And they're basically arguing that suicide is unethical. I have to argue with them and say that the solution that I am proposing is not suicidal. And I have to force myself on them to make them see this viewpoint. But I think that that's a very important lesson to remember: that it's not that these people are bad, although some of them probably are—there is always that percentage who are simply evil, and they are really enjoying this—but that's really a very small percentage. The vast majority are people who feel that they would endanger our survival if they would even allow themselves to feel for the Palestinians. And so they refuse to feel. They refuse to see Palestinians as human beings because it's easier for them if they don't.

Maybe the other important thing to realize, that keeps me going, is that human beings can change. Even if I look at somebody whose viewpoint is completely opposite from mine, I don't think it's a waste of time to talk to him. Because his ideas can change as well as my ideas can change. I think maybe that's the greatest cause for optimism. So when people ask me, 'Are you optimistic or pessimistic?' my answer is, 'I'm neither, I'm working.' Because if I meet somebody or something that I don't like, I think maybe I can change it.

N O T E S :

1. The Final Solution was Hitler's program that led to the killing of six million Jews during World War II.

2. Knesset is the Israeli Parliament.

3. Orthodox Jews cannot drive on Shabbat.

4. On December 30, 1989, 20,000 people—Palestinians, Israelis, Europeans, Americans—formed a human chain for peace around the walls of Jerusalem's Old City. As participants started returning home, Israeli police violently attacked the non-violent demonstrators.

Photo by Susan E. Dorfman

FREEDOM FIGHTER

Suha Hindiyeh

DECEMBER 1989

"I don't believe in one hero, because you can learn from the people more than you learn from one person...He or she might be good in...several things, but not in everything. I believe...collective work brings success—more than one person's work."

Suha Hindiyeh is the lively and multiskilled co-founder and current director of the Palestinian Women's Studies Center, an officially licensed institution by the Israeli government, which documents and compiles information on Palestinian and other Arab women's movements, as well as other international women's movements. Currently the Center is focused on developing a women's library, publishing a women's magazine, organizing marketing for cottage industries and working on pressing social/domestic issues, such as assistance for battered women. When I first spoke with Suha in December of 1989, the Center was situated in a modest house just outside Jerusalem. (It has since moved to a spacious five-room flat.) It had the usual desks, file cabinets and typewriters, and hummed with the bustle of women running in and out.

Suha juggles her administrative responsibilities at the Center with her teaching duties as professor of sociology at Bethlehem University. She speaks in a direct and engaging style that compliments her vast knowledge, her deep sensitivity and her quick and ready smile. I caught Suha just before she was to escort Archbishop Desmond Tutu on part of his tour of the Occupied Territories.

At the time of this interview, the Center was part of the Palestinian Federation of Women's Action Committees; currently the Women's Studies Center is an independent organization. Although the Palestinian Federation of Women's Action Committies is only one of several Palestinian Women's Committees organizations, the information included here is true of most of these organizations.

PENNY: *Suha, can you give me some background information on the formation of the Women's Action Committees?*

SUHA: The Palestinian Federation of Women's Action Committees was established in 1978—the first grass-roots women's committee to be established in the Occupied Territories, the West Bank and the Gaza Strip. When they started the Women's Action Committees, it was about eight to ten women, largely from cities, who were educated—well let's say, petty-bourgeois. They found out that large numbers of our women are still socially oppressed, and there are many social problems they're facing, in addition to the national oppression that we are going through as a whole.

Given that, they started going into villages, refugee camps and cities, undertaking house-to-house visits, talking to the women to see what their needs are. Also, not only talking to women, but to the family as a whole. Because we cannot deny the fact that we are a traditional society or, let's say, semitraditional society, and probably ninety percent, if not more, of our women living in villages and refugee camps are socially oppressed, illiterate and so forth.

Why did we talk with the family as a whole? Because when a woman wants to make a decision to join a committee of her own, the family should know about it—the father, the husband, the brother— and the idea should be accepted. Of course, it wasn't easy at the beginning to recruit women into units and committees of their own, because there were objections from their male partners. It took some time until they understood that when a woman is recruited into a committee in a unit of her own, undertaking different activities and programs, it will benefit her as a person, and it will benefit her family as a whole.

When we asked women, 'What are your needs?' they said, 'If you want us to be recruited into committees, we have to find somewhere to put our children.' The need for kindergartens and nurseries was raised, and then they started establishing kindergartens and nurseries all over. The other need was that a large number of our women are illiterate, so literacy classes started to open. It has taken us some time, but now there are over 220 units of women's action committees, consisting of fifteen to thirty women each. You find them in every village, in every refugee camp and in the cities. The total number now exceeds eight thousand women members all over the West Bank and the Gaza Strip.

PENNY: *In addition to the kindergartens, nurseries and literacy classes, don't these committees have economic projects as well?*

SUHA: Other projects were going ahead, projects such as sewing and knitting, because women used to ask about these skills; they wanted to learn them. We know that large numbers of women, not only in our country, but all over the world, do knitting and sewing—it's part of their domestic work. We went ahead with training in these skills for the women and eventually found out that indirectly we were reinforcing the traditional role of women. Given that, we've started thinking of new projects that won't be as traditional.

For example, we started food-processing projects. Somebody might argue that food-processing projects are also domestic, women's work. But actually when women undertake a food-processing project on premises of their own, in a small factory, it won't be considered a traditional role because they have to come in contact with merchants to sell the product which they are producing and to go into the market to buy the raw materials. They are getting involved with the society as a whole.

One of these projects, in fact, is the Abasan Biscuit Factory. It's an especially interesting project, and we're really proud of it. Why? Because in Abasan Village, in the Khan Younis area and the Gaza Strip, we have a kindergarten. Women there used to make biscuits in a small oven for the children, and eventually some of these women came up to the executive committee here and said, 'We want to expand biscuit-making to be able to start marketing it in the village, in the Khan Younis and Gaza, and eventually to sell all over the Occupied Territories.'

Of course, as a grassroots organization, we cannot afford to buy them high-technology machinery. We gave them as much money as we could, and then they put in some money from their own pockets. They went on their own to the market to buy a large oven, which is for the Abasan women a big step—to go into the market here in the West Bank or in Jerusalem, to buy a large oven and transfer it to Abasan. And they have rented premises, and now, after about four to five years, the project is going on very well. They've started to be an income-generating project, being able to pay the salaries of the women workers, pay for the rent, electricity, raw materials, whatever is needed for this project. Now, I would say that it's one of our best projects, and they've started marketing in the Gaza Strip as a whole.

Another project that we have is the Isawiya village project. It is a brass-engraving and enamel-work project, which is considered a big step forward for women, because brass-engraving and enamel-work have never been within the realm of women's work. Not only, I would say, here in Palestine, but in general it's considered male work.

PENNY: *So how did that get started?*

SUHA: In one of our exhibitions, a male artist was exhibiting some of his works. Women members of the Women's Action Committees from the Isawiya village in the suburbs of East Jerusalem got interested in this skill, and they asked us if they can be trained to undertake such a project. We asked this male artist, and he's now training them. Now, I can say that they are really trained, and the enamel and brass-engraving work is being sold here and even exported abroad.

Another project which has been established during the intifada is a baby food project, which is a pioneer work among grassroots organizations. A nutritionist working with us found out that in villages and refugee camps, among low-income people, children are either malnourished or underweight. All the baby food that we have here is either imported from abroad or is Israeli-made, and it's very expensive for these families to buy.

The nutritionist started thinking of legumes and similar foods that we do have here in this country in abundance. She found out that chickpeas and whole wheat mixed together have a protein that is almost like meat protein. This baby food is now being sold in the clinics and childcare centers and has been sent abroad for testing so it can be marketed internationally. Another project involves raising goats and making lebena, strained yogurt.

And of course all our projects are run and managed by women. At the moment, women workers and women coordinators of production for the Women's Action Committees are taking a course in management, accounting and bookkeeping to be able to run these projects efficiently. And these production projects do have a simultaneous aim: to bring women into the production sphere, to earn a living, because we believe that women are equal to their male partners and our program activities are going in that direction.

The other aim of these projects is to be able to boycott Israeli products and, at the same time, to help build our Palestinian infrastructure for the coming state, because our infrastructure has been destroyed during the years of Israeli occupation.

As a nation, we're approaching, hopefully very soon, having our own independent state. Given that, we have to start thinking of laying the basis for a strong women's movement. That's why we're planning to undertake the search and attempt to put forth women's legislation in every aspect—family law, women workers and many other issues related to women—drafting these legislations and discussing them with the other women's committees, with the Palestinian women's movement as a whole, so as to present it to our government when it comes, hopefully soon.

As Women's Action Committees, we have a simultaneous aim to raise the socio-economic consciousness of women on a feminist level and to make women aware of our national problem.

PENNY: *So a woman is trained, for example, not just how to do the brass engraving, she'd also have courses in...*

SUHA: We train them to become leaders in the community, to be able to ask for their rights, to go to school. From a feminist point of view as well, we want our women to be decision-makers in every aspect. On a social and political level.

PENNY: *Do the men want that?*

SUHA: Well [laughs]...no doubt there is a change in men's mentality. But still, you do understand that it's not only our men who do not want women to be equal to them; it's the case all over the world, and we have to fight for equality, as women.

Our offices here coordinate work with the different units all over, and I should here mention strongly that just because there is a director, it doesn't mean that our work is not done collectively. We do work collectively—it's not one person's decision. It's eight thousand women's decision.

In terms of structure, several women are elected from every unit as representatives of each of the eleven districts in the cities, villages and refugee camps of the West Bank and the Gaza Strip. These representatives participate in the Executive Committee, which then sends representatives to the Higher Committee, composed of about 150 women. Along with the collective structure, there is a president and vice-president of the Women's Action Committees.

PENNY: *And then does each unit decide what project they're going to do?*

SUHA: Yes, according to the needs of their community. And that's why we say that we do not impose on them what we want—because they live in this village, in this area, and they know what their needs are. They come up and say, 'Look, we need this project, if possible, to be implemented.' We ask, 'Why do you need it?' We discuss it, and then if there is a possibility, the project will be implemented.

PENNY: *What effect have the Women's Action Committees had on the intifada, and what effect has the intifada had on the Women's Action Committees?*

SUHA: If it weren't for the structure and the organization of the Women's Action Committees and the other women's grassroots organizations— organizations working for the last ten to twelve years among women, in the field, in the city, in the village, in the refugee camps—women might not have been able to be as effective in the intifada as they are now.

We do not deny the fact that Palestinian women have been involved in politics and in the general national movement since '48, if not pre-'48, in military actions, in demonstrations, and so on, but now it's taking a different perspective, a different vision. It's not only that they are going out into the streets demonstrating, it's not only that they're going into the Red Cross or any other institution doing sit-ins. It's not only that they are going to hospitals visiting the wounded, or distributing contributions, food, whatever is needed if a village or refugee camp is under siege. It's more than that. They are participating in the struggle as equal to men, which no doubt, indirectly and directly as well, is bringing social change.

But, as we know, social change does not come out of the blue moon, just in a minute or two. It has to take time…and we can feel it now, among our women, that social changes are taking root. In addition to demanding their national political rights, they are demanding as well their social rights. But it's all mixed together.

PENNY: *In the United States, during the Second World War, the U.S. needed women to work in the munitions factories. And then as soon as the men returned, they sent the women back home and the men got their jobs back. I know that in Algeria, women during the liberation struggle were very active and then [laughs]…so you understand what I'm asking—how will you keep that from happening here?*

SUHA: Well, a nation, any nation, should learn from the experience of other nations, and we do say we do not want another Algeria, in respect to women's issues. We do not want another America during the Second World War. We're not ready to go back home after the independence, and we know that the struggle is going to be harder when we're going to have our state. Okay, it was said in the Palestinian Charter for the Palestinian State that men and women are equal, but it's an elastic word. We have to work hard for it, to attain this equality.

Here I would like to say that there is a difference between Algeria and Palestine. Why? Because—this is my own personal analysis—in Algeria during the revolution, there was not a strong women's movement. Here in Palestine we do have a strong women's movement, but it still has to work even harder in respect to women's rights, women as decision-makers, as equal to their male partners.

PENNY: *Does this movement cross class lines, and does it include women who—I've seen women who appear to be more traditional, maybe in their dress—does it include those women as well?*

SUHA: Among the members of the Women's Action Committees, you'll find women who might wear the Islamic dress—long dresses or shawls on their heads—but it doesn't mean that they are traditional in their mentality. Okay, it takes time for them to be able to put aside the Islamic dress, maybe, but through our program we try to make them understand that it's not the way you're dressed that shows whether you're decent or not.

And at the same time, it's a sensitive issue that we're going through at this stage of the national and the women's movements. When these women are socially aware, they come to understand: 'As long as I'm wearing decent clothes, this is what counts.' We are trying to talk with our women from within the social context in which we're living. We should not impose on them western values. We have our own values. Given that, we have to be aware of all these issues—how to bring women into understanding how to attain their rights. This is the most important thing to us at this stage.

PENNY: *Right now in this period, what are the two or three biggest problems that you're trying to deal with in the Women's Action Committees?*

SUHA: On a national and a political level—that we are under occupation. As Women's Action Committees, or any other grassroots organization, whether it's women's or not, we are facing harassment and brutality from the occupiers. This is the biggest problem that we're working on. We're struggling to attain our freedom.

The other problem is making women aware of the social problems that they are experiencing. And this is what we're trying to do through our different projects and programs, and our discussions with them, to see what their problems are—whether social or psychological—and to train them in different fields. In this respect, it's not only our women, but the nation as a whole.

Because for the last twenty-two years, education has deteriorated, health has deteriorated—all aspects of life have deteriorated as a result of the occupation. It's not easy when you come to think of building up a state after having been under occupation for so many years, and at the same time, as a nation, we've been going through this problem for the last forty years as well.

PENNY: *Some of the Israeli women I've spoken with who are active in the peace movement have said to me that they're realizing the priorities for them in their work are to be working with Palestinian women, to be building those relationships. Is that anything that's important to the women that you're working with?*

SUHA: Now and then we do have meetings with Israeli women from different organizations, and we're attempting to discuss issues frankly with each other. It's not an easy situation, but we have to work on it as hard as possible, and not in one meeting or two meetings. It takes time to be able to open our hearts freely, but it's going on.

PENNY: *Could you tell me some of the lessons that you've learned about what's worked, what hasn't worked and what's important right now?*

SUHA: In any field you work in, you learn a lot. But maybe, as a woman myself, I've learned even more—how to struggle for our rights as women and for my rights as an individual in the society and how to be able to work with women. It's not easy going into villages and refugee camps to be able to talk and convince them, myself being a Jerusalemite living in the city and having been brought up in a Western way. They've taught me a lot.

I recall an incident with a village woman, talking to her about farming. And I asked about the male farmer. She said, 'Look at my hands; I'm the farmer.' You come to know that our women—ninety percent of them, if not more—are working in agriculture. They are the supporters of the family, especially during the intifada, when their husbands, brothers, fathers are being hunted or are in prison. The women are the main breadwinners of the family. Having myself not passed through being on my own, I realized you can learn a lot from them. You learn how to be strong and struggle for life.

PENNY: *Who are your heroes, your heroines?*

SUHA: All Palestinian women. I don't believe in one hero, because you learn from the people more than you learn from one person. The Palestinian nation as a whole and Palestinian women are the heroes that I look for. And not for an individual. I don't believe in charismatic leaders.

PENNY: *Why not?*

SUHA: Because nothing is done by one person. He or she might be good in one thing, or several things, but not in everything. I believe in collective work, and collective work brings success—more than one person's work.

PENNY: *What do you feel has been your greatest victory so far—either for yourself or for the Women's Action Committees—your greatest achievement, your happiest moment?*

SUHA: When I work among Palestinian women, in the village, in the refugee camp, when I see their sufferings, and from these sufferings, they still do have hope and yearn for peace.

PENNY: *What message do you have for the women in the United States?*

SUHA: That we Palestinians are a nation that have suffered a lot. As women, all over the world, we've suffered a lot and we're still suffering, and women of the world should work hand in hand for a better universe. And we are a nation who do have rights, and we should attain our rights. We do not ask for pity, we ask for real work—among all the nations of the world.

PENNY: *How can we support your struggle?*

SUHA: When you understand our suffering, I think you can find the way to help.

Photo by Catherine Busch-Johnston

Deena Metzger

JUNE 1991

"The challenge is...to be available to bring the beauty through...to open the eyes, to open the heart. To feel compassion on a regular basis. To strip myself down to wherever I have to go. To suffer whatever it is I have to suffer, in order to know what I have to know. Not to be afraid of that, even though it hurts a lot. Or to be afraid and not let being afraid stop us."

Midafternoon, Summer Solstice: shadows stretch their sleepy necks across Lake Vera, as our canoe rests lightly against a log in a small inlet. Deena silently beckons me to catch on my tape recorder the throaty bellow of a bullfrog beginning its song. Our interview over, she gently brushes a paddle through the water, as we absorb the awesome sounds of the place we inhabit.

Deena Metzger is visionary and teacher—thinker, therapist, poet. On journeys through Europe's concentration camp memorials, Greece's ancient mystical sites and the golden-lit stonescape of Jerusalem, she packs a bag of courage and compassion. Deena speaks slowly and deliberately, often using multi-layered metaphors. I'm riveted by the power of this tiny woman, filled with the sense of a world more vast than I have barely touched.

PENNY: *I know you, Deena, as one of the most integrative, compassionate and creative teachers I've had. You've taught me about peeling back the layers to reveal the tyrant of self-hatred inside, and then you've* *shown me ways to diminish that tyrant. You've helped me learn to imagine, and thus project, how the world could be—to envision very concretely what I'm trying to change. These times feel so dark, and you've been such a guide through the darkness. As women in these troubling times, what do you see as our greatest challenge, right now?*

DEENA: The *only* challenge is saving the planet, whether it's the challenge to us as women or the challenge to us as people. If we don't do that, everything else is academic. For me, the question is: how do we reintegrate ourselves as human beings into a world society, into an ecological society? Because it seems that our *differentiating* ourselves *from* the rest of the natural world has actually led to the destruction of the world.

PENNY: *Do you want to go into that?*

DEENA: Sure. It has always seemed important to human beings that we experience ourselves as different from animals and plants. We have wanted to appear superior, more closely related to the angels or the gods. And in that thrust of religious and political systems, we have completely lost our balance and lost our place. It's very interesting to try to unlearn all those beliefs, to come back to another kind of wisdom in which we are simply another creature—*no more important.* And in part because of the way we have distinguished ourselves, possibly less important; because we contribute *less* to the world as a whole than any other creature. We have removed ourselves from the community, and by doing that, we are destroying the base in which we live. Ultimately we will discover that we cannot feed on ourselves. We will have devoured everything else, and we will be alone in an empty world with our hunger. And then it will be over.

PENNY: *So that's the problem…*

DEENA: That's the problem.

PENNY: *Where do we go next?*

DEENA: I don't think we have to *go* somewhere. I think we have to stop. Everything that we do each day that's *less* than what we did before is probably useful. In the sixties, Dan Berrigan[1] said, 'Don't just do something. Stand there.' He was talking about being a witness, about that moment when you assess what needs to be done. Part of what we have to do is to stop long enough to find out what to do. But also, every time we don't do something, we're not using up resources. It's very simple, you know? The greed that we have for accomplishment, for manifestation, for success, for presenting ourselves, is insatiable. We have to find ways to be like the trees or the wolves, to live in that kind of relationship with the planet. It is a shock to our ego to think about that. We don't like it. Because we're always thinking about better and better, more and more.

PENNY: *Well, I wasn't thinking about that so much, as being an activist myself—and given the scope and the depth of the problems in the world—it feels like there is so much 'to do' to create peace, end homelessness, feed people, provide health care...*

DEENA: Those arguments are very compelling and very logical. I don't know that I really have an answer. I mean, I *know* I don't have an answer. All I know is that there is a kind of—and I feel it myself—*hysteria* about doing something. And that's the wrong way. At this point, we must think about qualitatively and drastically changing the way we live—but we can't do something till we know something. And we don't know *anything*. We're not as smart as we thought we were.

PENNY: *But if we don't do anything, won't the Right Wing take over even more and destroy everything in a very short amount of time?*

DEENA: You know how often we've elected people and it became the same story? We couldn't understand it. We thought, 'Oh, if we only got A into office, or B into office, or C into office, it would be different.' But once they were in office, the system was so pervasive that things went on as usual.

When we talk about being activists—and I certainly have been in my life, and probably still am—we're so often motivated out of terrible concern for what's going on and pain at what's existing in the world. And anger. And hate. And that is no longer motivation that serves us. Like it or not. So the question is, what would we do if we allowed ourselves to feel enormous, unbearable love for the planet? We would know more what to do if we stopped to feel that. If I'm sitting at home all the time trying to protect these trees that I never get a chance to see, and I'm writing hundreds of letters on pieces of paper made from these trees—I think there's a problem. How can we get back to those very basic feelings of connection with the universe? With the planet? With the creatures? And lastly, with the humans, with those people that we don't know. With the strangers. And try to protect them.

PENNY: *How do we do that?*

DEENA: It's a desperate process of going inside. You really have to break off the layers of culture and intellectual ideas. It is about coming to love the Other. If I only protect my family, or my friends, I'm going to make choices on their behalf that may very well hurt others. If I worry first about people that I *don't* know, if I try to open my heart to them and make decisions and say, 'What's good for that person, let it also be good for my family,' then I'm in another place. It's very hard to do.

It has to do with scrutinizing ourselves to discover the place where we make enemies. Where we live out enemies. And actually where the whole notion of enemy is within us. Because to a great extent, we define ourselves by who our enemies are. 'I'm against the loggers.' Or, 'I'm against [George] Bush.' I don't think he wants to go down in history as the man who destroyed the planet. I really don't. And I think about how we demonized Saddam Hussein, how we demonized the Arab people. Or whoever it is that we don't like. And the way my people have been demonized—I mean people literally thinking that Jews have horns, you know? We do that to each other. We can't do it anymore. We just can't do it anymore.

And we cannot look at the planet as the means for supporting human life. Nor can we look at animals, or nature, as being expedient because they support us. Now we're thinking about ecology, because we realize we're not going to survive without an ecological under-standing. But we're still trying to figure out which plant we can do without and which plant we can't do without. We look at the rainforest and say, 'We've got to save the rainforest because it's useful for medicine.' *No.* We have to save the rainforest because each one of those plants is precious. And maybe they offer themselves to us in some way. But then we have to make an offering *back* that's equal.

A long time ago, I had what I suppose was a vision, an audible vision. I was driving in my car, and I heard a voice say: 'Forgive those who have died young, or whom you feel have left too early. Maybe they were pulled out. And maybe they didn't volunteer to be here at the end.' I thought to myself, 'Well, I certainly haven't volunteered to be here at the end.' The voice continued and said that some people, like it or not, have volunteered either to make a difference or to be a witness to the end. I was very interested in nuclear disarmament at the time, and the voice said: 'Even if you [meaning the species] disarm completely, if you don't change your ways, we will stop you. Because we're not going to allow this consciousness to go out into the rest of the Universe, as you so intend at this moment.'

So the task is *not* to *do* something. *The task is to change conscious-ness.* To do whatever we can to change consciousness. To come to the place where we know how to live in balance with everything around us. There is a universe we're living in that's made of enormous beauty. And if there's any quality that's universal in the natural world, that is its beauty. Very recently I was looking at this extraordinary canyon, Canyon de Chelly, and I was aware this beauty comes from a great heart. There's a relationship between beauty and heart. The things we *do* are not necessarily of such beauty. Sometimes we manage something of beauty, but not as often as the natural world has managed it. And sometimes we manage things of great heart, and it's very moving. But not as often as the evidence of the great heart in the world.

So we have to become very humble. In the Greek tradition, monumental pride was the flaw that brought everyone down. Hubris. We are being brought down by our monumental pride. We can do something about that.

PENNY: *Thank you. As women, in terms of our role in this, we clearly have to be in touch with our power. Specifically in this country right now, what do you think are the main obstacles keeping us from accessing the power we need to take the leadership, to bring about some of these changes?*

DEENA: Well, I can give you a political answer that you know very well, and so I won't go into it. Because you are certainly aware of the limitations on women, of the oppression of women, of the lack of access that women have. It's tedious to repeat it. But because women have been so disempowered, we forget what it is we know, and we go after that which is going to kill us like it's been killing the men. As women we have to remember what life is all about. [We have to] give up those newly aroused ambitions, newly aroused because of the advent of the women's movement and the possibilities. Those ambitions will ultimately destroy us.

I myself have been a woman who tried to raise children, and have a career, and be a friend and a lover, and be a writer, and be out in the world. I worked from early in the morning till late at night, and I was driven. Am still sometimes driven.

That's not the way to live a life. And it's not good for the planet. Because it's part of that same escalation, which is misguided. And which very often is involved with ego.

PENNY: *But the work that you've done is so powerful, Deena. It's helped me and probably thousands of women to get in touch with our power, feel good about ourselves, really go deep—and also be out in the world.*

DEENA: It's a tough one, isn't it?

PENNY: *That's why I saved it for you [laughs].*

DEENA: It's a tough one. If everyone lived their life the way I did, it would not be a good world. My task is to find a way to make an offering and to live my life with integrity. You would get the offering by what I said, and also [you would get the offering] if I said nothing, but you just watched me. At this point, I wouldn't want you to watch me quite so much [laughs]. Because that integrity isn't there as much as I would like it to be [sighs]. I work with so many people who are driven, and we don't have time to *think.* And not having time to think, we don't act properly all the time; we act out of expediency or we act out of desperation. We don't have time to sit with nature and learn from it. It's easier to learn from a book about the birds than to sit and watch them.

It takes time, and real stillness, to sit and listen to the voices that want to speak to us from other realms. Because, you know, we're not going to figure it out by ourselves. And there are inner voices, deities, sacred spirits, that would guide us if we had the peace of mind to listen to them. I watch someone like the Dalai Lama, or Thich Nhat Hanh,[2] and I see how rigorously they pursue the contemplative and the meditative, as well as try to make political change. Thich Nhat Hanh says that he would be nowhere if he didn't take the time to plant his lettuces. After the Vietnamese War when he was filled with a rage he could not bear, he went into retreat for six years, until he could deal with that anger.

PENNY: *You're talking about balance…*

DEENA: I'm talking about balance. And we're out of balance when things seem so desperate. I'm talking about going the *other* way, slowing down so we can do something. And it feels like the wrong time to do it. But it's the *only* time to do it. I wrote this small poem that several people have put to music:

> They are trying to set fire to the world
> We are in danger
> There is time only to work slowly
> There is no time not to love.

All these things that I'm talking about feel either indulgent or heartless. How can you take time to sit on the lake when the world is burning? When people are starving? When people are in pain or being tortured? But if we don't sit on this lake, this lake is going to disappear. And the torture in part (not entirely) comes from being disconnected with the lake. Of course we have known people who have been very much involved in nature and yet have been very cruel. The Nazis came out of a very big back-to-nature tradition. But it was a certain kind of back to nature, a romantic, bucolic, sentimental view. And the Nazis were full of hubris; they were full of seeing how different they were, how special, the 'best race,' et cetera.

PENNY: *Somewhat like Americans…*

DEENA: Like Americans. And there's another view that comes when you really sit with the trees or the birds for a long time. Suddenly your own sense of superiority dissolves. It's like, I'm thrilled when I write a novel or a poem that I think has beauty. But I really know *I* didn't write it. I sat long enough to bring it through. And I'm really really not speaking now. I look at these trees, and I think, I couldn't get *close* to this. Yet none of what we're looking at would really fulfill our notion of beauty if anyone asked us. We don't think of beauty as dead brown leaves floating gently on this lake, or those odd bare sticks sticking up over there, or that dead tree that's fallen. It's not perfect.

PENNY: *But the light that shines through them makes them look beautiful.*

DEENA: It's the light that shines through, and it is glorious. But I guess what I wanted to say is that we don't know what beauty is. We learn by watching it. But what we would *do*, which we see in our malls and our skyscrapers, doesn't come close to this. If you look closely, you'll learn that you have to learn.

PENNY: *I'd love to hear about what you think has been your greatest challenge?*

DEENA: My greatest challenge is to live the daily life. To create a life that is aware, when all of us fall into unconsciousness all the time. To bring some modicum of consistency, of heart and caring, to every moment. And I know that if I'm exhausted I can't do it.

And the other challenge is to render this. To be available to bring the beauty through, or bring awareness through. My own and then others. To open the eyes, to open the heart. To feel compassion on a regular basis. To strip myself down to wherever I have to go. To suffer whatever it is that I have to suffer, in order to know what I have to know. Not to be afraid of that, even though it hurts a lot. Or to be afraid and not let being afraid stop me.

I'm sitting here and I can't bear it that this might go. I *just* can't bear it. And I worry about all the people who've never seen this, because we've built the world up in such a way that they've never seen it; they don't know what they can lose, or why they're losing their lives.

I'm writing a novel now called *The Other Hand*. It's about the stars and about Nazis. And it's about light and density. And the more I write it, the more I'm aware that there really is a mystery that we've got to fathom. Our consciousness has the possibility of understanding the whole relationship between stars and life and God and this tiny little planet. I mean, there are billions of galaxies, and in each of the galaxies there are billions of stars. We're one tiny tiny bit of dust—imagine! Moving around a very minor star at the edge of a small galaxy, lost somewhere in a probably expanding Universe. What an extraordinary thing! Who could even fathom it? And yet we don't stop to try to understand it. If we did we would be *so careful*, because there's probably not life like this anywhere else. Nor such beauty.

And so the greatest challenge is to save the planet.

PENNY: *Back where we started…A minute ago you said part of your challenge was to not let the fear stop you. That's an issue for me and many women I know. Do you have anything more you can say about how to work through the fear?*

DEENA: Find it exciting. Find it interesting. Use your imagination however you can. Find a myth that makes it okay, so that you're in the myth; say you're Artemis, or Demeter, or Odysseus.[3] Find friends who support you and understand what you're doing. Keep in touch with the gods. And hold onto love as a great passion. If you keep your eye on what you love, it's like a mantra; if you keep your eye on what's precious, the fear goes away. It's like, if you see your kid running in front of a car, you run out and you get that kid. Because your eye is not on the car. *Your eye is on the kid.* So that's how you do it. And…it's only fear [laughs].

PENNY: *Who are your heroes, your heroines?*

DEENA: Some of my heroes or heroines are people that I have had the fortune of knowing. They were glorious people, and they were also wonderfully ordinary and flawed. The closer you get to anybody, the more you see how we're all so flawed [laughs]. It's amazing we get anything done…ah, literature, you know? Stories, novels. The imagination. That's what feeds me. Poetry. Timberwolf that I lived with for fourteen years, and now Isis, his last mate, and Owl who's the new wolf puppy. I really hold onto them, they're completely magical.

PENNY: *One last question. Where's the light, Deena?*

DEENA: I would answer it this way: and where's the dark? Because this is the century of being destroyed by the light—by the bomb, by our minds. We've been blinded by the light. Where's the dark? Where's the place of dream and unconscious in its richest sense? Where's the balance between the light and the dark? We need to spend a great deal of time honoring the spring Equinox and the autumn Equinox. Those times of balance. The light is just next to the dark, and the dark is just next to the light.

PENNY: *Anything else you want to say about women and power?*

DEENA: The power is in the life force. And if women want to be empowered, we must be ruthless and rigorous in our affiliation with the life force. That is true empowerment. And nothing else matters next to that.

N O T E S :

1. Dan Berrigan [1921–] is a former catholic priest and activist for non-violent social change.

2. Thich Nhat Hanh [1926–] is an exiled Buddhist monk, highly revered peace activist and writer from Vietnam who travels worldwide, teaching the importance of combining meditation with social action.

3. In Euro-mythology, Artemis is Protectress of all young living things, Goddess of childbirth and also a skilled huntress.
   Demeter is Goddess of the earth, agriculture, fertility and grain. Her daughter, Persephone, was kidnapped by Hades, God of the Underworld; Demeter went on a relentless search until she found her daughter.
   Odysseus is the hero of Homer's *Odyssey* which represents the human journey through life for fulfillment and self-knowledge. With courage and determination, he never abandons his goal of returning home, and faces many formidable obstacles and setbacks.

Photo by Happy Hyder

MEDIATOR ON THE MOVE

Ying Lee-Kelley

"I have to believe that each one of us can make a difference. Because if I don't have that faith that my work matters, and matters a great deal, then I can't get up in the morning."

A sharp and probing, yet reflective mind; an animated energy that enables her to juggle more projects on a weekly basis than some people take on in a year; a passionate heart that consistently confronts injustice; a fine ear that negotiates through many viewpoints; a vibrant down-to-earth way of speaking that naturally motivates and inspires—these are several of the qualities that drew me to Ying Lee-Kelley. During the Gulf War, I asked Ying onto the radio several times, trusting not only her analysis, but especially her ability to express outrage and *feelings* at a time when so many were discussing military logistics. The following interview, however, was conducted more than a year earlier.

PENNY: *Ying, I'm familiar with you as the Co-Chair of the Oakland-Berkeley Rainbow Coalition but I know you also run Congressperson Ron Dellums' Berkeley office, you've been on the Berkeley City Council and you ran for mayor. You're also in Berkeley's oldest women's group—and you're a mother...In terms of starters, what keeps you going? What keeps you sane?*

YING: I don't know that I'm always very sane. I agree with whoever said that whoever can be sane in this society must be crazy. Like everyone else, I have great ups and downs. I go through manic periods, and I go through very very tired periods which I don't understand and try to figure out. I think it comes from taking on more than I can reasonably do. If I think about it, as I was able to do when I had my last holiday, I think, 'Here I am, tired on my holiday, and when I'm back at work I do all these different things.' I keep going; I think it's mostly from *faith*, which is a funny word for me to use.

PENNY: *Why?*

YING: Well, because I was raised as a Christian, a pretty evangelical fundamental Christian—'rice-bowl Christian,' if you will—a war-time World War II Christian, when people were really desperate and they needed hope. And the Christian Church had something to offer in terms of hope and faith. As I got older and took classes I would ask, as all reasonable children ask 'Why?' I wanted evidence that there was a God, because I didn't believe that a God could be so cruel. I was told that you've got to have faith, and I didn't accept that. I said I don't *have* to have faith.

Well, here I am in my fifties, and I begin to think that I have substituted in some ways my political and my social commitment for religion. It's an article of faith for me, that I *have* to believe that each one of us can make a difference. Because if I don't have that faith that my work matters and matters a great deal, then I can't get up in the morning. There are thousands of terms, I suppose, that can be substituted for faith. Perhaps another term is to say I want to be *alive*, and I want to be alive in the kind of world that I would like to see as a loving, giving world. And I think that there are *enough* of us that share this faith, this commitment to working for a more generous world that we know *can* be possible, that keeps us going.

By the way, I didn't start out like this. I started out as a flash in the pan. I started out as an anti-war activist, just absolutely furious about the war. It was *anger* that drove me, and drove me in a very crazy, very manic way. I wanted to end the war, I wanted to stop the killing. And in the process, I got educated and realized that even though that particular war was over—I'm talking about the Vietnam War in Southeast Asia—that the *causes* of the war are what we need to deal with. As I realized that, I took many deep sighs; I realized I had to readjust myself—that I wasn't going to flake off after the war was over and go back to my private life of family and novels and dinners…a 'well-ordered home life.'

PENNY: *I was going to ask you about that, because I know that you went to Vietnam?*

YING: Yes, in 1973.

PENNY: *What do you see now as the lessons of that time period, of that struggle?*

YING: I think there are thousands and thousands of lessons. What I gained from it, I suppose, is a recognition that as an American I have *tremendous* responsibilities to make sure that—I used to say that we do *good*; now I'm happy to say [that we] do *less damage*. I'm fifty-seven going on fifty-eight—I don't *feel* it, that's my chronological age—and one of the fascinating things about living more than five decades is that history is alive for me. I have seen the world change tremendously and I am constantly trying to make sense of these changes, to understand what they mean for us and how this [knowledge] can direct my life on a day-to-day basis.

PENNY: *Backtracking even farther, I understand that you were born in China? And that you walked out?*

YING: I was born in China in 1932, and I mention that because that was the beginning of the Japanese attack in Northern China, the Marco Polo Bridge attack. Up until 1945, when I was just thirteen, I had never known peace. And I can remember…you know, the war years are very very much impressed upon me. The privation, the unnecessary hunger, the misery, the destruction and the sheer *brutality* of the war is something that I think is very deep within me.

This is why I found the Vietnam War so painful. In the war by Japan against China and the war of Hitler against Europe, it seemed a little more clear who the evil people were. Everyone else was a victim. But for the United States—who we had all seen as one of the 'good guys,' the home of constitutional law and idealism—it was extremely cruel to think that we could go into Vietnam, and in an even more brutal way because it was so impersonal, drop the napalm and the bombs and clear out villages as if…I mean, it's even hard for me to talk about; I just found it totally unbearable. I think it was because of my education—my political education, if you will, my social education as a child in China—that I said, 'As long as I am human, as long as I've got a mind to say that this is wrong, I have a responsibility to do something.'

In this way, living has been enormous fun. And it's been hard. I think I had a tough childhood; but I feel that childhood has in some ways made me a more understanding, more sympathetic person. That's not to say that I can't be a whole lot nicer and better. But the thing that makes me want to do good things and be kind and loving and, I hope, tolerant, is because I've seen too much meanness and cruelty. I don't want to add to it; I want to take away from it, subtract from it.

I've always resented adults saying to children, 'This is the world that you're going to have, and we hope you do better.' I feel that that's a rotten thing to say to kids. As long as you are alive and you hope to do better, *you* should be doing it and asking the kids to help, rather than saying we're passing it on to them. And as women, I don't think we're superior because of being second or third class citizens—though it may make us a little more sensitive, less arrogant...hopefully!

PENNY: *I actually wanted to ask you a little more about this famous women's group that you are a part of. I believe it's been going sixteen or seventeen years?*

YING: Since 1973, for me. And for the other five members it's been going since 1971.

PENNY: *What specifically have you learned about power and control from your experience in that group?*

YING: I think that one of the biggest lessons particularly concerned those of us who were raised in families that said, 'Don't talk about your problems, *especially* don't talk about your problems to a large number of people—that is, more than one or two.' I was taught very early that you don't talk about your *family* problems, your problems with your husband or your parents or your children. Those are really really personal and you have a psychological and a familial loyalty. But I think part of the reason why I'm sane and why most women are sane—and this is one thing that the women's group did for me—is that I've always had one or two friends I could unburden myself to. Up until very recently I couldn't afford therapists and psychiatrists, and I think I was relatively healthy mentally because I had friends to whom I could talk.

And the women's group is politically based. When I was on the City Council and when I was campaigning for Council as well as for Mayor, I could talk about my tremendous anxieties, about whether I was doing the right thing and whether I was presenting myself correctly. It's amazing how now in retrospect one can be so foolish when one is young. I say this, you know, from the distance of great age and wisdom [chuckles].

Even in my late thirties I think I was afraid to admit to vulnerability. It was good to have the women's group, because each one of us had political values that we shared with the others, and we were activists. We acknowledged that we were not therapists; that was not our task nor our function for each other. We were supporting, intelligent, listening friends who could acknowledge each others' fears and say, 'I think you're wrong in this case, think it over!'

PENNY: *When you're depleted now, Ying, how do you fill the empty well?*

YING: Well, let's see, what do I do? Now I belong to *two* groups! In fact, three or four. It's funny, this word 'spirituality'—I've never accepted the word spirituality, mostly because I felt burned by the Church. Spirituality always sounded very mystical, and wishy-washy, and undefinable and if you will, sloppy. Intellectually sloppy. I'm not a mystic and I didn't understand it. But I think that as I've struggled to keep myself from being institutionalized, to keep myself vulnerable and human and approachable and capable of approaching others—I suppose one way to describe that is to say that I value spirituality. And I still don't like the word. I think I prefer humanism.

I just finished reading Riane Eisler's *The Chalice and the Blade*. And I was totally blown away. I not only felt absolutely fed in a personal way, intellectually and emotionally, but I felt that someone had given me a tool with which to look at history. And anything that reinforces my faith in the basic goodness of people—and if you will, the basic goodness in myself, and in people as a part of myself—makes me feel good. I came back just bubbling and saying, 'You've got to read this book, and then let's sit down and talk about it!'

Because I feel that we're in a very desperate race to survive as human beings, as one of many many living species. These lovely warm days that everyone talks about—well, the lovely warm days aren't lovely to me. They strike terror into my heart; I just don't think it's right to have this many warm days. Since the recorded history of weather, there are six years in the 1980's where there have been more hot days in this world than ever before. So I think we've got a lot to do. But it's nice to know that we have got some tools, and that we are capable of saying that 'this is the way the world is, and this is what we need to do.'

PENNY: *Well, what do you think are the priority struggles right now, especially for us as women, today?*

YING: That's the good thing about the Eisler book. One of the concepts that I learned was the 'cooperative society' versus the 'dominating society.' We've all heard these terms before, but I think she gave it a historical precedence that I had never before appreciated. When I look at it, it's *true*. What is *wrong* with so much of what we try to do is that we try to dominate and we try to crush. *Power.*

I tend to see now that the way the 1980's particularly looked upon power is a way whereby one person or one group may exceed that of another. It's oppression and subordination, it's domination and subservience. And I think this is horrible. We do this not only within every institution, it seems to me, but we do this with our physical world. We try to dominate agriculture, we try to dominate our water system, we try to dominate the supply of fuel...

PENNY: *Control it...*

YING: Control it and manipulate it and exploit it and use it, and we don't feed anything back. This has got to end; we've *got* to have another model. And I think this is where women of power, men of power ...we're all powerful, if we would just ACT.

PENNY: *We're leading into the process of leadership, Ying, and that's actually why I most wanted to talk to you. Working with you in the Rainbow Coalition, I've admired your leadership; you're firm, you're clear, yet you keep an openmindedness and a sense of fair play. Can you talk about how you take a stand, while maintaining your integrity and staying open?*

YING: I grew up in a hierarchical, male-dominated, class-dominated, sibling-dominated—you name it! I was bottom of the totem pole. And because I moved so much, I was always the social outcast. So it's easy for me to take a position of subservience, it's easy for me to accede to someone else's desires. And I think that very very often it's the case that then when you are in a position of power, you want to dominate. I always try to integrate, integrate, *integrate*, because there's an intellectual side of me which says 'This is what I want to do,' and then there's the emotional side which may be very blind and do things that I don't want to.

What you've described is what I *try* to do. So it's good of you to mention this. I think that it really comes from having respect for people, and having respect for myself, and saying that I don't ever want to fall into the dominating and dominated pattern—because I despise that pattern. I think that's a good thing about the Rainbow: we try to be as democratic as we can and still function. And you know it's a constant tussle between the democratic process, which is so very very time-consuming, and the authoritarian model, which is very efficient but which no one trusts. As inefficient as democracy is, we've got to scale down so that each one of us understands the decisions that have to be made and either makes them ourselves or delegates that responsibility. I think we're all in the process of trying to develop that model still.

PENNY: *Which is another power and control issue: letting go of power, letting go of control, trusting...*

YING: Yes. But I think that even in my very short twenty-year life in politics, I've seen too many cases where we've handed power over to a person only to see that it really corrupts the institution as well as the individual. We're still too eager to have leaders, and even those of us who do not want leaders feel that we need them for the larger society, because leaders with charisma can command large audiences, can command the media—or we think can command the media.

If there's anything that we can do in terms of education, it's to figure out a way to decentralize power—to take away some of the mass media's power to force icons upon us, and to force the sort of hierarchical behavior that makes us give up our power to an icon, only to be disappointed somewhere down the line.

PENNY: *Do you have any ideas?*

YING: I think it means lots of us talking and creating ever larger networks. It's a slow process, that's the frightening, painful thing about it. But it's happening. My children are better educated than I am, not because I was a better parent than my parents were, but because there's more information. There's far more information on how to raise children and how to talk to your children—I didn't talk to my children as much as I ought to have—but they're going to talk to their children more than I did and talk to each other a bit more. As long as we can talk as equals, and get more information, that may be a path.

'Democrat' is not only a capital 'D' but also a small 'd'. We have to remember that the democratic process is very very new. I've just been reading about the British Revolution—Cromwell and the Parliamentarians, and the struggle that they had to go through to spread power a bit. That was only in the 1600's, so we're very new, in terms of human and social evolution. I think we're getting there. We're talking about it increasingly, and we're talking about the need to change in order to survive. So we've taken the first big step, and, hey, we're all still alive, thanks to Mr. Gorbachev and all the anti-nuclear activists.

PENNY: *Before I talked to you, I spoke with a group of different folks who have worked with you and known you over the years. You have been called 'rigorous,' 'responsible in your use of power,' 'a great mediator,' 'thoughtful,' and 'a splendid human being.'*

YING: My God!

PENNY: *That was just a random survey…I wondered, Ying, what's been your greatest challenge?*

YING: Challenges…I think probably my biggest challenge was learning how to act politically. What got me into politics was the realization that all those people being killed in Vietnam were Asian and that this was a racist war, and that I as an Asian had a responsibility to let people know that *those were human beings being killed.* That was a tremendous tremendous challenge for me; I was a teacher and just *barely* was used to talking to groups of thirty or forty, not to several thousand. But it was anger, I think, that motivated me—and that's not *always* the best source of energy. For me, the challenge is still there—to figure out what is the best way to do what we have to do.

I want to see a world that is environmentally sound. I want to see a world that is free of racism. I want to see a world that is free of these tremendous economic differences. I cannot stand that there are wealthy people driving around in incredibly fancy cars, living in mansions, and that there should be people who are homeless and who have no security from minute to minute. In the twentieth century, almost going into the twenty-first, this sort of primitive difference should no longer be with us. I think it's all of a piece; what we do to the environment is what we do to our society. If we have a more just society, our behavior toward the world will be more just, so the environment will be more just.

So that's the challenge, a challenge that I think we're all trying to meet. How do we *do* it? I think there are thousands, I hope hundreds of thousands of us, who are trying to figure this out. That's why there are all these conferences and so on—we're trying to understand how to reach out to each other, how to develop a process and an institution that can bring this about.

If I had one hope I think it would be to figure out how we can have a *single* coalition whose manifesto would incorporate the best of the Greens, the best of the Democratic Party, the best of all the women's groups, the best of all the idealists in the Third World, all of the nationalists. And that we could say, 'We're all so small and we each have these agendas that are so *similar.*' [My hope is] that we *can* get together and—you know, give up something. When I think of the stack of mail that I have, two feet high, from all these wonderful groups—if I ended up giving to every group, it would be five dollars each. So I try to give fifty dollars to this one, or twenty-five dollars to that one, and it's still peanuts. I wish I could give several thousand to one group and say, '*That's* the one that's going to do it.' And, you know, that's the way I give my life. I'm looking for that, as I think many of us are.

PENNY: *Maybe you could organize it?*

YING: No, I'm not going to organize it, WE'RE going to organize it.

PENNY: *We're going to organize it. Well, on that note—do you have any personal heroes or heroines?*

YING: When I was going into politics, my heroines and heroes were the people from the United States who fought in the Spanish Civil War [against fascism].

And there were Mao Tse Tung[1] and Chou En Lai,[2] the Communists in China. They gave what I did not—they gave their lives. They gave thirty, forty years. And I think in terms of Tienanmen Square right now…we hear from a lot of the dissidents. What happened there was horrible. But I just saw a television program on women in Chinese villages, and this woman said she had been sold by her parents to her husband for some silver. Her husband mistreated her for forty, fifty years. But she said, 'But I'm a person now. My life is so much better than it was when I was a child.' Now, she can't be sold. I think we have to look at one billion Chinese people who have some dignity today because of what these incredible people did in the '20's and the '30's and the '40's. Lots of bad excesses, and I'm against authoritarian rule, but the Communists then created a dynamite of a revolution, and they made a difference in the lives of hundreds of millions of people. They're my heroes.

N O T E S :

1. Mao Tse Tung [1893–1976] founded the People's Republic of China in 1949. He had also been one of the founders of the Chinese Communist Party in 1921, and he is regarded, along with Karl Marx and V.I. Lenin, as one of the three great theorists of Marxian communism. (*Academic American Encyclopedia, vol 13. Danbury, CT:Grolier Inc, 1982.*)

2. Chou En-Lai [1898–1976] a colleague of Mao Tse-Tung's, while a student in Europe he founded a branch of the Chinese Communist Party in Paris. In 1931 he joined Mao Tse-Tung and his guerilla movement in Jaing Xi province. After Mao became party chief, Chou En-Lai continued to support his policies. He was prime minister (1949–76) and foreign minister (1949–58). He also helped to build up the Red Army. (*The International Dictionary of Twentieth Century Biography, NY: New American Library, 1987.*)

Photo by Maureen Murdock

Flor Fernandez

JUNE 1989

"I always correlate power with a sense of joy and happiness…Anytime you smile and you feel joyful…that allows you to be creative and to inspire other people."

Flor Fernandez carries a light in her eye that warms and brightens—a soft sparkle of compassion and joy. Flor is the drum to so many others' dance, the calm and steady heartbeat that stimulates, heals, guides and comforts. With intuitive skill she appears with just the right word at the moment we need her. Splashing in the lake at midnight, dancing the salsa, tending the fire or making an offering, her reverence and care shine through. Flor's power is her humility; her light is a lesson of spirit.

PENNY: *Flor, you're a Doctor of Transpersonal Psychology and you work with abused women and children. You're also a shaman, a psychic healer and a carrier of the Sacred Pipe, as well as a teacher of vision quests and empowerment. How do you use these different tools on a day-to-day basis?*

FLOR: I try to understand your own personal story: where you come from and what you have to share with others, as well as what is it you need to heal for yourself. We work from that in terms of life purposes, to help you manifest your own vision as you work through personal and collective pain.

PENNY: *How have you drawn from your own personal experiences?*

FLOR: Well, I grew up in a family that gave me a lot of love and support. But my parents were wounded in their ability to love themselves and to express that to to me. When I was eleven, I was removed from my family and taken to work in the fields, in Cuba where I grew up. This experience was part of the whole process of the new system under Castro's government. The philosophy behind it was that basically everyone needed to contribute to the community. But there was also the process of brainwashing the children, of separating them from the elders so they wouldn't be able to know and understand the storytelling of the other past-times, of the system that was in Cuba before Castro.

By experiencing the pain of separation from my family as a young child, I needed to become a very mature person at an early age. In psychology we call this a very 'pseudo-mature' child, a caretaker. As a result, that's the main role I've played in my life, of always understanding what other people wanted from me.

My pain is based around that and being able to let go of that pattern. It's a pattern we all need to let go of, personally and collectively—the caretaker, the warrior, needing to be active and role playing all the time, being on stage, taking care of business so we don't fall apart.

The pain came from my wounded child, because my child never really got to play or to have fun, to feel love and support from the grown-ups. That wounded my own sense of trusting that what I do is right for me to do, trusting my own inner wisdom and knowing. Part of my lifetime has been healing that inner child, so I can accept her innocence, and can trust that I'm okay—no matter what I'm doing and no matter where I'm standing.

PENNY: *So how do you heal others and still take care of yourself?*

FLOR: Part of healing others is learning to take care of myself. You cannot really take any energies from an empty well. You need to constantly nurture yourself and build a community of people around you who can support your work, who can support you as an individual and embrace you so you can give to others.

PENNY: *Can you give me an example of how you, in your daily work, integrate your transpersonal psychology and the shamanic traditions?*

FLOR: Most of the time it's a very individual process, but recently I have been working with a lot of people who in traditional psychology are considered to be having nervous breakdowns. What I find most of the time when I work with these people is that they are beginning to get in touch with that inner knowing. They are getting in touch with their vision, which comes in dreams—many times terrifying dreams—because they don't have a sense of their own power. A lot of times it happens that people receive information that they don't know how to integrate into their frame of reference, and we label them right away, because their behavior does not fit into what we expect to be 'normal behavior.'

One example would be someone who recently had a psychotic breakdown, who was going through a tremendous amount of changing and transitioning. They don't have the resources to integrate that, so they fall apart. When they come to me, we begin to look into all the symbology and metaphors they're being given. We begin to integrate the information and make some sense out of it.

Another situation is when I work with children who have been abused, especially physically and sexually abused. These children oftentimes don't have a sense of self, so a lot of the rituals and ceremonies that I use—for example the power animal dance—allow them to get in touch with their own power. Most of the children only know a sense of helplessness and powerlessness, so I do a lot of work with power animals. They draw or paint their symbols of empowerment on shields: like 'my kitty-cat' or 'my dog', or animals they feel very connected to, and where they feel a sense of support.

PENNY: *What is a power animal or shield?*

FLOR: A shield is a concept taken from Native American Indians. It's supposed to represent—and I will use psychological terms—the concept of the spirit, the self, and your journey through your own lifetime. It's supposed to symbolize your power. When you paint your symbols on the shield, you're actually using symbols that will remind you of your own personal power and that will give you a sense of protection from the spirits that could harm you—or from other people that have bad thoughts toward you. It's like a mandala, a mandala of the self.

The power animal is an archetype. In the tradition of the South American, the power animal symbolizes your connection to the earth, your connection to your power. The issues that are reflected are manifested in the archetype of one animal that you feel connected with. As you begin to work with that animal, you begin to become aware of your own powers as a human being. You become aware of your own connection to the earth, to other kingdoms, and you gain a sense of not being alone in this universe—that you have other kingdoms and other people supporting you.

PENNY: *So which spiritual traditions hold meaning for you?*

FLOR: To me, what holds meaning is any tradition that focuses on working with the earth, with simple principles of nature—connecting with the spirit of the rocks, the spirit of the mountains, things that I can see and feel. Most of my life I have connected with that tradition because my grandmother was a healer. She taught me a great deal about herbs and about using energies to heal, about the use of ritual in ceremony to do healing, and about the use of prayers to heal. She also taught me the use of inner power, which means going deep into yourself to find your own powers, so then you can help others.

PENNY: *How would someone do that?*

FLOR: It's a whole journey. For example, in reconnecting with the essence of the trees, you choose a tree to connect with that has some meaning for you—a symbol of a part of yourself that is reflected in the form of a tree, in the shape and the way the branches are going out, or the shape of the trunk. It's a reflection of yourself.

I work with the concept of mirrors a lot. Everything that you encounter, every person that you attract to you is a mirror that you look at to learn from, because each one of us brings different gifts to each other and all the other kingdoms as well. For example, I oftentimes do the mirror work where you can just look for a piece of rock, or a stone. If you focus on the shape of the stone, you will find an aspect of yourself that you are not familiar with, or that you have neglected to look at. There is a teaching in everything that we encounter, whether it's a rock, a tree, or other humans.

PENNY: *It seems like you've done some pioneering work in integrating various traditions and academic disciplines. What guides you in that?*

FLOR: I think what guided me to explore different traditions was my feeling and belief that we are all unique and different individuals and that what worked for you may not work for me. I usually feel like I have to carry a bag of tricks, or a bag of different techniques or medicine powers to help different people.

My own personal curiosity about other people and differences has taught me that we are all coming from different places with different knowledge and that it's important not to neglect anyone in the picture. We all form a big mandala, which is the Medicine Wheel, and each one of us comes from a different direction carrying the powers of our ancestors, whether you're Irish or Jewish or Native American. Each one of us has something to offer, to heal, to find and to reconnect with the harmony and the balance that we have lost in our planet.

PENNY: *Isn't it unusual for a woman to be a carrier of the Sacred Pipe?*

FLOR: It is unusual in the Native tradition. The way that I became a Pipe Carrier [is that] I did all the traditional ceremonies. Now I feel we are moving into a new time where we need to let go of some of the teachings. Even though I am not a Native American, I was taught to carry the Pipe with a sense of integrity and never to misuse it, and I honor that tradition. But I feel that the Pipe is an instrument now that reflects our need to find power outside ourselves.

My philosophy at this point in time is that we need to become the Pipe, as a nation and as individuals. We need to begin to focus inward for teachings rather than outside. To go inside and become the Pipe, or become the Drum, or become the Medicine Wheel. We are It. We have all the knowledge that we have to know, and the feeling that I have been getting is that we are recycling knowledge at this point in time.

When I do my workshops I find that people know the information, but what they're searching for is something more meaningful that goes beyond words and beyond information that is written or intellectually passed on. We're looking now for the New Myth, and the New Myth is something that can only be found in experience, in your own feelings, your own sense of connection to you and to others and to the land. It's not anything that you can find in the written words.

It's something that is transcendental, that goes deeper. It's a journey of the soul to deeper places where we don't know yet what it's going to be like, but we've got to trust that it's going to be there. I encourage people to go deep and find their own New Myth and what they need to share with other people, coming from their ancestors as well as their own personal knowledge and experience through life.

PENNY: *Flor, I'm really concerned about the uses of power in this society, and I'm wondering if you could comment on how you see power being used in this country now—in healthy ways, in unhealthy ways?*

FLOR: I feel power has turned into weapons at this point in time. I was thinking in particular about the Alaska oil spill. It became clear to me as I was listening to everything that was happening there that the universe is giving us metaphors. For example, I was thinking about the metaphor about the Captain of the tanker being an alcoholic. Alcohol abuse is one of the major diseases that is killing our nature and taking our power. I see how the oil, our shadow, has spilled over that beautiful land killing many creatures and causing a lot of grief and sadness to the children of the Valdez town [Bligh Reef; the town nearest the accident involving the oil tanker named the Valdez]. It's a sad metaphor of how we're misusing power, because what we're doing is using power to destroy, without the conscious awareness of what is sacred within us.

That tanker carrying all the oil, to me represents a shadow that we need to embrace—that as long as we continue projecting that shadow to others and to the land, we will continue using power to destroy rather than to create. Our basic challenge is to go back to the Feminine, to the journey that is inward, to really honor the shadow dancer inside us—the darkness inside us—and to stop projecting that to others and to the land...so we can regain some balance, and stop alcohol abuse, child abuse, drug abuse, the killing of so many people, like in China [the Tienanmen Square massacre]. Until we do that and starting walking in our own shadow and embracing that shadow, we will continue using power to cause harm.

Power to me is not an active concept, it's a concept of being *receptive*. It's the power in my tradition and my teaching of *allowing*, rather than controlling or mastering. It's not power over nature or power over the people, but it's basically allowing yourself to be in a position of power—to be in synchronicity with the energies around us. To be attuned to the messages that we are given, so we can make a decision based on choices rather than on the need to control other people, to be on stage, to be the 'star' people.

We need new heroes and heroines, because so far the heroes that we have are very active and shining stars, very direct, very controlling. We need a new image of heroines and heroes that work more on the concept of quietness and stillness, focusing inward.

It reminds me of the myth of Creation from the Navaho people, where we have two archetypes, Salt Woman and Spider Woman. Salt Woman is the aspect of the supernatural and the natural in us, but she is also that element of solitude and retreat. She teaches that we need to take care of our own personal garden before we can go out and help other people, to heal the pain and the wounds that we've been creating.

Spider Woman is the weaver but she is also the small voice, the small self, that oftentimes we refuse to listen to. Because we're looking for Big Voices, for Famous Stars, rather than listening to our own inner little selves telling us what we need to do and how to empower ourselves. Which could be very simple—it could be like Spider Woman weaving her web, or being a teacher or a housecleaner, but doing it with a sense of connection rather than disconnection.

PENNY: *So many of us in this society are so cerebral and so busy. How do we find that inner voice?*

FLOR: You have to *make time*. You have to stop and find the place to be alone and to be with yourself, and that I think is the most difficult thing for all of us to do. Because we have lost the memories of how to do it. In our traditions they made these times ceremonial by doing a Vision Quest, or by sending people out in the night to begin to take a look at themselves. In our society we don't have time—we have TV all the time, we have Nintendo games for the children to play, we have the radio, we have all sorts of stimulus separating and distracting us from knowing ourselves, distracting us from really going inside to learn more about who we are and how to love ourselves rather than hate ourselves.

PENNY: *How does everything you've been talking about relate specifically to women?*

FLOR: I think women at this point play a very important role in our society, because we are the container, we are the vessel. We are in a position where we have been growing very fast and receiving a great deal of information. Our task is not to become masculine and become the active forceful leaders, but to really honor our feminine nature and nurture ourselves—to be like Spider Woman, the weavers of our society; to be like Salt Woman, the medicine woman who knows about the dark powers. By dark I mean the shadow powers: knowing your pain, knowing your sorrow and making the space for you the woman to deal with the sorrow, as well as making the space for other people to deal with that sorrow.

I also think we are becoming Changing Woman in the Navaho myth. Changing Woman has a lot to do with that essence of us that keeps changing, like the cycles, like the seasons, like the moon changes. We are right now like the anchors of the society, and we are the Rainbow Dancers in a way, the Changing Woman.

There are so many aspects of the Feminine that need to brought back into our culture, that have been neglected and forgotten for so many years. The whole concept of the quietness and the stillness that we were talking about before—how do we become quiet—that's a Feminine aspect. How to go inward is another aspect of the Feminine that has been pretty much neglected and ignored. Also the aspect of nurturance and truly nurturing ourselves without the need to use or abuse people.

The image that I get is like the ocean, to be in a sense of movement with the changes—not trying to control those movements, but going with the changes and the New Myth that we are creating. I believe that Woman is the myth-maker in our society at this point.

PENNY: *So you're saying women shouldn't be forceful?*

FLOR: Yes, I believe that Woman should honor her feminine qualities and not be forceful. The power of the woman comes from really being who she is. If you try to be forceful, you will be going into the masculine or the male role of forcing things to happen, and that's not the Feminine way. The Feminine way is allowing things to happen, with the right time, with the flow of the energies.

I believe that she should take responsibility for not becoming the victim. We need to move from a place of passivity—which is different than receptivity—to making our own choices about what we want to be.

PENNY: *For example?*

FLOR: I think women have been told many times what they need to be like. As little girls, we were totally enculturated about how we need to look, what we need to do with our lives: 'You need to get married, have children.' That's fine if you choose to do that, but it's important that we know we have other choices and make some room to take our own power and create what we need. Such as maybe choosing not to have children, and write a book—that's another way of giving birth. It could be choosing to go on a journey around the world, rather than staying home and being a housekeeper. Just the idea of making choices and taking responsibility is a different concept than being forceful. It's taking care of yourself so you don't become a victim.

PENNY: *Using what you've been talking about in the uses of power, do you think it's possible for someone to be President of the U.S., for example, and not be forceful, but allow things to happen?*

FLOR: I think we are working on that concept, but it's going to take a long time. It's an ideal, but it's not impossible. The process that we're going through right now is taking care of our own personal shadow, our own personal issues with power, and at some point in our evolution hopefully we'll be able to take care of that shadow and embrace it so we don't have to project it.

I feel very hopeful that we are going toward balance rather than destruction, even though our universe is giving a lot of metaphors that seem to be the opposite. With the Harmonic Convergence [August

1987], we opened a new cycle of cleansing and healing for our universe. A lot of people were of the belief that we were going to enter into a cycle of more harmony. It is true that we are working towards harmony, but what we are experiencing right now is a healing, on all levels. Physically, Mother Earth is healing, and personally, we are healing. Before we can have a presence that will be more balanced, we need to begin to work with our own personal selves and manifest that to the universe.

PENNY: *Can you tell me a little more about what makes you feel hopeful about the future? I think many of us are in need of reasons to feel hopeful right now.*

FLOR: One thing is that I see a lot of people doing their own personal work. I see women especially seeking experiences that will allow them to heal their wounded child, to heal the victim/offender inside them. We are seeking not so much knowledge, but we are seeking the *experience of healing*, and we are creating more experiences for women and men of that nature—retreats and workshops that allow them to really think and to experience their own healing.

I feel hopeful because I think what we're going through at this time is the shadow work of our universe, and if we can make it through this cycle, then, like the Mayans say, we'll get to the Heaven cycle. But right now we're going through the Hell cycle.

In the myth of Quetzalcoatl, the Plumed Serpent, Quetzalcoatl has the realization that he has created a culture of decadence, a culture that is dying. In order for him to create a transformation for his culture and for himself, he needs to go look at the mirrors. The dark mirrors are those aspects of ourselves that we don't want to see, because we're scared to see, or because it's too painful. Quetzalcoatl is forced to look into those mirrors, and go into the underworld to face those monsters and enemies, to find allies that will help him go through the process of transformation that we're going through. It is a journey towards unconsciousness, bringing what is unconscious to consciousness, so we don't have to continue creating the structure around us as a way of living.

PENNY: *So it's possible for men to go through these changes too?*

FLOR: I believe that it doesn't have anything to do at this point with being a man or a woman; it has to do more with the personal self. I think we're all pretty much in pain in having to go through the transformation process. We've been getting the call and it is up to us, whether as men or women, to make the choice to go through our own healing.

PENNY: *You mentioned earlier heroes and heroines, that we need some new ones. Who are your heroines and heroes?*

FLOR: My heroine was my grandmother, my paternal grandmother. She taught me a lot about being quiet, and being in the presence of your own essence, rather than stepping out all the time to search for power. She taught me about the beauty of honoring and making sacred everything that you come in contact with.

And she taught me about the idea that we are all in this world to learn from each other, to touch each other—that anytime we step outside that concept and become inflated, feeling we are better or more powerful than others, we break that balance and cause ourselves pain and other people pain. She was my heroine from a very early age.

PENNY: *Anything else you want to add, Flor?*

FLOR: I think this is a time to tell the stories, and the best way for you to learn is to really take a look at your own lifetime, your own stories, and see what they have to offer you. It's a time to go inward, not to go outward.

I recommend that people take more walks in nature, to really focus their awareness on what it is they're doing that is taking them away from their own power, from their own sense of happiness and joy. I always correlate power with a sense of joy and happiness. To me, *that's* power—anytime you smile and you feel joyful—that allows you to be creative and to inspire other people.

Photo by Michael Porter

Vivienne Verdon-Roe

JULY 1990

"I used to think that I was a teacher and
I had a message. I would formulate the
message and go out there and throw the
words at you. I've learned that you teach
what you need to learn yourself."

Vivienne's almost demure countenance belies her razor-sharp mind
and gritty persistence. These qualities have forged Vivienne Verdon-
Roe into the toughest of adversaries. Beware the nuclear power pro-
ponent, the housing developer or the Star Wars advocate. Falling into
activism almost accidentally, Viv has taken to it with relish, mesmerizing
audiences with an astonishing delivery of statistics. However, it is her
vulnerability which is so compelling; it helps us imagine that possibly
we ourselves could self-actualize, could risk our own journey into the
realm of becoming...

PENNY: *Vivienne, you're a film producer and director, a community
and international activist and an Oscar-winner for your documentary*
Women—For America, For the World. *When I think about you, I have
this very strong impression of a storyteller. You're a wonderful storyteller,
and you speak all over the world. One of the things that's so inspiring
about your story is your journey in a few short years from housewife to
winning the Academy Award for your documentary, a product of your
activism against nuclear power.*

    *You strike me as someone who's not afraid to fight City Hall—
again, and again, and again. And sometimes you win, and sometimes
you lose, but you make fighting City Hall seem—so natural. As one*

individual, you're not afraid to go after some of the biggest guns out there, like the nuclear industry. Where does that fearlessness come from?

VIVIENNE: I don't know that it's fearlessness. I think it may be sheer bloody-mindedness, rebelliousness. I was a very rebellious young person; I got into trouble a lot at school. It came from growing up in a very dysfunctional family, being unhappy and not wanting to accept the status quo—which in my case was not acceptable.

PENNY: *Is there anything from your experience doing this that you can teach those of us who feel like we keep ourselves back, keep ourselves from fighting the kind of fight that you're waging in the world?*

VIVIENNE: My experience of women has been that many of them don't recognize the strengths and the skills that they have. It's not so much that they need to go out and do Political Activism 101. It's really more that they need to find within themselves the strengths and skills that they haven't recognized up to this point and polish them up.

I feel that I've been coming from a place of male energy. And when I say male energy, there's really nothing wrong with it. I'm talking about the energy that gets things done in the world. It's very determined and aggressive and almost self-righteous. It's very focused, and it gets things done, goddammit! I feel that I've been coming from that for quite a long time, until very recently when I've wanted to change it around and deepen something else—my female energy.

PENNY: *Where did you learn that 'male style' of accomplishment? Because for a lot of women that does not come easily—it sounds like it comes easily for you.*

VIVIENNE: Well, my father definitely would rather have had a son when I was born, and he treated me in many ways like a boy. I was encouraged to be extremely competitive. At school the thing that my father would look at on my report card was the place—I had to be first. The grade I got didn't matter, but I had to be top of the class.

And I've really seen in myself a very competitive streak, which I'm working on right now. Because it's totally inappropriate for the kind of work I do. I think I'm beginning to get a handle on it. But I do see how much my energy has been male, and how much I really want to soften that, and spend more time being, rather than doing, all the time. I sometimes feel like I've been a 'human doing.' And it's been great, I mean I've gotten a lot done, but I feel the need for balance in myself.

PENNY: *Before we move on to the 'Feminine,' you said you'd been doing work on your competitiveness. What kind of work?*

VIVIENNE: You feel that competitive edge in everything if you've been brought up that way. It's really almost on a cellular level, and you have to really become aware of it. Once you become aware of it, you can laugh at yourself and say, 'Oh I see, I want to be top of *that*' or 'I want to come first in that.'

When I started to notice these things, the hardest part for me was to see how judgemental I had become—because I was also criticized a lot, and I've internalized that voice of criticism, of judgement. I'd say, 'Oh Vivienne, god you're so competitive, how ugly and how horrible!' and give myself a hard time about it. When I changed that into 'Oh Vivienne, there you go again,' it became much easier to recognize, because I wasn't giving myself such a hard time. And I think it's more valuable in the long run.

PENNY: *It sounds like you started treating yourself with more compassion.*

VIVIENNE: I find it much easier to be very compassionate towards other people in the world than to myself. That's really been a big lesson.

PENNY: *And how are you working with that?*

VIVIENNE: Well, I had a car accident six months ago which jolted a lot, including my back and neck. I've had to spend a large part of the last six months on my back, and that's been very interesting—it brought me to a standstill. Whereas for the last eight years I've been going like a train rather out of control. So these months have been a time of reflection, which is a word I never thought I would use. I've learned an enormous amount about myself. I can say I've come to like myself, which I didn't before.

I know that the process I've been going through will have a profound effect on my future work, because I've changed my view of the world. I've realized that for the last two years I've been very depressed—very. In fact, more than depressed, I've felt despairing that we weren't going to make it, and that all our work to end the arms race and to restore and preserve our environment was going to fail.

I didn't realize I felt like this until the accident, until I had time to really just stop. What's happened over the last six months, through spending a lot of time in nature, is that I've changed. And it's not my belief. I was coming from belief and faith a lot of the time before. I changed my knowingness about what's happening.

I didn't really have a vision of the future before. I knew what we didn't want: we didn't want nuclear weapons, we didn't want nuclear war, we didn't want a devastated environment. But I didn't know what we did want. And I'm now beginning to get a picture of the world as it could be. Riane Eisler's work helped me with that *[The Chalice and the Blade]* when I heard that there had been societies before patriarchy, before the last 5000 years—when women were revered. At the same time we weren't the dominant sex, but people worked in partnership. When I heard that and started to read about it and realized it was true, that not only could people live in partnership, but it actually had happened—and that that knowledge has been repressed and removed from our history because of the coming of patriarchy and the suppression of women—I felt, wow, this is not just the way it could be, this is the way it's been. And therefore we've got a vision now. I mean this is not idealistic, this is absolutely possible!

I also began to look at the cup as not half-empty but as half-full. I began to see how much we've done, and how many pockets there are now of good stuff that's going on in the world. So my attitude about the future has profoundly changed. I feel like I'm not a cheerleader trying to get everybody's spirits up for the last battle, which we might not win. I really feel now that we're going through an evolutionary leap, in the evolution of this planet and in the evolution of the consciousness of the human. And it's going to be very hard. I don't belittle that. We're going to go through a great deal of dying, because in order for the new to come through, the old has to die. And it's clear we're going to lose many species and maybe many people, and maybe much of the environment. But I think we're also going to lose the old ideas and the old way of being. And that we are going through a period of upheaval and transition. It's both very frightening and very exciting.

I mean, what a time to live! What an opportunity to be part of the new that's coming through. You know when people say, 'I'm not sure I have time to be a political activist or to write letters,' I almost don't understand how you can be on the sidelines when you're living in this era. What an exciting thing to do, to participate, to be part of it—it's not a choice for me, it's just fun!

PENNY: *You started this off by talking about using the male model of power and then the female model emerging for you. So now, as you use your power, as you live your life, as you're an activist, as you're a human being, a woman—do you feel like you've switched modes? Is it an integration? How does that all shake down for you?*

VIVIENNE: I think I've started listening much more. I used to think that I was a teacher and that I had a message and I would formulate the message and go out there and throw the words at you. I've learned that you teach what you need to learn yourself. And I've learned that the people who I am teaching usually have something very important to teach me. It's important for me to listen, much more than I used to.

So I think I'm much more receptive. One thing that's really beginning to change is that I was so goal-oriented—which is a perfectly good skill to have, as long as you don't go overboard. I would decide on a goal, and I'd head for it and if I won, great, I came first. And if I lost, it was terrible, I was a failure. This became really clear for me last year, when I was thinking about the work that I did.

I worked on four different projects which I felt failed. I worked to try and stop the Galileo Plutonium Shuttle from going up, which it did. I worked to try and stop a developer from destroying a piece of the Oakland Hills where I live, and I failed. Even though he was breaking environmental laws and we went and testified before the City Council, we failed to stop him.

And I worked with Witness for Peace trying to get the story out last year about the Contras using the so-called humanitarian aid that Congress had given them—50 million dollars—to buy supplies and hide out in the hills and kill the Nicaraguan peasants. The Contras claimed that if people voted for the Sandinistas [the revolutionary government of Nicaragua at the time] the killing would continue. So the Sandinistas lost the election because the mainstream media in this country refused to cover the real story.

And there was a fourth thing that I worked on, the Alameda and Marin County Nuclear Weapon Free Zones Initiatives which we attempted to pass and which were opposed by the military contractors—to the tune of 600 thousand dollars—a heck of a lot more than what we had to play with. And they defeated us.

I looked at these four issues that I'd worked on, and I realized that in each case something unexpected had come out of them—not the goal. For instance, in the environmental issue in the Oakland Hills, I tried to get the neighbors involved. It was very difficult. A lot of the people involved were little old ladies who'd bought their houses years ago and didn't feel you could fight City Hall.

Eventually, I got a few people together and found another neighborhood group that had just formed. We amalgamated our forces and formed a neighborhood association in the Oakland Hills which has 300 paid-up members and 1000 on our mailing list. And the ringleader of this organization has pushed through a tree ordinance and done all sorts of incredible work, as a result of the impetus to try and stop this particular development. So although we failed to stop this development, in the long run the energy and work that we invested has come out in other ways.

In each case I found that in fact my goal hadn't been satisfied, but that something unexpected and positive had come out of the energy that I'd put into those projects. Which is I think a very different way of looking at success—'did I succeed in my project?'

PENNY: *So that's a real change for you.*

VIVIENNE: Very much so, very much so. And it's part of really stopping this 'I've got to control everything in my life,' which comes from being a very insecure kid. I mean basically that's it—I've got to control everything in my environment because I feel so panicked and scared.

So many of us really have that very controlling edge, and it's so nice when you're able to let it go and allow things to manifest. So often things happen that you never dreamt of, and which turn out to be much more positive than the goal that you originally had in mind.

PENNY: *Some of what you're saying is reminding me of when I've heard you speak about your recovery regarding alcoholism, food issues and your being an adult child of an alcoholic family. Has the recovery affected your emerging sense of a whole new kind of power?*

VIVIENNE: Yes, this introverted work that I've been doing over the last six months, really finding myself, definitely started when I gave up alcohol after twenty years of drinking alcoholically. I also finally managed to get the beast of food compulsion out of my system after fifteen years of anorexia and bulimia; my body is in remarkably good shape considering the kind of abuse that I've poured upon it.

I don't know which was the hardest, dealing with the food disorder or the alcoholism—probably the alcoholism—that was the last thing to go, a couple of years ago. I went to Adult Children of Alcoholics meetings, and I found just going to those meetings once a month for about six months was very helpful. I didn't really make a big thing out of it, but it helped me over the beginning of coming out I suppose—to break through the denial and deal with the problem head-on, seeing that other people were in the same boat, who were good people and weren't lacking in willpower, and weren't shamefully depraved or all the things that I feared.

After about a year of being a dry drunk, I still wasn't happy. I felt very tight, and I obviously was still under the demon of dependency on alcohol. It was still in my system. But then, around the time I had the accident, I don't even know how to describe it but I suppose it is my spiritual side, started to flower. And it really got sparked off by the time I spent in nature. Just the awe I began to feel, like when I was a child, falling in love with the trees and the little insects and the little wildflowers.

Not being able to walk is a very interesting experience, just literally having to lie around. And I lay on cliffs by the ocean. I would look at a patch of grass for about three hours; I really couldn't do too much else. That was such a change for me, from working fifteen hours a day nonstop, just filling up every single minute with something so I didn't have time to think about myself—because, 'uh-oh, there's a lot of undealt-with stuff in there and I don't want to bring it to consciousness.' So I'd keep super super busy and drink alcohol to numb the pain.

It was really extraordinary to have the time to really get to know myself and nature again. It's so wonderful how being out in nature brings you back to your core, the center of your being. The connection is so solidly there, you can't miss it.

I got a real burst of love in my heart, which seems to have been happening on a fairly regular basis for the last six months. One time I actually felt the muscles in my heart stretch—I even heard clicking going on in there. And I have been really asking that my heart be opened up, because what I believe now is that the only way we are really going to change the world is through love. I know that sounds a little idealistic or cliché, but if we don't come from love, it won't be change, it won't be transformation. The only way we can change the world in the radical way it has to be changed—it has to come from love.

PENNY: *So as women, empowering ourselves and bringing that out to the world, what's the most important thing we can be doing for ourselves right now?*

VIVIENNE: The whole experience of the women's solstice camp has been for me exactly what I think every individual woman needs to do, which is get in touch with her female power. And in a way where it's safe for her to feel a lot of anger. Five thousand years of patriarchy has done something phenomenal in terms of building up a reserve of anger in women's psyche at what's been done to us. It's righteous anger, but it has to be transformed, because there is no place for it in what we do.

I think places where women can be together and talk, and tell stories—which of course is our way of being together, that's women's culture—is extraordinarily valuable, because we can transmute that energy and that anger into compassion, into understanding for each other's pain. And into understanding the pain of the men, which is a very important part of this. Patriarchy is not just repressed women. I know it seems like it's stuck all those white guys at the top of the pile, but look—look at their psyches and what's going on with them, and how dead they are. And how unconscious they are. That's painful, to live like that. I'm not saying it's the same; I'm just saying that it's really valid that we remember and acknowledge that men have their pain too.

The important thing for women to do is get it all out, get out the shadow side, really look at yourself. It's amazing how if you bring it to consciousness and vocalize it, talk about it—admit it to someone like your best friend, your therapist, yourself—how it changes.

One of the things that has made me feel most ashamed about myself, that I was an evil person, that I was bad—I really carried this for a long time and I know it's therapeutic for me to say it again—is that when I was nineteen I trained as a Montessori kindergarten teacher. And I only taught for one term. Because during that experience, I became so horrified and scared at the violence I felt towards those little children when they frustrated me, that I quit.

I got a dog about two years later. I think I wanted to test myself again. And I kicked him three times. When I saw what was in me, I gave him away to a family that wanted him—and that's been one of my darkest secrets. Only recently, when I started to go back over my past and deal with some of the experiences that seemed to have really negatively impacted on me—a polite way of putting it! I realized that the beatings I received as a very young child have profoundly influenced me, causing enormous amounts of rage and helplessness, which were stuck down in my center, to come up.

When I really got in touch with that experience of being beaten and relived it, I was reminded of my violent feelings, and I put the whole thing together; I understood that if you are treated violently as a child, you will repeat that behavior. That is something which our legal system does not sufficiently understand—our prison system certainly doesn't. I don't know what to do about it, but I think the recognition has got to become so much more visible and talked about. Just understanding it and admitting that I've had those feelings, and even acted on them, has released me of some of the guilt I felt and made me realize I'm not an intrinsically bad person. There was a reason for those feelings.

It's really been a cleansing too. I got another dog four years ago, and Michael and I weren't ready to make a decision about a family, but...well, we were ready to make a decision about a family—Oscar's definitely our family at the moment. And those violent feelings have not gone on with this dog. I've really treated him in a totally different way.

In fact he's turned out to be this bundle of loving life—he's a really beautiful dog. That's such a joy to me, to see that you don't have to go on repeating the past. If you bring the past into consciousness, you can change it around. And in fact what you're doing when you do that is so incredible, because you're not just changing around your life, you're changing around a pattern which has come down through the generations. Because of course my father was an alcoholic and violent, and his mother was too—he was treated that way, and it's always the case.

So that's been really wonderful for me to see that we can change. And if we can change on an individual level, it's clear that the planet can change.

Top photo by Chris Gilbert, bottom photo by Jane Scherr

Barbara Lubin

SEPTEMBER 1991

"I think it's really important that women hang in there for women and speak for women, that we are vigilant about our rights and about justice for women. If we don't, we'll lose everything."

The telephone calls are incessant: "Will you help us raise money to bring a wounded Palestinian child over to the U.S. for medical treatment?"... "Mom, can you watch the baby while I go to the dentist?"... "Will you sit-in with us to protest U.S. policy in El Salvador?"...

Off she runs with slide show and projector in hand, to a school in San Jose, a shelter for street people in San Francisco's Tenderloin District or a benefit for a women's newspaper in Sonoma County. Wherever she speaks, Barbara Lubin tells the truth as she sees it—sometimes directly, sometimes through anecdote, always with humor and heart. She trudges with young children through the muddy streets of Jabalia refugee camp in Gaza; she emcees a peace rally on a makeshift stage outside her downtown Berkeley office; she hosts a barbeque in her backyard to help social change artists fund their work. Barbara Lubin exudes charm with a dash of daring. She lives life on its precarious edge, just keeping balance; fully absorbed, she plunges through the tragedy, the comedy, the journey for justice.

PENNY: *Barbara, of anyone I've interviewed, you're possibly the person I've known the best, so it's somewhat different today. There's also a lot I don't know about you. I'd like to talk today about what you've done in your fifty years, but also about how you've done it and what you think about how you've done it.*

I know that you were a high school dropout at fifteen, you had two young daughters soon after that—you experimented with drugs and you were a draft counselor during the Vietnam War. You now have four children and two grandchildren. When your son Charlie, who has Down's syndrome, wasn't allowed in California's public schools, you successfully fought to create programs in the mainstream schools for kids like Charlie, winning a lawsuit that set a national precedent. And Charlie just graduated from Berkeley High this June. In the meantime, you taught about Down's syndrome to student doctors at Harvard Med School. You've also headed the Berkeley School Board, and most recently you co-founded and currently direct the Middle East Children's Alliance, which has raised over a million dollars in humanitarian aid for children in the West Bank and Gaza, and now Iraq.

You see the need to do something and you just do it. You take that power, and you move from your heart. Where does that motivation come from?

BARBARA: What's left to say, Penny? Except when you gave that history, or herstory, I was struck by an omission. In fact I don't just have four children; when I was very young and dropped out of school, I had a baby. I wasn't married, and I gave it up for adoption. So that's a piece of that history.

I guess most of what I've done throughout my life has been motivated out of anger. For example, when Charlie was born, I was really furious; I felt I had really been dealt a bad hand, because I had a child with Down's syndrome. There was a sense of, 'I'm not going to let this get me down.' I thought I had two choices: one was to buckle under in the depression I was feeling and do nothing—maybe even place him in an institution, as we were told to do by the genetic counselors and doctors who came to see me. But I couldn't do that. Because I had already given up that one child earlier, and there was no way I was going to part with another baby.

I was actually shocked at the response from everybody around us when Charlie was born. I should say everybody except my own mother and family, who always believed that we would never place Charlie [in an institution] and felt very strongly that we would keep him. I was shocked that doctors and social workers and rabbis all felt that my son's life was not worth much, because he was mentally retarded. That was just an amazing idea to me.

We traveled around in those early days looking at all these private institutions on the East Coast. At each one I saw a group of kids who were very happy, who really looked like they would be perfect in society, and those were the kids with Down's syndrome. I thought, 'Why are these kids here? Why aren't they home with their families?' I felt this was no place to put a child of mine. Or anybody's actually. If I went back and looked at those places again, I would feel even stronger about this decision; and I would expand it to not just the children with Down's syndrome, but to all of our children, no matter what's wrong with them. They all deserve to be given as much as they can be given at home with their mothers and fathers and siblings, and to be loved.

Much of what I did then, and before then, was out of a sense of anger at the injustice. And that has carried me through. I was involved as a draft counselor in the anti-Vietnam War movement in Philadelphia for five years, with my two little baby girls, and I was in and out of jails demonstrating.

But I certainly was blind to the injustice around Palestine. I can only blame that on the fact that I grew up in a Jewish Zionist home—not very religious, but I went to Hebrew school three days a week. I remember going with my mother to vote in national elections in Philadelphia when I was little, and she would let me come into the voting booth with her. Most of the time she would just go up and down the ballots, and she'd check off the names of everybody whose name was Jewish or sounded Jewish because, in fact, 'it would be good for Israel.' And this was the bottom line that I grew up with: 'Pass the salt at the dinner table—is it good for Israel?' Our first allegiance was to the state of Israel—because I was told all my life that when they came for us here, like they came for the Jews in Nazi Germany, if we kept Israel strong and secure, we would all have a safe place to go.

When the massacre at Sabra and Shatila[1] took place, I had just been elected to the Board of Education in Berkeley. And I can honestly say that I did not believe what I was hearing about the role Israel played in that *horrendous* massacre. A year later I was asked to speak at a Sabra and Shatila memorial, and by the time they got to me I couldn't speak; I felt that everything I was hearing was due to anti-semitism. I was very upset—I thought it was Israel-bashing. The same kinds of things that many people say about me today, I said about the progressive Jews who were principled enough, even back in 1982, to stand up and speak out.

I can remember the first time I was at a demonstration with progressive Jews in Berkeley. I was on the Board of Education. There was this beautiful little woman walking next to me with a sign saying Jews Against the Occupation. I asked her, 'What do you think about this?' She told me how there should be two states, one state for the Jewish people [Israel] and one state for the Palestinian people. I said, 'You're *Jewish*. How can you talk this way about Israel?' And she replied, 'It's because of my love for Israel that I do this work.' Her name is Suse Moyal and now I love and respect her; she's a member of Women in Black[2] and the Jewish Peace Lobby. But I was shocked to hear her talk that way back then. So I've grown a lot myself.

I guess my real growing took place in February of '88, a month after the intifada began. I had met Palestinians while working on Jesse Jackson's Presidential campaign, and I became interested in their plight. So I organized a delegation of North Americans to go to the Occupied Territories as guests of the Palestinians, to see for ourselves what was going on. We were the first American group to go there after the intifada began, and there were about twelve of us; we ranged in age from very young to Maudelle Shirek, who's on the Berkeley City Council and just had her eightieth birthday. We were locally-elected officials, we were clergy, we were Black, we were Latino, we were women, we were men, we were Catholic and two of us—Osha Neumann and myself— were Jewish. I think it was the most painful time Osha and I have ever had, because we really were shocked to see the brutality of the Israeli soldiers. We were shot at, we were tear-gassed, we were body-searched; anything that could have happened, happened. We also met with members of the Israeli peace movement. They were really wonderful, and they talked about the need for those of us in this country, especially American Jews, to speak out against this horrendous occupation.

I was just blown away by the trip, and when I came back we held a press conference at the San Francisco Press Club. My friend Howard Levine, who had been the editor of the *Daily Californian* when I was on the school board, was in the audience. After the press conference he asked, 'Now what are you going to do, since you're off the school board?' I said, 'Well, I really want to do something about this issue. I've always worked around issues with children—whether it was writing laws for disabled childrens' right to education, starting summer pro- grams for disabled and able-bodied children…and I am particularly struck by the effects of this brutal occupation on the children.' He told me he was very interested in this issue also; at the time he was a journalist for the *San Francisco Examiner* and said he was fed up with it. As a result of that meeting in May 1988, we started the Middle East Children's Alliance. So I guess all of what I do in life has come from this sense of seeing injustice.

And it's hard for me to say this because our politics are pretty opposite on most levels, but I have to think back to my own mother. Whatever her politics were, she was always taking care of people. If a neighbor was sick, if a relative was sick, she was the one who was there at the hospital feeding them. She was the one that was making the food for them when they came home from the hospital and shopping for them and bathing them. I come from this background of caring people. So in some ways my life has been wonderful, because I've been able to live on this level of being involved in what's most important in life.

And a lot of it's been very painful. I had one sibling, a sister, who committed suicide four years ago. She was fifty years old, four years older than I am. And that loss was very difficult. There've been a lot of losses in my life. My father died when I was sixteen. And being a mother has not been easy; I have been one of the funniest mothers, but probably not the best mother. I believed in Summerhill[3] and the right for kids to just grow up and be whatever they want—and they certainly have. And I have wonderful children; I'm proud of all my kids. I can't believe I'm a grandmother. Of course I don't let them call me anything that sounds like 'Grandma,' 'Nana,' 'Bubbie.' They will call me Barbara...or else!

PENNY: *I've seen that sense of humor accompany everything that you do. And I just wanted to backtrack a minute; could you describe your famous—infamous—action at the draft board in Philadelphia, about twenty years ago?*

BARBARA: I never thought that would come back to haunt me. But in 1967—it's *more* than twenty years—one of the young men that I was counselling was supposed to go for his physical, and he wasn't going to go. We decided that it would be very funny—we were always looking for great theater around that time—if I got dressed up in drag as a young man, and he gave me his draft notice, and *I* showed up for the physical. And I did! I actually crammed a whole lot of flyers into my pants, and when they told us to strip down in the draft board—there were about seventy-five young men and myself—we all stripped, and I started leafletting and counselling the young guys there. It was really hilarious, because the draft board didn't know how to handle it. They were completely enraged. They came with bayonets fixed, and I was led out of there and arrested, half-dressed, half undressed. But it was quite a moment. You had to have been there in the sixties to have appreciated all this.

PENNY: *How did the other draftees respond to you?*

BARBARA: Actually I counselled one of them and he left with me. Many of them were angry, but everybody thought it was very funny.

PENNY: *If you were writing your autobiography right now, what would the title be?*

BARBARA: 'God Works in Mysterious Ways.'

PENNY: *When you were talking about your kids, you said that you weren't a very good mother, but you were a funny mother. What makes you say that?*

BARBARA: I don't know, I've just always seen life with this tinge of humor, because so much of it has been so awful and so painful and sad. My way of dealing with life has been to see the humorous side in it. One of my daughters and myself were talking the other night about the days when I would wake them up and say, 'Please don't go to school today. Come on, let's stay home and play, we'll go shopping, we'll go to the movies, we'll go out for lunch. What are they gonna tell you at school? What do they know?' And the kids used to say, 'No, I've gotta go to school, Mom.' And I'd say, 'Oh, okay.' But there was a lot of humor in all of it. And there were a lot of hard times in it. Much of what we did in the sixties, much of the drug culture that we were involved in, turned out to be a nightmare for our kids. I'm not sorry that I was involved in smoking marijuana and doing LSD. I loved it. But I'm sorry for what kids today are going through. And I don't know if any of it's connected to that or not.

PENNY: *But why weren't you a 'good' mother? What is it that you didn't do, that you think you could've or should've done?*

BARBARA: In my second marriage we were always fighting. We never agreed on anything around the kids. It's hard for kids to have parents who each have a different view on *everything*: from, 'do you have to sit down at the table to eat or can you eat upstairs?' [to] 'Do you have to put the napkin on your lap or don't you have to put the napkin on your lap?' I personally don't care whether somebody has a napkin on their lap or not. There just seemed to me to be other issues that were more important than that.

In terms of my son Alex, I think I drove him crazy. I was not ready to have another child eleven months after I had Charlie, my son with Down's syndrome. I just couldn't believe that there was nothing wrong with Alex. If he'd cry, I would take him in and make them do an upper GI, or a lower GI[4], or have hearing tests. Children's Hospital in Oakland said that my children had more hearing tests than any children they'd ever seen in their lives. If I called them and they didn't hear me immediately, I'd put them in the car and take them for a hearing test. Alex couldn't hear me say, 'Come on in here for dinner,' or 'Come on in here and do your homework.' But if I was to open an M&M wrapper four rooms away, and he heard the crinkle of the candy paper, he was in there in thirty seconds. Selective hearing.

Life was a struggle. And I was struggling. I was unhappy to be at home, and yet I hadn't gone to school, and I felt like I didn't know what I wanted to do with my life. Here I was at home when I really wanted to be out. And I wasn't prepared to have all these children. I guess I was a good mother in some ways, but in a lot of ways my kids got a raw deal. They had a mother who threw herself into the limelight of politics in Berkeley, and that didn't just start with my being on the school board, it started...

I'll tell you a story. From the time we moved to Berkeley in 1973 when Charlie was four years old, we lived around the corner from a soda fountain named Ozzie's. Every day for twelve years, Charlie could walk around the corner to Ozzie's late in the afternoon, he'd sit down on the same stool every day, and he'd order the same thing: tuna, chips and a Coke. It was the only place he could go by himself at all in life and it was two hours of respite that I had every day. Now any mother who has a retarded child, or any disabled child, will know that there's nothing more in life that you cherish than respite time.

One day in July 1981 Charlie came home and said, 'Mom, Ozzie's has been sold.' I jumped up and ran around the corner to Ozzie, and said, 'What do you mean it's been sold?' He told me that a group of unscrupulous speculators had bought the soda fountain and three stores next to it for a very exaggerated price. And the name of the buyer was Mr. Wright. I said to Ozzie, 'Are you gonna fight this with me, Ozzie? You cannot leave this store.' He said, 'I'm in it with you Barbara.' I ran home, I called Mr. Wright, and said, 'Mr. Wright, you don't know me, my name's Barbara Lubin. I have a son who's retarded, he's just a little boy, and he eats at Ozzie's every day. I need this soda fountain to stay there.' I forgot to tell you that they were going to raise the rent 400 percent. I said, 'I will buy back the pharmacy. I understand you paid $780,000 for the property. Tell me what you need to make a quick profit, and I'll raise it.' Of course, I had no idea how I would raise it, but I've done things that I never thought I could do before, so I thought I'd just go out and get the money. There was this silence. And then, Mr. Wright *laughed*. He said, 'You must think I'm crazy, that I would

give up a deal like this for some crazy woman and her retarded son.'
I then said, 'Mr. Wright, you have just made the biggest mistake of your
life. You will *never* develop that property, ever.'

The next day I set up a table in front of Ozzie's, and two weeks
after I [had] called Mr. Wright we called for a neighborhood meeting at
my house. At 7:30 that night no one was there, and I said to Ozzie,
'Well, I guess nobody cares.' At 7:45, there were over 400 people on
the front lawn of my house, and we had the first meeting of the
Elmwood Preservation Alliance. For the next year, we worked on
saving Ozzie's, the soda fountain. I was at that table seven days a week
for a year, from early in the morning till seven at night. My kids and I
and Ozzie leafletted our neighborhood of 5,000 homes about three
times a month all year. It became a big national thing. Midway through
the year, Ozzie and I realized that even though we had gotten the City
Council to pass a moratorium on unjust evictions and unfair rent
increases, that unless we had commercial rent control there was no real
way to save the merchants. So with the help of two consultants, we
wrote the first commercial rent control law that America has had since
World War II. There was commercial rent control in New York City
during World War II, but that's the only time. Ozzie and I and all the
folks from the soda fountain formed a little campaign committee and
raised $8,000 for this initiative. The other side, Goliath, or the spec-
ulators and landlords in Berkeley, raised hundreds of thousands of
dollars to fight this. We were on all the national television stations, and
the *Wall Street Journal* would come and interview me—they all thought
I was crazy, and it was really very exciting.

I'll never forget the night of that election when we won. We got
73 percent of the vote. It was the first time in America that there was
commercial rent control in any city. We had it for four years until, I
think it was the California Supreme Court ruled that a city couldn't have
commercial rent control. But that threw me into the limelight.

My children had been eating at Ozzie's for the last ten years, and
most of the time they didn't have money, and they'd just say, 'put it on
the tab.' It was sort of this joke, and I just thought Ozzie was being nice
to me. Then one day I was sitting in there, and he said, 'The tab is
getting very big, Barbara.' I said, 'It is? You've kept track all these years?'
'Yeah', he said, 'it's about $4,000.00.' I said, 'You're kidding? What can
I do?' 'You can work here two days a week and pay it off,' he told me.

So I became a soda jerk and worked at Ozzie's two days a week.
It was like being a stand-up comic. All of these regular folks and
television people came in, and it was from the counter that I ran my

campaign for school board that next summer. I ran for the Berkeley school board, even though I hadn't graduated high school, hadn't gone to college. But I had been at every school board meeting in the city for the last ten years, fighting for special education, suing the school district—and I was elected very handily.

Two weeks after I got on the school board, we were told that because they were millions of dollars in debt, we had to close four or five schools in Berkeley. The next four years were a nightmare. People were fighting us, setting up pickets around my house, screaming. They had petitions on every street corner to recall us when we closed the schools—we, the first progressive school board anywhere. We felt that we weren't going to just close the schools in the flatlands, and in fact we only closed one school in the flatlands, but we closed four schools in the Berkeley hills.[5]

It was difficult for me to go from being the neighborhood sweetheart, because of my commercial rent control and saving the soda fountain, to being the enemy of the neighborhoods because I closed their schools. We had the same number of school sites open in 1982 with 8,700 students that we had open ten years earlier with 15,000 students, but in 1982 the schools were all half empty. I had gone to all those school board meetings for years, saying it was irresponsible to leave all the schools open. Once again, the good folks of Berkeley supported closing the schools—until their school was named—and then they became the anti-school closure people. I saw opportunism and racism, and I became very disgusted; I learned why people down in poor neighborhoods are messed with, and not those up in the hills. Because people who live in the hills have all the time and energy and the money to pay the legal bills.

The final thing I did on the school board, which was very difficult, was serving on a public housing committee formed by the Mayor. The City of Berkeley had gotten seven million dollars to build fifty-one units of four and five bedroom public housing units, and we held hearings in all the neighborhoods. We had a committment to do 'scattered sites' where there would be no more than twelve houses on one site. And it was really a shock to me that all these good progressive folks supported public housing—'but not in *their* neighborhood.' It was a major battle to build these units of public housing, and we lost about twelve units. When I see families on the street today who are homeless, I think, my God, I don't know how people who fought the public housing can sleep at night, *knowing* that they're responsible for at least twelve of those families not having homes.

While I was doing all this, I became involved with Gus [Newport], then the mayor of Berkeley, and that influenced a lot of what I've done in my life and helped open my eyes to the Palestine issue. I first met Gus when I set up that table in front of Ozzie's. I had never met him before, because I was only interested in disabled rights; if you weren't disabled or the mother of a disabled child, I didn't care what you had to say. I got to Ozzie's late one day, and Gus was sitting there. I went in to Ozzie, and asked, 'Who is that jerk sitting at my table?' He said, 'That jerk's the mayor of Berkeley.'

I've opened up to many things because of Gus. I remember going to a meeting with him in 1984 to pick delegates for Jesse Jackson to the National Democratic Convention. By the end of the day, I'd been elected to be one of the delegates. It was right after Jesse had made that very unfortunate remark about New York being 'hymie-town,' referring to Jews as 'hymies.' I thought it was important that somebody who was Jewish and progressive stand up and support Jesse. I didn't like what he said, and he certainly has apologized for the rest of his life for it—but I felt that the politics and the progressive voice that he had were far too important to throw out because of his stupid remark.

I then started an organization called Jews for Jesse Jackson. And all of this while I was a soda jerk, on the school board, a delegate for Jesse, and in the midst of this horrendous divorce, with four children.

PENNY: *Do you see any of these decisions as mistakes?*

BARBARA: Yes, I do. I think that there was a lot wrong with my marriage and I should not have been as frightened to leave it as I was. I should have been more principled; I should have left it before I became involved with Gus. Whatever differences I had with my husband, he didn't deserve that. He wouldn't have done that to me.

PENNY: *Listening to you talk, I hear a lot of qualities I'm familiar with: the determination, the courage, the outrageousness. To me that all connects with a sense of power and a fighting spirit. When I first met you, less than two years ago, I walked into your office and you spent two hours talking to me—about being a Jew, about anti-semitism, about the intifada and your experiences in Palestine and Israel. I was amazed at your vulnerability and your accessibility with me, someone you didn't know at all. Since then I've noticed that even though you're a widely-respected public figure who's on a first-name basis with many world personalities, who's called by the mainstream media as well as by the alternative media, who takes your work very seriously—you lack a sense of self-importance that separates you from other people. During the Gulf*

War when you were very much in the spotlight, you consistently made a point to share that spotlight with the others organizing with you. You just don't seem to use the historic, what I'll call 'male model' of achieving power through domination or through intimidation.

Instead, you come from the heart. You're accessible to whoever walks in the door of that office or calls you on the phone. And more than that, you have an ability to empower others. You believe in us as if it's the most natural thing in the world, and so you help us to believe in ourselves. I wanted to bring this up because I have found it to be a rare approach, and I wonder where that comes from in you?

BARBARA: In my family, the women were very smart in a lot of ways and very controlling in other ways. So I grew up with this feeling of 'you're a woman, you've got power.' In terms of my wanting to share the limelight, I think that whatever was wrong in my family, I was very much loved—and I have a pretty strong ego. I don't need to be the person who's in the front line, who provides leadership. To me it's a relief when there are other people who come forward. I think that the movement has for too long operated around people and personalities. And that's what's wrong with all of it—we haven't brought other people up. There are people out there who are just as good as I am, and even if they're not strong on this issue, they can learn. That's our role. For those of us who the media does listen to, when they call and say, 'Who else can I talk to?' it's our role to tell them to call the organizer from the Chicano Moratorium, to tell them to call the soldier's mother who spoke out against the war. These are the people who need to be talked to. Like our friend in high school, who organized teach-ins at his school, who marched with us in all those demonstrations. To me that's what's important. Now he's going to Harvard. If we can empower young men, young women, old men, old women...I don't want to be the person who's out there. I'm just as happy to be marching with the people in the crowds, as to be up on the stage.

But I don't have very thick skin. When I'm attacked publicly, I do take it personally. I'm very sensitive to the Jewish community in particular, especially the progressive Jewish community, when they criticize me. One after another they take me out to lunch and say that I'm doing such good work *but*...but I'm not balanced, I'm not this, I'm not that. That's very painful to me, and it's very difficult to continue on the path at times. None of those people feel any stronger about Israel and its future than I do, or care about being Jewish any more than I do. If they really cared about the future of Jews and Israel, they would take their cue from the Israeli peace movement. They'd stop this brutality that's going on there and would make Israel the democracy it claims to be.

PENNY: *You traveled to Iraq a week before President Bush started bombing Baghdad, and you returned to Iraq a few months after the war 'ended.' We worked together against the war, and I know we both felt an incredible amount of despair that what was happening was exactly what we had been spending our lives trying to prevent from happening for so many years. Have any lessons emerged for you about that period of time?*

BARBARA: I don't think I'll ever forget those months, during the war, in the Middle East Children's Alliance office with you, Penny, me and Howard—while everyone on the street in Berkeley walked in. Next to having Charlie and those early months of trying to deal with a retarded child, those were the most intense months I have ever had. Instead of being on the fringe, as most groups who work around this issue of Palestine and Israel are, we were thrown into the mainstream of the peace movement—because the peace movement had been caught with its pants down. They had no Middle East platform, because nobody wanted to criticize Israel. So, who was there? Who had the platform? It was us.

And it was a really intense time, on every level—the vigils every night that we organized, for example. I'll never forget, every evening turning around and asking, 'What time is it?' and you, me or Howard would say, 'It's 5:00.' Knowing that at least two of us had to take that huge banner downstairs and stand outside with our candles, in either the rain or the cold—but *doing* it. Organizing those demonstrations and rallies…and being some of the only people in this area who, from the very beginning, condemned Saddam Hussein and his brutality and the invasion of Kuwait—*and* who called for the end of *all* the occupations. Who brought the occupation of Palestine by Israel into the discussion of what was going on in the Gulf. Who stood up and recognized that you can talk about 'Bring the troops home!' all you want, but if you don't really have a peace conference and address all of the issues of occupation of the area, there will never be peace there. It was very frustrating; I think it will be a long time before I can evaluate all of it. I really was burned out.

When you and I went to Palestine, with fifteen women[6] the end of December [1990], you *know* that every Palestinian, *and* every Israeli, said there would be no war. The same was true for me when I went to Iraq. It was a little bit like being on the deck of the Titanic, for us as

American women, knowing all too well what this government and this President could, and in fact did, do.

Everybody says, 'I'm so wiped out, we didn't stop the war. Look what happened, it didn't mean anything.' Well, it *does* mean something. It means something to each of us to be out there. Some of the demonstrations that you and I went to were really wonderful. In particular, the dinner that we organized just before the war. Three hundred people showed and we had expected about seventy-five. We were watering down the soup in the kitchen. Then the next morning, getting up at 5:00 AM to go to the BART [subway] and seeing *everybody* we knew going with their banners to the Federal Building. We were so wonderful—all of us. Old people, young people, women, gays, lesbians, clergy, kids—hundreds of us got arrested that day. And then to be locked up in that room with ninety people for the entire day at the police station, and the two of us standing up with this captive audience, giving a 'report-back' from our trip to Palestine and Iraq. That was the best! And that woman who contributed $600 to our humanitarian aid campaign as a result!

When people say 'we didn't do anything,' and 'what's the use,' I am reminded of Nelson Mandela who languished in jail for twenty-seven years, struggling for the end of apartheid and for justice in South Africa. For us to throw in the towel after a few months of demonstrating out on the streets, that's pretty ridiculous.

I personally am not willing to throw out socialism, and I think that we have to regroup, to start again. I was never a member of the Communist Party, although for the four years I sat on the school board I was accused of being in the Party and never denied that; but I think it's important to look at what went wrong [with Communism] and to be able to criticize. We have to evaluate, to be able to be critical and to stop finger-pointing. There's a lot of middle-of-the-road people who really believe in peace and justice, and whose voices have to be heard. These are the people, we're the people, who need to build a movement. And we need to do it *now*. So that when, and if, the next war takes place, the people who are in the ultra-left don't take it over. *We all* need to be in the leadership.

PENNY: *When you say 'we all,' you mean...?*

BARBARA: I mean the women. I mean the groups that I've worked with during this war: the progressive Jewish groups, the churches, the labor groups, the women's groups, the lesbian and gay groups. People who have a full agenda, and not an ultra-left agenda. That's what I mean.

PENNY: *So what keeps you going?*

BARBARA: I've always gone between being depressed and sort of seeing the folly and the beauty of life. What keeps me going is my children, and the responsibility I have to them to keep on going and to be strong. And to try and build a better world for them and their children, and for all the youth in America, and in the world. I feel very strongly that we as older people have that responsibility.

I also have a lot of really wonderful friends. And I have Howard, who is really there for me and is my very best friend. He is eighteen years younger than me, and when I first started seeing him, I didn't want anybody to know because I'm so much older. It took me awhile to calm down. I was constantly thinking, 'What will it be like when I'm older and he's younger?' [But I realized] I don't know what it'll be like; I don't know what anything will be next year. I don't know what it will be tomorrow.

And my sense of humor keeps me going. Life is hilarious. Whoever thought that I would be having dinner with Yasser Arafat?[7] Would be sitting in a meeting with Hafez Assad of Syria? Would be having breakfast with King Hussein of Jordan? It's all very funny and very wonderful. And very unpredictable. You never know what's next.

PENNY: *Do you have any heroes or heroines?*

BARBARA: I guess Emma Goldman[8] is one of my heroines. I've loved women who have stood up and spoken out. Virginia Woolf[9] and Sylvia Plath[10] are two of my very favorite people. And I really loved Martin Luther King[11] and Malcolm X. Because they did it all. I just loved Malcolm's anger and his truth. I think you have to be angry.

Yesterday I met with the head of the Buddhist Peace Fellowship, and he asked, 'Do you believe in non-violence?' And I *said* I did, but after he left, I was thinking I don't know…I *believe* in non-violence, but I also believe after awhile people have a right to take up arms and struggle. If I were a Jew in Germany or in Poland, I wouldn't have believed in non-violence. I think that people in this country in the movement who sit and talk about non-violence speak about it from a very luxurious position. Most of them speak about it with white skin. They're not people who ever will have to make that decision on a real important level, like the African National Congress and people in South Africa. Like people who are struggling for freedom. I think you get to a point where you just finally have to *do* something. I certainly would have done it in Germany.

I'm mesmerized by the evilness of what happened there, the twelve or thirteen million people who died at the hands of the Nazis. And people saying, 'It could happen anywhere.' I don't believe that. I don't believe that every one of us has that in us. *I* don't have that in me; I can be angry, and I could probably kill someone if they were going to hurt someone I loved and that's what I had to do. But I couldn't do *that*. If I had lived in Nazi Europe, I would have been one of the people who took up arms. I could see myself in the Warsaw Ghetto getting into a lot of trouble.

PENNY: *But what about Martin Luther King and Ghandi?*

BARBARA: I don't think I would have had it in me to do it that way. Although I marched in the Poor People's Campaign in Washington, D.C. and heard Martin Luther King at the Washington Monument, and loved him. I think what he did and the movement was very good, and I certainly think that the first obligation is to do everything possible through non-violent means and through conflict resolution. But at some point, people have to stand up. That wouldn't have worked in Germany. It wouldn't have worked in South Africa. Martin Luther King was moving and realizing that there were times when non-violence doesn't work, and he was changing a lot politically. And that was one of the reasons he was killed.

PENNY: *I just have one more question. You have two granddaughters, one of whom is just six weeks old. What lessons would you most like to pass on to them about how to live in this world?*

BARBARA: It's a very hard time to grow up. It really pains me to think of the world our grandchildren are growing up in. I want my grand-daughters to grow up to be very strong women. I want them to love themselves. I want them to respect other people, to respect the earth, and to trust people. I want them to go to school so that they have all the tools they need to make the decisions they need to make in life. And I want them to wait and have children when they're older, so they can really find their way in the world. I don't want them to take any shit from any man or woman, ever.

PENNY: *So even though I can look at your life and see how successful you are, you don't want them to do the same things you've done?*

BARBARA: I want them to do more. I don't want them to get married and have a lot of kids because they don't know what else to do.

PENNY: *Anything else you want to say, about women and power?*

BARBARA: I remember when I was living in Philadelphia and I had these two little baby girls. A friend of mine knocked on the door—this was in 1965 or '66—and said she was having a meeting at her house. I said, 'What kind of meeting?' I was a draft counselor then, we were all involved in the anti-war movement. She said, 'It's women.' I said, 'What do you mean, *women?*' She said, 'Well, we're talking about forming a women's organization, an organization for women.' And I said, 'You're kidding!' You know, it just never entered my mind. I was really tuned in to all these strong domineering women around me—I thought we controlled the earth on some level. So I went to this meeting, and it was one of the founding meetings of the National Organization for Women in Philadelphia. I went to a lot of demonstrations, I burned my bra. I'll never forget that. It was great.

I've always operated in both worlds pretty comfortably, with men and with women. I hope my granddaughters are more involved as women and are more identified as women than I have been. Because I have a hard time hanging onto that, and I sometimes lose how important it is to see it as a woman instead of just as a progressive person. I have to fault myself in that, because I think it's really important that women hang in there for women and speak for women, that we are vigilant about our rights and about justice for women. If we don't, we'll lose everything.

NOTES:

1. In 1982, thousands of Palestinians were killed in massacres at the Sabra and Shatila refugee camps in Lebanon.

2. 'Women in Black' is a weekly one-hour vigil of women against the Israeli occupation of the West Bank and Gaza. It began in many cities soon after the intifada started, and is now observed by women in cities all over the world

3. Summerhill was a private, experimental child-centered school program started in Great Britain soon after World War II.

4. Upper GI/lower GI (gastro-intestinal)—tests designed to detect any problems in the upper or lower gastro-intestinal tracts.

5. The flatlands refer to the area between the San Francisco Bay and the Berkeley Hills, primarily populated by working class and poor people. As with most cities in America, the hillier areas are reserved for the more affluent.

6. The U.S. Women's Peace Brigade to Palestine and Israel, sponsored by the Middle East Children's Alliance.

7. Yasser Arafat [1929–] is the current Chairman of the Palestine Liberation Organization.

8. Emma Goldman [1869–1940] was an anarchist and advocate of women's rights. She was imprisoned at various times: for distributing birth control information, for opposing the draft and for advocating that unemployed people steal bread if they were starving. She was eventually deported to her native Russia. Goldman is well known for statement, "If I can't dance, I won't be in your revolution."

9. Virginia Woolf [1882–1941] was a British novelist, critic and early feminist. She is author of two well-known novels, *Mrs. Dalloway* and *To The Lighthouse*, among many other novels, collections of essays and short stories. In her fiction she was interested in revealing the inner essence of her characters, and is often quoted from her famous essay "A Room of One's Own," in which she states the need for a woman to have space and adequate resources to allow for her creative process.

10. Sylvia Plath [1932–1963] was an American writer, best known for her autobiographical novel *The Bell Jar*, which centers on a woman's struggle with 'madness,' and points to the impact of socio-environmental mores and conditions on women's mental health. Her *Collected Poems* received the Pulitzer Prize for Poetry in 1982.

11. Martin Luther King [1929–1968] was a Baptist preacher and a Civil Right's leader, assassinated in Memphis, Tennessee. He led the March on Washington, organized many sit-ins, and was jailed in Alabama for the peaceful march he led there. He organized and inspired many such nonviolent protests against racial inequalities and advocated integration. He was awarded the Nobel Peace Prize in 1964.

For information on Malcolm X, see notes following interview with Maudelle Shirek.

Photos by Darryl Klegg

Hi-ah Park

JUNE 1991

"When we learn something, we always think we're learning something from outside. That's why our mind is so busy...Transformation is not difficult because it's too far away; it's because it's so close."

Light as a bird's feather, she leaps and twirls in a sacred dance devoted to the death of ego. Earlier, at a dawn's purification ritual, she led us naked into the mist-covered lake, emerging again without a sound. Late that evening, eating dinner after the day's fast, she chats spiritedly with friends at the table, often throwing her head back and laughing until her small frame hums with energy. Hi-ah Park defies any preconceived image of shaman. Her tremendous power neither intimidates nor marks her as superior—rather, her easy laughter, tireless energy, and body-oriented focus draw her to us. Hi-ah conveys a profound sense of flowing completely with the life force.

PENNY: *Hi-ah, in 1963 you were the first woman chosen as a court musician and dancer by the Korean National Classical Music Institute, and you've been called 'the greatest dancer in the Korean tradition for this generation.' I know your initiation as a shaman in 1981 sparked a national renewal of respect in Korea for this ancient indigenous Korean spiritual practice. What was the process that led you to shamanism?*

HI-AH: Why did I choose to be shaman instead of a nun? Christianity is overwhelming in Korea right now—and there is a Buddhist monk nun too—and there are many other paths of spirituality. When I look back in history, the first real Korean indigenous women were shamans. But in patriarchal society, women are not supposed to be powerful.

Shamanism looks like a religion, but it's not—it's a way of life. That's probably why I am drawn to it. And I see shaman as the original artist; probably that's another reason I'm a shaman.

PENNY: *As I've experienced you working, I've been especially moved and affected by how you integrate body, mind and spirit, along with art and ritual. Is this integration the source of your power?*

HI-AH: It's a life process. When you really search towards that longing place, there's no other way. It's genuine integration, not a concept or perception. It's a real life force. In other words…integration is love [laughs]. I cannot explain. It's like when you feel joy, you know, energy just springs up.

PENNY: *In your workshop, it seemed like you were mainly trying to get us out of our heads. You kept doing bodywork with us and saying, 'I still hear your voices [inside your heads] talking.'*

HI-AH: I'm not putting down intelligence. What I'm talking is spiritual intelligence. There's no separation between right and left brain. It's whole being. That is integration to me, you know? How could you have a whole being? You have to love.

PENNY: *And you feel that as the source of your power?*

HI-AH: Whenever anybody talking of power, I become quiet.

PENNY: *Tell me about that.*

HI-AH: Because power has been abused in history. The only power I know is love. And spiritual power. But out there, there is power which is not service but manipulation.

PENNY: *You said to us, 'Anyone who says that they heal other people, be wary of them. What a real healer tries to do is create an environment where the person heals themselves.'*

HI-AH: Right. Many people think somebody can heal other people. Yes and no. What I mean yes, is that healer can create special environment to trust so person can feel safe. Like a midwife preparing the place for the baby, delivering the baby. That's the healer's job. And so healer/healee can come meet together. Our organism knows how to heal itself. Healer's job is to create that safe place, to witness and to listen.

PENNY: *In the ritual you performed last night, is that what you were doing with several of the women who needed healing?*

HI-AH: In this case, theater is healing. Because theater is not something to show. Whatever *is* [in you], bring it there. It's expression of your stagnated emotions, and in that moment between healer and healees, communication becomes play.

PENNY: *Tell me more about using ritual theater to express stagnated emotion.*

HI-AH: In ancient time—I never studied, but somebody told me—near Turkey and Greece, there is one time people gather at a healing place; and in a month the patients process their unknown fears and terrors, all their suppressed emotions. It becomes theater, and that is the healing ceremony. And the more I do shamanic ritual, this is what it is.

PENNY: *And yet, you have a profound simplicity and humility in your work, a lightness—so that even though it's very intense, you just do not take yourself too seriously. You have such a strong aspect of fun in your teaching, and I guess that connects to your Clown. That was very new for me to experience.*

HI-AH: Unless you have that quality, it's too heavy. You will drown in it. Because people are so attached to suffering. And that's why shaman has to have this clown quality. Otherwise, it's almost impossible to handle this kind of situation. You have to [figuratively] die. And after that process, you recognize these tragedies and you're no longer attached to it.

The Korean Female Shaman is called Mudang. I like to include five meanings of MU (무). One is MU (巫)—Shaman: two persons are doing the Ritual Dance between heaven and earth. MU (舞)—Dance; MU (武)—Warrior; MU (無)—Emptiness; and MU [Hi-ah had no character for this MU]—Clown. These are the qualities of a shaman. MU-A (無我) is the context of a shaman's work—meaning literally, No-Self/Ecstasy.

In the MU meaning Sacred Dance, dance transforms fear into primal spirit. In the MU meaning Warrior—in this case, woman warrior—the warrior doesn't mean killing the other's head in battle, but dealing with your own fear. Shaman's job is defeating this fear. Almost all problems, if you look at it, the cause is fear. The warrior asks for the death of ego, to change your life according to your true vision. But you have to prepare this clean ground; that's why all the rituals require the purification ceremony. The moment you are purifying your emotion you become like a child, innocent, so you surrender to the God. And that is the death of ego.

When you manage the death of ego, you get into the point of Emptiness, nothingness. This is long process [laughs], but it can be fast—it's not a rational process. When you reach that point, you are empty, empty of separation. Because the fear comes from separation from the God in you, right? That's why you fear...

PENNY: *What do you mean, emptiness?*

HI-AH: It's a paradox, very difficult to understand. When you are empty of the garbage, you are really full with wonderful feeling. Because you are empty of separation. That's the MU-A, Ecstasy. If you reach that point, you are no longer attached to tragedy, and this release helps you laugh at your life. It helps to have a sense of humor about yourself. So the tragedy becomes a comedy. That's the Clown.

The shaman understands this process, and when they meet all the tragedy and drama, they have a great compassion. They know the source of suffering is fear, so they learn how to laugh at it. Also they have the ability to feel what this patient feels. When you have that pain, it's genuine. It looks so real. But the faster that you touch it, the faster you can get out of it, like a dispersing. The shaman already had previous experience like that. They know what that pain means. It looks horrible, terrifying, but they know this is a good thing that is happening because you are moving into that liberation.

PENNY: *So the point then is not to get stuck.*

HI-AH: That's right. And ritual is rite of passage to deliver that.

PENNY: *Does that go along with fear being our ally?*

HI-AH: Yes. If you're not honest about this fear, it becomes poison. But if you're one hundred percent honest about the emotion, in this case your fear, there is nothing bad and good; there is truth. That is the terror, the terrible beauty. No matter how terrifying, better be honest about it. Through this catharsis, you will experience grief or joy, what you call this ecstasy. And that moment your heart is opening. But it comes when your heart is dying...

What does that mean, heart is dying? Most of the time, heart is not focusing on one point because of conflicts—duality, good and bad. When it is not divided and has *one* focus and concentration—that's the shaman's ability. That's the only time you can really integrate.

PENNY: *That's what I find so difficult: concentrating and turning off that voice. Is there anything more we can be doing to quiet our minds and concentrate, so that we can access that power?*

HI-AH: That's why the Yoga is a discipline—Pranayama, or practice of the breath, you know [laughs]. How to quiet your mind? First, watch the mind. And not fight with it. Manage stillness. That's what I mean, you have to die. When you die, this becomes quiet. But don't fight with your internal dialogue. The more you try to stop it, becomes more noisier, right? That's why breath is important. Breathe in and breathe out. If you focus on breath, eventually your mind will become quiet.

PENNY: *The first time I went to your workshop, you proceeded around the circle and looked each of us in the eyes for several seconds. When you looked at me, even though it was from quite a distance, I felt this incredible heat. I had been feeling not very with myself, but when you looked at me, I felt very seen. I felt the heat, along with this great sense of intimacy. It was wonderful, and it filled up that yearning place inside me. The question in my mind was, 'please let me learn whatever I should learn.' What are you doing, when you work that way with us?*

HI-AH: It's ironic. What I'm doing is *not* doing [laughs]. And already Westerner will be lost...but the Oriental philosopher Chuang Tsu,[1] a very unknown philosopher, wrote many poems about this undoing. Doing, Not Doing. Modern education is so focused on *doing*, doing, doing; you have to do it, do it, do it. But the sitting...when I gaze at you, it is complete stillness. This is like a minor samadhi [dead] state. I make myself completely empty. When I am in that place, I become like a mirror. How can you become busy when you looking at the mirror? So what I'm doing is helping you slowing down. Slowing down. Slowing down. So what you're actually learning is unlearning, if that makes sense to you.

When we learn something, we always think we're learning something from outside. That's why our mind is so busy. But what I was trying to do is to find the truth in you. You keep saying, 'I, I, I'—but you never touch that 'I,' as long as you are so busy. Transformation is not difficult because it's too far away; it's because it's so close. When I'm sitting down and gazing you, it's to remind you of the nearby. By my being there, you reflect yourself in me.

PENNY: *So I was really feeling my own heat?*

HI-AH: Right. When you are in that place, you connect with Kundalini. Spiritual heat. It's there waiting for you. But most people have been so busy looking outside, their heat was wasted. I'm giving you one moment witnessing your own heat, by me being present that moment. I just become a mirror for you [laughs].

PENNY: *Thank you. Another thing you said in your workshop intrigued me. You were talking about how in Western culture there is such a focus on each of us trying to be so extraordinary...*

HI-AH: That's right. You think this heating is belonging to an extraordinary person, but you all forget, *you* have it. In order to find your own spiritual heat, you actually lose it sometimes [laughs]. This is the difficult tendency of spiritual materialism, trying to build this 'spiritual force.' It's like a material greed, you know. You think you can *get* it or *buy* it. One thing; you have to really give up this attitude of *grasping*. If you're not greedy about 'extraordinary,' if you really integrate 'ordinary human being': that is the real extraordinary human being. And we *are* extraordinary. But you think you have to be *really* extraordinary, like a medicine man.

In a restaurant in Italy they introduced me once: 'This is Korean shaman Hi-ah Park.' And the others look at me and say, in Italian, 'But she's so normal!' [laughs] When I heard that I was very glad. This is a vast compliment for me.

Real jade, real gemstone, doesn't have to be on exhibit. You know? That is a commercial stone they trying to shine. You shine when you need to shine. But most of the time you need to be wrapped. Like the stove burner—you don't turn on all the time. Then you would lose the real energy. The sharper the sword, you have to keep it in the case. You only pull out when you need to use it, and the rest of the time put it in and turn off. Ordinary. That is the real extraordinary.

PENNY: *Last night you said you found it exciting to work with groups of women. Do you have any special message for us as women?*

HI-AH: I been watching men, how they work...They are wonderful too. But I found that women work a little differently [laughs]. How I can say? Their sensitivity is different. And they understand more women's feelings. Spiritually, you need this kind of sensitivity in order to see the invisible, in order to touch the intangible, in order to hear the inaudible.

I think this is a very important time. Women need to learn from women. I didn't think that very seriously until recently, but the more I work with women, I'm discovering how many women terrified to touch their own power.

PENNY: *What do you think it is that makes us so terrified of touching our power?*

HI-AH: Because in history, they have been teaching that women not supposed to be powerful. In the eleventh century, there was a magician, a healer—I think her name was Hildegarde Nun.[2] She was really a saint. You know that time was patriarchal society; after almost ten century later she finally got the title, saint. That's why witches have been cursed, you know, along with those shamans in Korea. When I was performing in [the province of] Trento, in Italy, they told me that 1500 witches were burned there—only 500 years ago.

Men don't want women to have power. So women blindly believed the power belonged to men. That's why all the shaman women, before they're initiated, they all go through death. Otherwise they couldn't accept the power, with ordinary consciousness. But I think we are living in a century for the women awakening. Especially now the dawn of the twenty-first century, women have a special work to do.

PENNY: *What is that?*

HI-AH: *Awakening* [laughs]. And accept who we are. *As* we are; as women. One of the biggest mistake is woman imitating a man. Woman is powerful because she is woman. And it applies to me, because one period of my life in the 1970's, I was just depressed at being identified as a woman. Because this was before my initiation—I think unconsciously woman identifies as powerless, and I couldn't take it anymore.

PENNY: *Well, what changed you?*

HI-AH: After initiation…no, that's not true! The other way around. Woman is powerful because we are *women*. But that doesn't mean women have to be weak and look like a madonna—though the madonna is powerful too. But there is another terrifying beauty. In India they call it Kali or wrathful side of Dakini.[3] And we have to remember that power, but not by threatening others. We have to touch that inner energy life force, that is the real empowerment, and we have to learn how to balance these two sides. We must learn how to be neutral and grounded. Until then, we cannot use this power properly.

PENNY: *But how do we learn that balance?*

HI-AH: [laughs] When you accept who you are.

PENNY: *I'm still not sure what you meant when you said you changed your attitude, in the mid-seventies?*

HI-AH: That was a time when I didn't want to wear makeup like a woman. I didn't want to please, you know? Woman's sexuality felt like a prostitute to me. In a way I was rebelling against the way I saw women had to sell their love. I wondered what women supposed to be, you know? But after I touched this area, now I want to be beautiful.

It's okay, it's wonderful. Goddess have to be beautiful. But not before I touched that real genuine woman power.

PENNY: *Of accepting yourself.*

HI-AH: Right. I feel very uncomfortable when I see women in high heels flirting to men. If that is all coming from a whole place, it's alright. It's also powerful. However, just pleasing men, I'm not satisfied with that. Should be the other way around! [laughs] And believe it or not, when women are powerful, men go around that woman and men are floating. But women should recognize their power. They don't have to buy men's love. When they love themselves, men will come to them.

N O T E S :

1. Very little is known about Chuang Tsu and what is known is inextricably woven into legend. It is said that he was a contemporary of Mencius, an official in the Lacquer Garden of Meng in Honan province in China around the fourth century B.C. He developed the doctrine of Taoism (the belief system that all things come together in an indefinable harmony) with rigorous logic. His fables and humorous writings are imaginative and poetic, reflecting a brilliant and original mind.

2. Abbess Hildegard of Bingen [1098–1179] born in what is now Germany, has been called "one of the most creative personalities of the Middle Ages." She was a visionary, naturalist, poet, playwright and composer, as well as politician and diplomat.

3. Kali is the Buddhist divine aspect which governs our time, as the female aspect of the principle of destruction. She is seen, in a positive sense, as destruction of the ego.

Dakini are the messenger forces in Tibetan Buddhism which appear to highly awakened lamas.

For information on Kundalini, see notes following interview with Vicki Noble.

Photo by Bev Ramsey

FROM THE HEART

Fran Peavey

APRIL 1990/MARCH 1991

"When someone on the street asks you for spare change…look in their eyes and make some connection. Give them something. If it's not a quarter, give them respect. Give them a blessing. Touch them on the shoulder and wish them well. Build a connection. Take your heart…and touch that suffering and take it in. Don't hide from it."

Jammed into a dank, low-roofed parking area beneath the San Francisco Federal Building, several hundred of us wrestled out of our plastic handcuffs. After being arrested for non-violently protesting the newly-announced U.S. trade embargo on Nicaragua, we were gathered into a temporary holding cell. We could be there for hours.

Off to one side I heard a boisterous voice regaling the crowd with jokes and stories. Squeezing through to get a closer look, I found a thickly-set woman with dancing blue eyes. That was my introduction to Fran Peavey: "Atomic Comic," photographer, poet, television producer, author, gardener, carpenter, thinker, furniture designer, artist, organizer, lover…a woman who astounds and provokes, challenges and enlightens. Who pushes us until it hurts and loves us through every fall. An original mind, a soul who lacks the fears socialized into many women, Fran Peavey, who never had great expectations for her life and so finds her achievements a continual surprise, is herself a constant source of surprise and joy.

PENNY: *Fran, you've done such powerful work. I just know about some of it. You've strategized on housing issues with street people in San Francisco, and you've built a park together. You're working with people in India to help clean up the Ganges River. You've written one book,* Heart Politics *and another about a woman grappling with the AIDS epidemic. And you've been doing all this for over twenty years. I'd like to draw from that experience and talk about how to create positive social change in the most effective, powerful, humane, creative, respectful and balanced way. How to do the work and stay whole in the process...*

You told me once that at any particular point in your life, you choose what you think is the most important question for you to answer at that time—and then you find work which will help you address that question. I wondered what that question is for you right now?

FRAN: I guess the question that I ask myself every day is how can I help the earth survive? And then I listen to the spirit of life inside of me and try to do, as often as I possibly can, what it suggests.

PENNY: *And what is that suggesting for you today?*

FRAN: I've just come back from India, and frankly I'm spending a lot of my time in my garden. I'm preparing my heart for some changes in my personal life. And I'm doing some writing on Strategic Questioning. Some workshops that I gave in Australia and New Zealand have broken loose a lot of questions that I really wasn't able to grapple with before. Now I'm ready to look at those issues in my writing.

PENNY: *Tell us more about Strategic Questioning.*

FRAN: In the old days, politics was a matter of being closed. You had an ideology and you were moving that ideology on every agenda, every issue, through the world. Now we have a new politics which is much more a politics of openness, a politics of collaboration. It *has* to be. Confrontation is often very important but if you only have confrontation, rather than real collaboration where we all work together to get out of this pickle in the best way possible, we're going to miss a lot. How do we ask ourselves questions that bring forward the most powerful, the most substantive changes that we all long to make? We all know we're in trouble—we're not sure exactly how much trouble we're in—but we know that as a species, as a planet, we've got to make some changes. And we're going to have to make those together. All of us.

PENNY: *But how do we do that if we disagree? I mean on big things? For example, how do we do that in places like Israel and Palestine where there are such different opinions?*

FRAN: In a situation that is as tight and as vested as Palestine, we need to find where are the dissonances? Where are the unresolved questions that have the possibility for some motion? If we question and we get only ideology, we get old, dead answers and everything seems tapped down. Then we're not dealing with places where movement can happen. We have to find those plates that can shift, those questions that aren't resolved. Then we can find ways of resolving them together, of building new trust, so that new possibilities can occur, rather than staying at the static level. So we're going to have to go deeper.

PENNY: *Can you give me some examples of how you might do that?*

FRAN: A group that I know about had a team that went into Palestine and into Israel and asked questions. They tried to ask questions from a neutral point of view, to move things forward in a number of different ways, not working from a vested interest. One of the questions they asked the Palestinians particularly is why Palestinians cannot recognize Israel?[1] Palestinians would give the historic reason and start reciting the crimes of the Israelis. Well, it had to get deeper than that: 'What does it feel like inside of you to be at a fixed position? What would you need to recognize Israel?' A Strategic Question creates an answer that you didn't know existed inside of you. Our whole human mechanism is to get everything static, to get everything *controlled;* a Strategic Question goes down to where it isn't controlled, where everything isn't tapped down, where things are still living and juicy, where creation is still happening. A Strategic Question finds the motion that can help life survive, that can help us live dynamically rather than statically.

PENNY: *Doesn't that process require a real level of trust between the questioner and the person being questioned?*

FRAN: Yes. The questioner needs to come from either a neutral place or be able to discipline herself to keep her own position to the side in the relationship and not secretly try to sell her own position. It is an ethical issue how one uses Strategic Questioning. And it's not a shortcut process. We've had a lot of time for shortcut politics. We're going to have to develop real relationships. We're going to have to take them very slow. We're going to have to test each other: are we reliable, can we do what we say we'll do? Can we proceed one step at a time, build the kind of bridges that a whole people can walk across?

PENNY: *Can you give an example of how this process might be used today in the United States, especially on an issue with women?*

FRAN: I think almost every woman is at least unconsciously saying, 'What can I do in my home to help the earth survive? What are the products that I'm using that are killing the earth, or are dangerous to my family, dangerous to myself?' Asking ourselves that over and over again, we can give ourselves more powerful responses every day. Because new information is coming to us. Once we're recycling our bottles, then we can work on our newspapers, and once we're doing that, we can start looking at our cleaning liquids and spray containers. Or, 'How can I improve my relationships at work, in my neighborhood, in my family, in ways that will propel people to be more the human beings that they need to be? How can I use questioning and be open, be *genuinely* open, to new responses in my relationships—so that I don't count on people being the same as they were yesterday, but know that they can be new people every day?'

Another issue of a more electoral political nature: 'How do we get more women in the public dialogue of this country?' Every time we hear more women complaining about an issue, we can ask the Strategic Question, 'What would it take for you to speak out publicly on this issue? How can I support you to take your position into a more powerful level?' If we made this a habit in our conversations, women would be more visible in the power citadels of our country.

PENNY: *That reminds me of a passage from your book* Heart Politics *where you discuss 'calling forth the humanity within each adversary,' about talking and* listening *to people. In this example you're speaking with a nuclear engineer, and you're trying to see the world through his eyes.*

As you're listening to him, you're also noticing the context of the world around you, such as the birds singing and how people are responding to you. That really made me think. For me at least, it would be very hard to even talk *with a nuclear engineer. But to be open...*

FRAN: True. But however we're going to get out of the radiation mess we're in, he and I are going to have to work on it together. We're not going to be able to just get rid of him. He is solving some energy problems in his way. We need to solve those problems, but probably in a different way. I think we have to start by not thinking of him as an adversary, but by thinking of him as a co-creator of the solution; and that we are also creators, and we come as proponents, together to find a way of creating energy that doesn't produce radiation and waste.

PENNY: *That sounds like a huge leap of faith [laughs].*

FRAN: [laughs] Well, what else do we have to do in this life, besides have leaps of faith and build trust? It also requires leaving the irresponsible position of opposition and growing into the task of co-creating. Alienation is a comfortable position. Relationship is tough—especially when you disagree.

You have to walk on one foot and then you have to walk on the other; you can't leap out too far until you build good trust, and then you leap a little bit further. Actually, each step is a small step. And I think that this is particularly a feminist perspective—that we don't just take a big leap. We take the small leaps and make them stable. We open the curtain a little bit, and we glimmer and we move. We don't jump with great leaps of bravado and shout, 'Here we come to save the world!' Nobody can save the world. But each of us can take a little step everyday, and go forward.

PENNY: *But what about those of us who love drama, Fran?*

FRAN: Well, then we're setting ourselves up for great frustration and great feelings of inferiority. This is one of the problems I think with this period. Each of us can do our very small piece, and that will move the world forward. When we see that the problems are so massive, sometimes we think that we have to be massive people. Whereas in fact each of us has to be willing to take the biggest step we can take today, make the biggest grounded change we can make and know that tomorrow we'll make another one, and that we're on a path.

PENNY: *And yet it seems like the work that you're doing in the world is really massive.*

FRAN: No, it just *seems* that way. If you got up every morning with me the way you get up every morning with you, you'd see these *little* things that I do every day. Today all I had to do for the Ganges River was to mail one thing that somebody asked me for. I helped clean up the Ganges River this morning on my way here—I mailed one thing. Now I need to plant my lettuces because they're needing transplanting.

PENNY: *You're an Atomic Comic…How do you use comedy to change the world?*

FRAN: One of the most important things about facing what's happening around us is to stay whole, to stay alive. There's a lot of deadening things that you could get really grim and miserable about. And it's no fun. There is a particularly powerful posture in being able to see the human situation from enough of a removed perspective to laugh.

Whenever I laugh at the universe, I feel like I kind of lift myself up off the earth and into the clouds—and I take the perspective of the Gods and Goddesses—and I look back and say, 'Oh, those human beings. They are really in a pickle.' I find laughter and a healing kind of joy in that.

I'm only an Atomic Comic two months of the year. The rest of the time I do my social change strategy work. But I just love laughing *with* audiences. It helps me get through my year. And so I read the newspaper; I find the funny things in the newspaper, and then I just go and laugh. It helps me read the newspaper knowing that I'm also gathering comedy material every day.

PENNY: *I'd like to go back to something we were touching on earlier. A section of* Heart Politics *that struck the deepest for me was where you talk about connectedness as a political principle. And this certainly relates to what you said about Strategic Questioning and trust. You wrote: 'if we aren't connected to the people we're fighting for, there's an emptiness, a coldness at the center. It's the same coldness that's at the heart of prejudice, the coldness of separation.' Can you apply this to anything you're working on today?*

FRAN: This is something I've learned a lot in India. When I go there, the first thing I usually say is, 'What do you want me to do?' I've been working there about one month a year for ten years, and they always say, 'Be sure to spend a lot of time on the river. Take a boat trip every day.' I finally understood that what they were really saying is, 'You need to have a relationship with this river.' And I feel that the Ganges River—or as they call it in India, Gunga—is a *friend* of mine that I am caring for. That she and I together are working for her cleanliness and mine.

I came home this year with parasites, so I can see that my cleanliness and her cleanliness are interconnected. That we're dependent upon each other. I can feel her suffering, because I had my own suffering, and what it must mean for her to have millions of people along her banks who suffer from intestinal parasites, how that saps the vitality and kills the children.

Once you have a real connection with people or trees or whatever you're working for, you have to understand what the implications of that are. You and I have a responsibility to each other because we care about each other.

It's the same way when you love a tree: you have a responsibility. When you think, 'I'm going to be building a trellis, should I make that out of 4x4's or 2x4's?,' you have to think, 'Well if 2x4's can do the job, it would be better because it would take less trees. 'Should I xerox on both sides of the paper or one? It's an awful lot more work to do it on two sides, but it means less trees have to be cut down.' My friends, the trees, would be so much happier if I would stop the mass destruction of the trees. Friendship has with it obligations and responsibilities, in order to build trust, so that when you go back to the tree, you can say, 'Hello tree, I come to you with as clean a heart as I can. And I'm going to do better, and better and better, to prove our friendship, to prove my loyalty to you.' So I think connectedness is a very *in action,* very dynamic, way of living. This is just scratching the surface of what that means for my heart and my life. I have a lot of questions about even if I'm using a 2x4, how do I go to the trees and say, 'I'm sorry, but I need this 2x4 for this trellis.' It's one of the real agonies.

PENNY: *It reminds me of another thing that you say in* Heart Politics, *that 'allowing the suffering to ripen in one's soul is an essential component of appropriate action. One's feet move most determinedly when one's head and heart are both engaged.' Wholeness...just what you were talking about.*

FRAN: Not only suffering, but love. I think social change is about love. I don't think it's about ideas. If social change comes from the great and abiding love of life, it's a very important thing to do every day. Just a little bit. And to know that you're part of the flow of history: when you turn your xerox paper over and do it on both sides, when you choose the 2x4, when you say yes! when someone asks you for help in sustaining life. Whatever you do, whatever step you take, whether you're an AIDS caregiver or a xerox person or someone who tries to think how they can drive their automobile less. It's all part of openness to what is required of us for our planet to live. Just little steps.

PENNY: *Isn't it Che [Guevara][2] who said, 'The true revolutionary is guided by feelings of great love?'*

FRAN: He had a good idea there [laughs]. And he was a great revolutionary.

PENNY: *At the end of* Heart Politics *you write a letter to the people of the future which says: 'Work for all of us who went before you. Develop an analysis of what is happening and look for the best ideas. Fight your tendency to avoid pain and suffering. Accept your fears. Be informed by them, and learn how to set them aside. Develop an even deeper connection to the creatures you share the planet with. Enjoy the absur-*

dity around you.' You wrote that in 1986. What would you add today in 1990?

FRAN: Ask yourself questions and give yourself answers. And look for the questions and the answers every place, at all times. Test those answers. Prepare for new answers tomorrow. Care for life at every turn. Because in order for us to make it into that future, we're going to have to find those questions that will create the new and deeper answers that will move our feet.

And have FUN [laughs]. Be sure you find fun in your life.

II. MARCH 1991

The Persian Gulf War was a source of personal grief and of a deep sense of powerlessness for me, both as a peace activist and as a woman. I spoke with Fran again in mid-March, 1991 in an attempt to sift some meaning or direction out of the despair. Much of what she shared I think applies to any time of crisis.

PENNY: *Fran, you talk so much about connection as a political principle; I wonder how you see that applying to our situation right now?*

FRAN: During these times, I think one of the most important things is that we stay connected to each other. And that we build new connections to people in the Middle East, to the ocean and the animals and to the desert [in Kuwait, Iraq and Saudi Arabia] where the top is being crushed. That we share our shatteredness. In that sharing, a kind of composting happens, and that which was dead becomes alive and rich and feeds us in a new and deeper way—and our groundedness goes even deeper.

Every day of the war a group met at my house, a group of people that didn't even know each other before. Now we've become good friends, and we're writing together. We just talked about how we were feeling about the war. Sometimes we were feeling sorrow, sadness, anger. Sometimes we said, 'Hey, I'm not feeling anything, I'm busy now.' And we said that to each other, and then we'd wait, because we knew that was part of the process: to come in and go out, go inside, go outside, keep moving. We watched the war move through us, and we supported each other to do whatever came to us to do to stop the war. And we cared about each other in the process. Sometimes we'd say, 'Hey, slow down a bit,' and we'd say things to each other that acknowledged that we *felt* the connection and that we cared. It was an important part of the war. And we will come out of this time with new inspiration and new fuel and be ready to work even harder.

PENNY: *That's a powerful model. What ideas do you have about making those connections with the people in the Middle East?*

FRAN: I think we do it in a number of ways. When people say how many people were killed in the war, we don't number in the hundreds. We remember that there were hundreds of *thousands* of people killed.[3] When you go into a grocery store and say, 'Hey, where you from?' and the guy answers, 'I'm from Palestine,' you say, 'How is it for you?' We really say, 'I care about what happens to your grocery store. I'm next door; if you need help, come talk to me.' When we hear that a synagogue has been grafittied, we go to the synagogue and say, 'We know this isn't right. Please, what can I do to help you?' We put ourselves at the service of those people who are being damaged.

We listen to our heart. Our heart will lead us into connections. It will call us to go to slide shows or speeches or theater performances. It will call us to read poems and great literature by Iraqi poets. It will call us to go take a class. It might call us sometime to go there and to meet with the people. To sit down on the street and talk to the shopkeeper. To *witness.* Witnessing is an important act. Over and over again I have been told by people who were in very tragic situations that just my willingness to open myself to their suffering makes their suffering somehow more manageable. To take that in and to let it hit my heart as hard as it can. To not barrier myself off from what is really happening anywhere.

PENNY: *To validate.*

FRAN: Yes.

PENNY: *Barbara Lubin of the Middle East Children's Alliance was in Iraq just before the war started. She tells a story about when she was visiting a school there, a young woman ran up to her and thrust a tube of lipstick in her hand and said, 'This is all I have to give you. Please remember me.' And that's exactly what you're talking about.*

I know that Joanna Macy[4] is a colleague and friend of yours.

FRAN: In fact, Joanna Macy is just now traveling to Chernobyl with two weeks of gifts for those people, in terms of wisdom and compassion. She's going to witness and take in *that* suffering.

PENNY: *In the chapter 'Tales of Change' in* Heart Politics, *you talk about a prophecy that was told to Joanna by Tibetan Buddhists. It's about the* *physical and moral courage that's required of Shambhala warriors, where they must go right into the centers and corridors of power, 'into the very citadels where these weapons...are kept. There they must dismantle these weapons. Now is the time that the Shambhala warriors must train for this work. They train in the use of two weapons. One is compassion, the intense tuning to the sufferings of others. The other is a clear understanding of our profound mutuality, interconnectedness and complicity, the web of being, in which we all coexist. Without either of these weapons, courage will falter and burn out, strategies become confused, actions too partisan.'*

Is that our guide for where to go from here, as a peace movement?

FRAN: I think that one of the things about being a Shambhala warrior is that we never take ourselves outside the sphere of action. That we keep right in the midst of the suffering. We don't, by what we wear or what we do, say 'Oh, I'm good and you're bad; you're part of the problem, I'm not part of the problem.' We stay connected to the problem. We stay in touch with our families, where weapons manufacturers come to holiday dinners. We stay connected to the people who need to change. We build even stronger connections to the people who are doing things we don't feel good about. And we use that connection as a way of really talking to each other and co-creating a way out of this mess.

I don't know the way out. That guy doesn't know the way out. My brother, who at one time manufactured missile silos, doesn't know the way out. But together, if we stay open to each other and questioning deeply, we may find ways to move, *both* of us, into a more appropriate relationship to weapons that will free our earth from this suffering.

PENNY: *It sounds good, Fran...But it feels like this society is so polarized right now, and there's so much hostility. I mean, am I supposed to go up to somebody who I know has an exactly opposite view and say, 'Let's have lunch?' That's pretty scary.*

FRAN: This is a time of tremendous change. We don't know what match will set our society afire, but the fire is embedded in us. To the degree that we are involved in bridging, the changes will be able to be nonviolent, deep and lasting.

And you have to be prepared to change yourself. Because you will change if you are in good connection with another. You have to make sure that you have a good strong basis yourself and that you have connections you can come back to and say, 'You know, I was talking to so-and-so, and what can be said about this position? What's a new way of looking at it that will help both of us move into a more correct position?'

PENNY: *That sounds like your concept of Strategic Questioning...*

FRAN: It's close. Strategic Questioning is what one does *in connection*. But I just don't trust 'connection' in and of itself; we get so seduced into, 'I hope they like me' and the purposelessness of 'connecting.' Strategic Questioning has to do with how we ask each other questions that move us into a new place. Not to defend our old place, which is bankrupt because it's yesterday, and what was yesterday isn't today. There's always a poverty in only drawing on yesterday and not looking in *this* moment for today.

Strategic Questioning is looking forward. It's saying, 'How are we going to put these weapons away? How are we going to build the friendship bridges that will allow people in the Middle East and people in the United States to have connections?' And then just opening our heart to let the answers start coming. Just like we did in the Soviet Union.

Ten years ago when people saw the Cold War heating up between the US and the USSR, hundreds of people said, 'My government is not making the peace I want. I will have to go and see this evil empire for myself.' So we did. Ronald Reagan had to run to get around in front of us. He could no longer maintain that this was an evil empire; too many of us knew better. We had built real connections, and we came back home with the impact of those connections.

We don't have to kill each other, we don't have to have an enemy. [We can have] an advocacy relationship. Strategic Questioning is asking questions that there aren't answers to yet. But by the mere asking of the questions, answers can start coming forward and blossoming.

PENNY: *It reminds me of something that Naomi Newman says in her one-woman play* Snake Talk, *where she's talking about if you know where you're going, it means you've already been there, and you're just going to go back to where you came from.*

You said in Heart Politics *that it could take four to five generations for our species to learn how to make change without war. That was in some ways a relief for me to hear, because I had been assuming I had to 'finish it'...you know, accomplish that in my lifetime. But you're saying, we have a few more lifetimes to learn this lesson.*

FRAN: Which is what will enable us to do it well. We're not going to learn how to live without war by doing kind of quickie patch jobs. It's going to be a slow but deliberate process. This doesn't mean we should just not work at it, but that we need to do it thoroughly. We need to take care of every relationship, every part of the connection. I think if we felt we had to do it quickly, we might not do it with as long-term a view as is going to be necessary for us to really learn it.

PENNY: *How are we supposed to deal right now with the powerlessness many of us are feeling? I'm speaking as a peace activist, but I'm sure a lot of people who relate differently are having that same feeling.*

FRAN: This is a time when the powers of the world are making major moves out of our view. We don't know what's going on. The lies that we are exposed to are so massive that it's easy to feel overwhelmed and outnumbered. The thing we know as we look at history is that the essential truth will always come out. For instance, someday we will know the truth of why the Middle East war occurred.

But this is also a time of tremendous opportunity, when people who are open and have questions need to step forward in their most vulnerable and their most questioning way, so that we move forward with the *power* of our openness. That we don't hold back one inch from the rage we feel, because we know something is going on that we don't know about. That we call them on the carpet and say, 'We *must* know!'

PENNY: *That's hard.*

FRAN: It's not impossible though.

PENNY: *Especially for those of us who are compulsive* doers: *'I have to do this, I have to do that. Oh, my gosh, we have a war, I have to make peace, I have to stop the bombs, I have to save the people, I have to save the world.' Which for me can come from unhealthy impulses, but also comes from my Jewish heritage of tikkun olam, or 'repair of the world'—what can I do in my lifetime to make it better? It's hard to sit and wait. It goes back to what we were talking about before, not knowing.*

FRAN: I didn't say *sit* and wait. I said, work purposefully, bring all of your questioning, all of your not-knowing into every piece of work you're doing. Defend yourself not one bit. Don't do *more*. Do it *better.* Do it more openly. Bring more of yourself to fewer things, to fewer actions, but bring *all* of yourself—don't leave any at home in the closet.

PENNY: *But how do we do all that and still not let the well go dry?*

FRAN: That's part of good work, to make sure that we get the kind of spiritual and physical and emotional nourishment that we need. When we bring more of our unknowing and more of our pain, we also are opening ourselves up to more of the love and support that is in the world. Because even those who might appear to be our adversaries have much the same pain that we have. To the degree that we come unarmed, we disarm them. Even our busy-ness, our 'doing'...with 'I am the hero,' are a kind of an armament. Whereas if we bring ourselves with all of our shatteredness, all of our not-knowing, then everybody can let down a little bit and say more of the truth. The only way to fight lies is to tell your own truth—it either calls forth the truth from the other side, or shows them to be a sham.

PENNY: *Keeping an open heart is what you're talking about. It's very different from the way many of us in the United States have been brought up.*

FRAN: When you're on the top of the earth economically—not that we're on the top but we're close to the top—we have so much that we think we need to defend. We have all these policemen and all these armies that we hire to keep people out of our refrigerators and out of our bank accounts. One of the things I've learned from working so much in the Third World is that we are going to lose *something*. We're either going to lose our integrity or we're going to lose our cars. We're either going to lose our hearts or we're going to lose our addiction to big houses. I see people living on much less and living well, with lives of integrity.

Everything has taught us, in our world, to be afraid. And we, as Americans, have got to stop being afraid. That means really challenging our own arrogance. It means learning to walk as equals on the earth with other people. It means when it comes to what are we going to do about powers in the Middle East, that we come to the table as equals, not as the most powerful gun on the block.

PENNY: *You're talking about humility.*

FRAN: I'm talking about humanity. And finding ours. And it's findable. But it's not findable in a new refrigerator. You don't find your humanity there. The more things you have to have, the less of your life you have. Because you have to take care of all those things, and you have to defend them and you have to repair them, and you have to keep them dusted. I consider myself an economic dissident in a monolithic culture [laughs].

PENNY: *So what is the hope, Fran? Is there hope?*

FRAN: I no longer think that hope is an important gradient to live upon. What is, is. And there is good and *possibility* in *everything* that is. Dreams are important, but they can be changed from night to night. Whatever we have to let go of in order to be the greatest person or people or world in any given moment, we have to let go of that. I think this is one of the great gifts of the AIDS community: that hope is not relevant. Hope keeps us attached to something that was, rather than acknowledging what is and learning to live in this moment with what this moment brings. And to find happiness *now*. And meaning *now*—to work with what is *now*. A guy named Ronald Higgins once said in a book *The Seventh Enemy* that 'the only thing we have to fear is hope itself.' Because hope keeps us attached to how it *should* be, rather than allowing us to live in what is. And to find dignity and joy in what is. Right now. That's not hope—that's joy in this moment. Sorry…I know you wanted me to say something hopeful [laughs].

PENNY: *I didn't know what you would say, Fran. With you I never know [laughs]. It's helpful. I wanted to know what you're thinking because I'm desperate for a new way of doing my work, of being a human being, a woman, a peace activist and you're one of the more creative thinkers I know.*

FRAN: We are all looking for ways of doing our work, of finding ourselves proud enough to demand that things be better. I know we can't control history—but we can live by our light and add it to the sparks others have.

Behind hope is the basic denial that we're all going to die. And once we know that we are, then we can live in this moment and draw joy from this moment. Find the blossom in every pile of shit, something that is very fine and that can be delighted in. Even this moment of brokenness.

PENNY: *It will be transformed. There will be a new beginning.*

Looking at the peace movement during the Gulf crisis, do you think what we did made a difference?

FRAN: I don't know. I have deep questions about this myself. What is the appropriate institutional strategy, organizational strategy, for these times? I think clearly people around the world knew that there was not unanimity in the United States [in support of the Gulf War], that there were people here who were objecting. We have been somewhat bamboozled by the often-quoted polls that say we're a minority; I see these polls more and more as part of the brainwashing that is happening in this country.

Because I know *my* America. I have been across this country. I have family in the heartland of this country. My America is not a bloodthirsty America. My America does not take glee in bombing, and bombing, and bombing, when people aren't fighting. My America might be sick for awhile or might get off course with the cheerleading from the media. And the media might pick up on the most exaggerated parts of my America. But *I know.* And if you talk to somebody who walked on the Great Peace March all across this country,[5] they will tell you the same thing. We know our country. And our country is going through some very hard times.

And our country has a disproportionate amount of killing power these days. It's very dangerous, and the only force that can stop us is ourselves. It's like the addict—our country is spinning out of control with fear.

But we cannot let the media tell us about ourselves. It's like letting a schoolteacher tell you you're stupid—you'll never develop your brain if you believe that. The media has a vested interest in us not feeling good about ourselves, because they want to sell us something. They want to show us the misery, and then on the next page there's Macy's: 'You can leave your misery if you just get this coat.' The way it works is to show you the worst, and then relieve you with the advertising. So we can't believe what the media tells us about our country. We have to go find out ourselves.

There are alternative surveys that show that America did not support the war anywhere near to the degree that the media has told us. It depends on how you ask the question. 'Do you support the troops?' 'Oh yeah, I support the troops.' That's not a very deep question. It doesn't say, 'Do you support what they're *doing?* Would *you* do that? Would you want your child to do what those troops are doing?' Everybody wants to *support.* The way you ask questions has a lot to do with the kind of answers you get. We have been manipulated into thinking that our America is something it isn't. As a peace movement, we have a lot of deep work to do, to start bridging this polarization. We have got to go out and find our America and talk to it, and not huddle in our own comfortable areas.

PENNY: *How do we do that?*

FRAN: Well, it's a complex and multilevel strategy. But essentially I think each of us has to ask ourselves, and each group has to ask ourselves, what is our job in keeping peace moving? And then listen. Listen deeply. Question everybody: what can we do? And then *do* it.

And support what our friends are doing. We have to develop good alternatives and make them known. And we have to appreciate and feel good about ourselves and our brothers and sisters who are also trying to make peace.

It's been very hard on our generation. We've been locked out of power for a long time. We hardly even know what power is. And I think that very soon now it's going to shift.

Another thing we need to do is really formulate the ideas that we know and teach them to the young people—a lot of social change concepts have not been well taught to the kids in high schools and colleges.

PENNY: *I don't know. I was talking with a panel of high school and college students recently who were using a feminist process, a multi-racial process, a decentralized collective process, and actually those conversations gave me the most hope. Excuse me for mentioning hope, but...*

FRAN: [laughs] It's alright for you to hope, Penny.

PENNY: *You said that the power is going to shift back. Do you really think so?*

FRAN: Yes, I think the vision that is compelling the country at this point cannot go for very long.

PENNY: *I think I might disagree with you, Fran. I'm trying to dig in and accept that it might go on this way for a really long time—to figure out how to do my work with that assumption, so I don't keep getting my hopes up and then getting so discouraged...*

FRAN: See, that's the problem with hope...[laughs]. Yes, we have to acknowledge that we are really in the minority now, and that our ideas are not the compelling ideas. We've got to figure out how to work in this environment and learn to have a good time. But if you look historically at the life of ideas, they do not go on forever. The fifties did not last forever, even though they were terrible. There was a time when other visions, other questions drew the attention of people.

PENNY: *Oh, I know it will change. I'm just thinking it might be years and years.*

FRAN: It might be. And we should be having a good time now and finding ways of being really effective. We should be getting ready for the change and making sure that we build, at the *root*, good relationships, good processes and good institutions that will be ready.

PENNY: *Finding ways of being really effective—that's the trick. I feel like I don't know what that is anymore. I was just talking to a friend in the Israeli peace movement in Jerusalem who was depressed about the same thing. I hear everything you're saying, and I think it's valuable information that I want to integrate. But effectiveness—that's the key to me.*

FRAN: If we keep asking ourselves, 'At this juncture, what will be effective? How will what we're doing be the most effective?' we will be effective.

PENNY: *Fair enough.*

I also want to talk about the war at home. I just heard three to five million children in the United States go to sleep hungry every night. In some parts of the Bay Area twenty-five percent of schoolteachers are being laid off, and student councils are sponsoring bake sales and dances to earn money for basic school supplies. Vital services like childcare for student parents, as well as drug and suicide and pregnancy counselling, are being totally eliminated. And these are our kids. This is the future.

FRAN: One of the things that upsets me the most is that money for the state colleges and universities has really been cut. This is one of the greatest travesties of the last fifteen years, that people have not had equal access to the information that would allow them to have power.

Increasingly, it is people who have money or who have the confidence to leverage their future salary, who are able to go to college. That locks out poor people. It locks out Third World people. It locks out people who happen to have been born women and who are afraid to take student loans, because what if their hypothesized husband won't want them if they have to pay back student loans? We have a right to have access to happiness, and that means access to information.

PENNY: *So what should we be doing about this?*

FRAN: When we talk about connectedness, it doesn't only mean international connectedness. We should be building bridges to people in our own communities who are suffering. When someone on the street asks you for spare change, instead of just not looking at them, look in their eyes and make *some* connection. Give them *something*. If it's not a quarter, give them respect. Give them a blessing. Touch them on the shoulder and wish them well. Build a connection. Take your heart and put it out there. Go to a school and volunteer. Take some of your life and touch that suffering and take it in. Don't hide from it.

PENNY: *Connection. We're coming full circle.*

FRAN: Full circle.

PENNY: *My friend Betsy Rose, who is a singer and songwriter involved in social change, said something to me yesterday and I wondered if you had any response to it. She said, 'I see resistance not as a clenched fist but as an unclenched heart.'*

FRAN: I love what Betsy has said. I would add 'an unclenched heart with moving tennis shoes' [laughs]. Out working on the streets. It's not enough for a heart to be open in our living rooms. We have work to do in our lives that is so much bigger than our jobs—we have our life's work. And we need to think, as well as laugh. Our heart will tell us what to do and then we have to do it; an open heart does the work and has a good time with it. And music, I think, helps us do our work with a joyous heart.

N O T E S :

1. In November 1988, the Palestine Liberation Organization issued a peace initiative that included accepting United Nations Resolution 242, which implies recognition of an Israeli state.

2. Ernesto 'Che' Guevara [1928–1967] was a Latin-American guerilla leader who helped Fidel Castro acheive revolution in Cuba. He was born in Argentina, and was a doctor before he became involved in agitation against dictator Juan Peron. Che met Castro in Mexico; from 1956 till the taking of Havana on January 1, 1959 he fought as a member of Castro's army and helped to shape its strategy. He was minister of industry in the new Cuban government [1961–1965] but was more interested in using revolutionary warfare to spread communism in Latin-America. He was captured and executed by Bolivian forces in 1967, while on a guerilla training mission *(Academic American Encyclopedia, vol.9, Danbury, Connecticut: Grolier Inc., 1982).*

3. This statistic includes the Kurds and Shiites killed in 'post-war' strife initiated by the war, and includes the 100,000 Iraqi children under the age of five who died—in just 1991 alone—from impure water and lack of medication that were direct results of the Gulf War. (International Study Team to Iraq, September 1991)

4. Joanna Macy is a renowned writer, a practicing Buddhist, activist, a passionate and compassionate humanitarian. She works on issues with an approach she calls 'despair and empowerment.' She is concerned with our cleaning up of nuclear waste. Her most recent book (1991) is *World as Lover, World as Self.*

5. In 1986, over 500 Americans walked for peace from Los Angeles to Washington, D.C., talking to millions of Americans in towns and cities along the way.

Photo by Marilyn Humphries

Barbara Smith

NOVEMBER 1989

"What's beautiful about grassroots political movements and liberation movements, is that people who are viewed as being dispossessed, as being powerless, as being ignorant, as being outsiders—suddenly we tip the balance, we change the means of exchange of the coin of the realm. Suddenly *we* become people who define what humanhood is and what power is, and then the world turns over."

Barbara Smith's warm and pleasant face greeted me as she answered my knock on her hotel room door. She had just flown into San Francisco from her upstate New York home to deliver the keynote address at the Dynamics of Color Conference, organized to combat racism in the lesbian community. For years I had admired the strong and courageous African-American lesbian voice of leadership she raises to the world—a voice that challenges as it provokes, teaches as it encourages. In conversation, Barbara is ardent and articulate, mixing sharp intelligence with quick humor. I felt both her softness and her fire.

PENNY: *Barbara, you're an outspoken feminist, lesbian, writer, political activist; you co-founded the Combahee River Collective in Boston in 1974, a Black feminist organization that gained national recognition for your local organizing. You also co-founded Kitchen Table: Women* *of Color Press, which publishes and distributes numerous books by women of color. You've been active around abortion rights, sterilization abuse; you were on the Board of the National Coalition of Black Lesbians and Gays, and you've taught at nearly 100 different universities. And you've been published in feminist and lesbian journals, as well as the* Village Voice *and the* New Republic. *Where does that kind of commitment come from?*

BARBARA: Probably from my origins. I was born in 1946 to a typical Black family of that time. We were poor and we lived in segregation, even though I grew up in Cleveland, Ohio—theoretically the North. But as we say, when we talk about the South, we talk about south of the Canadian border, because of course the system of racism extends throughout this country. My family happened to be almost entirely women. I had a couple of uncles, but my sister and I did not grow up with a father. Just seeing how the women in my family had to struggle, how talented they were and how invisible they were—how disregarded as far as their great talents—that alone would make one want to struggle. They made many many sacrifices for my sister and myself so that we would have the opportunity and the option to live a life different from theirs.

But I think any Black person of my generation has a sense of struggle and also a sense of where the lines are drawn, because it was not nearly as nebulous as it is [in the] post-Civil Rights era.

PENNY: *So—what feeds you, what nurtures you?*

BARBARA: Having seen conditions change, having seen my status change within my own lifetime. As I say, I was born into segregation, and we're sitting up here at one of the most exclusive hotels in San Francisco. Thirty years ago, I probably would not have even been allowed to be a cleaning woman here, let alone to make a reservation and stay. These things seem small in relation to profound political struggle and change, but it's hard to calculate how demoralizing it was to live under that system unless one actually experienced it. This country pre-Civil Rights was much like South Africa. There was an official system of apartheid called 'Jim Crow'[1] and having seen those changes and having been a part of those changes really makes me feel like we can continue to struggle.

PENNY: *You were part of the Combahee River Collective, named after a guerilla action that freed 750 slaves, conceived of and led by Harriet Tubman in 1863?*

BARBARA: Yes, during the Civil War.

PENNY: *From what I understood, one of the main new concepts that your collective contributed was the idea of the interlocking oppressions: racism, classism, sexism, heterosexism—how those combine to create the oppression in women's lives, the lives of women of color. I know this is a big question, but how are those interlocking oppressions affecting women and women of color today? Has it improved?*

BARBARA: Well, I think it's really hard to weigh and measure that, because it depends on where you're looking. Class and economic oppression are extremely important when you consider people's objective conditions. I think that at the end of the Reagan decade we see tremendous deficits for women of color, people of color, working people. All kinds of disenfranchised groups have really suffered under that regime. So it's hard to talk about strides.

And yet culturally, we have a flourishing movement of Black women writers, for example, and recognition of writing by groups of other women of color. We were watching 'Oprah!' before we turned off the television and turned on the tape recorder. To my eyes, seeing someone like her and other Black people in a position of prominence…We just had an election this week and there's now a Black mayor in New York City and the first Black governor [in Virginia].

It's hard, as I said, to weigh and measure. I think generally the condition of people of color in this country has degenerated during this decade. On the other hand, we can see certain powerful political gains that we've made, often in the context of doing that multi-issue coalition-building type work.

PENNY: *What do you see as the most important work we can be doing right now—whether as women in general, as progressive people, as women of color?*

BARBARA: I like the phrase 'Think globally, act locally.' I think it's very important to figure out what is most needful where you are, as opposed to being overwhelmed by this whole political economy and a world situation characterized by incredible contradictions and also by wrack and ruin. We live in a context in which a moment could cause obliteration of the entire world and human population, and animal and vegetable population as we know it. So we live with the prospect of the reality of annihilation. Instead of being overwhelmed by that reality, not only must we work for peace and anti-militarism, we need to figure out what needs to happen where we are.

We need to figure out how to grapple with homelessness and find practical solutions. I believe in grassroots organizing; and I don't believe that you vote, and all questions are answered and all problems are solved. I think that voting and electoral politics are a part of a strategy for what we're ultimately trying to accomplish, which is a fundamental revolution. So I really think that people need to figure out what's going on.

I've watched the situation with the earthquake here very conscientiously because of knowing people and also just being struck by how vulnerable we are, both with Hurricane Hugo on one side of the country and then a few weeks later the earthquake here. I know those people who were most dispossessed to begin with, such as the people in Watsonville, are the ones who are hurting most now that the earthquake has occurred. I would like to think that people here are organizing relief efforts, and specifically doing that as women and as lesbians, really making links with people.

The problem of homelessness has been highlighted by the earthquake, but existed before. Another problem is the fact that most students don't have anything like a quality education or access to one in this country. And that the farther away you are from being white and male and middle or upper-middle class, the less likely you are to have something like a decent education. These are issues I feel we can work on very effectively. AIDS is another one, of course. But it's not about naming one issue as the most important. It's about trying to figure out how to work effectively in the context in which you live, and to work with people who are like-minded.

PENNY: *You mentioned multiracial alliance-building. When we're building these alliances, focusing on a particular task, how do we work on that task and not ignore the other 'isms—but not get diverted from our agenda? Which is what often happens around racism. For example, if I'm part of an alliance-building group, and we're working on this conference which is about fighting racism—how do we focus on that conference and still not ignore anti-semitism or classism?*

BARBARA: What you're asking is a complicated question and the only answer to it is having experience with multi-issued organizing. I'm a part of a group in Albany, New York, called the Feminist Action Network. This is a group of women of color and white women, of lesbians and heterosexual women, working specifically on issues of racism and homophobia. At our first meeting, we discussed that we are coming from a multi-issue perspective, which means that we're holding all those 'isms in mind. We do talk about the anti-semitic implications of whatever the issue is before us, we do talk about ableism and differently-abled women, we do talk about homophobia and racism, we do talk about the class implications of what it is we're doing. You can't juggle every ball perfectly, but you can have them all on the table ready to pick up when appropriate. It comes from experience. I can't really give you a formula for that. It comes with consciousness. It comes with doing. The more you do it, the more natural it comes to you—to deal with segregated schools at the very same time that we take into account that differently-abled students are not having equal access to those schools too.

PENNY: *Towards the end of the Combahee River Collective Statement, it says: 'We do not believe the end always justifies the means. As feminists, we do not want to mess over people in the name of politics.' Does the end ever justify the means?*

BARBARA: I can't remember what we meant when we wrote that… [laughs] I think it came out of some experiences with the white male left, and maybe with leftist males of color as well, who we saw doing work we could support but doing it in such appalling ways, and with such human tolls being taken, that we could not justify that as feminists. We're not going to be destructive to human people at the very same time we accomplish some very laudatory goals. It's another way of talking about the personal and the political, that each of them is important. It's also a way of talking about having ethics and being principled.

You ask, 'do the ends ever justify the means?' I think there are situations probably where the ends do justify the means, because you're talking about life and death. When you're fighting in the context of a struggle to liberate your country, in the context of armed struggle, where many people are dying around you, I think sometimes you have to make some very unlovely choices—choices that we're not even perhaps familiar with, living in this kind of post-industrial capitalist nation. But it's always unfortunate. It's always unfortunate I think when the human spirit has to be compromised; but sometimes saving a lot of people's lives and losing a few, maybe sometimes that does have to happen. It has happened.

PENNY: *Can you think of any examples of healthy uses of power?*

BARBARA: Well one thing we need to understand is that every human organism is inherently powerful at birth. I always talk about that moment when the baby first arrives. Every child born really has the potential to alter the world as we know it, to create beauty, to be kind, to be imaginative, to be incisive and brilliant, to be funny, to do all the kinds of things that make it worth it to be here together. But because we live in an unjust society, some children get to manifest their power and to maximize it, and most of us never do. So that's one thing to understand, that we all have power.

What's beautiful about grassroots political movements and liberation movements, is that people who are viewed as being dispossessed, as being powerless, as being ignorant, as being outsiders—suddenly we tip the balance, we change the means of exchange of the coin of the realm. Suddenly *we* become people who define what humanhood is and what power is, and then the world turns over.

PENNY: *Can you paint a picture of what the world you're building looks like?*

BARBARA: Well it would be fair, for one thing. It would be just. Everyone who came here would have the same opportunities to maximize. Everyone wouldn't *be* the same, because not everybody wants to be the same thing. I would no more want to be a nuclear physicist than I would want to be a tightrope walker. I wanted to be a writer when I was growing up, and amazingly enough I got to be that.

Because people know that I'm a feminist and a lesbian, and I'm apparently Black, people often think that I'm talking about taking away from one group to give to those groups of which I am a member. I try to explain to them, 'No, that's not what we're talking about. What we're talking about is enough for all.' There's a mentality in this society that there's only so much power and so many goods to go around; that there's a pie the size of a cupcake, and you are not even going to get a crumb. That's not the nature of power and of resources. I think it's infinitely available.

The society would not be organized around capital; it would not be organized around inheritance and people who came here rich and so-called powerful getting to keep it. Things would just be equal. There would be no violence. None. NONE. No one would be afraid to leave their house at any time of the day or night. Rape, hate crimes, homophobic violence would all go out the window.

You know there are some moments that we all experience in a certain context. It might be at a cultural event, maybe at a conference. There are just certain moments that we always remember, because they were so beautiful, and people were so connected to each other, and people were so full as human beings. You get a glimmer of 'Oh yeah, this is what it's supposed to be like.' That's how I imagine it would be all the time, after the revolution. The revolution that I would want to see would be a socialist and a feminist revolution.

PENNY: *But not a violent one?*

BARBARA: Who knows how it will come about, I'm not a seer. History creates its own outcomes. I would love for it not to be violent. I think a violent revolution will be, by definition, male. The feminist socialist revolution that I envision probably would not be violent, but how the power positioning and everything would come about, I really can't say.

PENNY: *It's hard to imagine a society without violence.*

BARBARA: But you asked me what I would *like* to see. Needless to say, I will not see that. I think our efforts with the battered women's movement and the anti-rape movement over the last twenty years—our raising the issue of incest and childhood sexual abuse—have all contributed toward making a different kind of world. Now you can turn on the TV and there's a public service announcement about battering and how that's wrong. I assure you, when I first became a feminist in the early seventies there was not a single battered women's shelter in this country. That's a change that we've made.

PENNY: *Who are your heroines, your heroes?*

BARBARA: James Baldwin[2] is a hero, because he made me want to be a writer; I was reading his work in junior high school. He was at the height of his fame and brilliance during those years and it just happened to coincide with my coming of age. I was very very fortunate.

I had always written and enjoyed it, and I knew that was what turned me on. But he was the model, because not only was he an incredible craftsperson, he also wrote essays and did political analysis. He was both an activist *and* a writer—and I fancy that that's why I've chosen to do the things I've done, because of his inspiration.

Then right out of high school, I met another hero, Fanny Lou Hamer, and I'll never forget that experience. I was involved in the Civil Rights Movement as a teenager in Cleveland, so I met her in that context. One of the reasons she was so special to me is because she was so much like the women in my family. She was from Mississippi; the women in my family were from Georgia. They could've been sisters, in physical appearance and in social and historical background. They were really of a piece.

Any Black writer that I read during those years was important to me. I was reading Langston Hughes[3] then too; he happened to have grown up in Cleveland, so that was a plus. There are probably a lot of people—but those people stand out.

Audre Lorde[4]...but see Audre's a friend of mine too, so there's one level on which I'm in awe, and there's another level on which we hang out. These are people who are beacons. Pat Parker[5], who is no longer with us...I lost someone very important when she died, because there are very few women like myself who will get on the radio, or anywhere else for that matter, and say, 'Yes, I am a Black lesbian feminist, and you just need to deal with it and relax.' Very few, very few—and she was one of the few. Audre's another. So these people are important to me.

PENNY: *When you look back, what do you see as your greatest victory?*

BARBARA: The fact that I got out of Cleveland, Ohio. No, really! I just flew through Cleveland today, and I thought, 'Here I am, on my way to San Francisco to talk to the people at this conference.' I had such dreams when I was growing up, and they were encouraged by the people in my family, but I am the product of historical coincidence. I could have been just as talented and just as full of passion, and if I had been born in a certain other moment, none of it would ever have happened. The fact that I was able to realize those dreams, and leave the place of my origins, and see a lot of the places I wanted to see—I guess those were victories.

Surviving as a Black woman has been a victory, with sanity intact, you know? I mean that's really great. I went to a ruling class school by fluke—the oldest women's college in this country, Mt. Holyoke. I still identify with the people who raised me. It did not ruin me. That's a victory. And I love the fact that I've been able to publish. And those are all personal victories.

I guess on a less personal level, the victory has been that Black women now have a place to stand. Because when I was growing up, there was so much shame associated with being who I am today, which is Black and female. So that's a true victory. People actually look at us with some admiration now.

PENNY: *Can you look back and pick three of the biggest lessons you've learned from your experiences, to pass on?*

BARBARA: Well one of the fairly recent lessons is that everyone who talks good doesn't necessarily do good. That being able to be articulate and present things in a very incisive manner doesn't mean you actually follow through. That was a hard lesson.

Another lesson which I think is really important is humility. That's one of the keys to people who are different from each other working with each other. I often say that to people who are working in coalitions together. You have to know you're ignorant, you really do. And I have to know that. People often think that because I have all these politically correct 'oppressed identities,' that I never feel unsure when I confront the difference of other people, and other women in particular. But I do. What do I know about being an American Indian? What do I know about being a Latina? What do I know about being Asian-American or Arab-American, or a poor white person from Appalachia? Nothing, really nothing. I have inklings, because of where I came from, but I face that sinking feeling—like the elevator's going down real fast—like 'Oh, my God, I don't know what's happening here.' I experience it. Humility is really important.

You want a third one? Let's forget about that, you got two.

PENNY: *In the work that you're doing, and the life that you're living, how can your white allies best support you?*

BARBARA: By committing themselves thoroughly to anti-racist organizing—with emphasis on *organizing*. I'm really not impressed by talk; I want to know what people are doing, and see what they're doing. There are so many opportunities for standing up, and there are so many ways that we can alter that power structure and that status quo by working together.

That's probably the third lesson: what we can do when we band together with each other. So really, what my white allies can do is demonstrate to me that they are thoroughly committed to anti-racist work, and that we can do that together.

N O T E S :

1. "Jim Crow" is a term which came into use in America in the 1880's, referring to "practices, institutions or laws that support segregation of Blacks from whites." (*World Book Encyclopedia*). Most of the laws were officially invalidated by the 1964 Civil Rights Act and U.S. Supreme Court decisions.

2. James Baldwin [1924–1987] an African-American writer well-known for his essays, novels, plays and short stories. Of a large family, he was raised in Harlem and began writing at an early age. Later he moved to Europe and lived there, primarily in Paris, as part of a colony of American expatriate writers and artists. His works include the novel *Go Tell it On the Mountain,* his collections of essays *Notes of a Native Son* and *The Fire Next Time,* two of his plays *Blues for Mister Charlie* and *Amen Corner,* as well as his frequently anthologized short story *Sonny's Blues.*

3. Langston Hughes [1902–1967] an African-American writer, his poetry, novels, plays and essays are now recognized as keynotes of the Harlem Renaissance. He did not hesitate to use the language of everyday African-American people, or to depict their lives and views. For this, as well as other of his standpoints, he received much criticism from both conservative and progressive political factions. His most famous poems include "The Negro Speaks of Rivers," "The Weary Blues," and "Montage of a Dream Deferred."

4. Audre Lorde [1934–] is a "black lesbian poet…a black woman warrior" *(Sister Outsider).* A pioneering African-American feminist theorist, through her uncompromising statement of selfhood and politically salient essays, poems, speeches and other writings, she has consistently led the way in the development of twentieth century African-American feminist perspectives. Her works include the two collections of essays *Sister Outsider* and *The Cancer Journals,* her biomythography *Zami: A New Spelling of My Name,* as well as numerous poems.

5. Pat Parker [1944–1989] a giant voice of early lesbian feminism, who died of cancer. She was a succinct describer of racism and sexism and a fierce promoter of equality for all people.

For information on Fanny Lou Hamer, see notes following interview with Maudelle Shirek.

Photo by Catherine Busch-Johnston

Colleen Kelley

JUNE 1989

"I have such a sense of women being able to somehow turn the tide. To step in, pick up their vision, have the faith to do it—and *do* it! It's time, it's really time for that to happen."

Shivering slightly in the morning dew on Buffalo Woman Meadow, before the sun's rays have quite filtered through, we kneel in a rough circle, attentive to our Sensei. She's dressed in the requisite hakama; her auburn hair gleams with flecks of red and gold. Centering herself, she leads us in the respectful bow-upraised arms-clap, to honor the beginning of our morning's aikido practice. Then looking up and flashing her wide smile around the circle, as if seeing us for the first time, she breaks into a metaphorical story about aikido founder Morihei Ueshiba (meaning Abundant Peace). We're held by Colleen's quiet power, her obvious reverence for spirit, her spontaneous bursts of exuberant laughter, her open heart. Teaching us to create our own power shields, drumming and chanting in ceremony or whispering by the lake, watching a turtle dive nearby, this same essence flows into whatever she does.

PENNY: *Colleen, I've just seen some of your talents. I know you're an aikido Black Belt, an artist, a ceremonialist, a leader of vision quests. And you've also spoken about being a political activist working to clean up nuclear waste in New Mexico. To me, you seem like a modern-day spiritual Renaissance woman. How have all these things come together for you?*

COLLEEN: As a little girl, I decided that I had a certain kind of work to do in the world that had to do with women and women's power and that I would devote my life to that. I'm now forty-five years old, and I've been in circumstances that have really allowed me to develop my talents; I was married for a period of time, and during that time I was free of having to earn a living, so I was able to develop my art and to study aikido deeply. The ritual part has come most recently for me, over the past eight years, and the activism has basically been just over this last two years.

There are all of these parts of me that I had difficulty with in a way. Most of my aikido community was very involved with body, and being embodied, and so the trance channelling work I was doing at the time was not really respected there. When I was with the trance-channellers, they weren't so interested in the body. So I felt like I had these many pieces. And my art took a back seat for quite some time, because I really didn't know how to integrate it in all of the other things I was doing.

It's only been over the past three years that somehow the activism and the aikido and the ritual and the art have all come together. The place where that happened was at a Council at the Ojai Foundation. It was called a Peaceful Cultures Council, and there were some Indian artists there from the Northwest coast. They described an action that they had just completed in which, through the use of ceremony and purification, they had carved this incredible figure. It was a thirty-foot-high totem—a welcoming figure. And they took it to Parliament [in Vancouver, British Columbia] in protest of this beautiful virgin forest that was scheduled to be cut down. When they took the figure to the Parliament Building, they had the Parliament members come out and help them carry it inside. This happened in protection of Mare's Island [off the coast of British Columbia], and they used it as a statement for protecting that site.[1]

When I heard this story, all of these pieces of me came together in one place, and I saw how that could somehow move into the world in a form. It was very healing for me, because I had felt very scattered and wondered was I just a dilettante at all of these things? I had real concerns about that—that I should just choose one thing and do only that. But now I've seen all the pieces come together.

PENNY: *So it's a lesson in having faith... You mentioned once that you grew up very streetwise, and you just now talked about having a sense,* *as a young girl, of wanting to work with women and power. Do these two connect in any way?*

COLLEEN: I hadn't made that connection, but there is a real connection there. I grew up in a neighborhood where there were some gang members on my street. This was Massachusetts, and it would have been the early 1950's. Now I was at the time in the Catholic Girls Choir [chuckles] and I was extremely devout, very religious, and had shrines all over my room. My parents weren't this way, but I was this way and I had friends, of course, who were this way. But at the same time there was this whole other aspect of these women on my street who belonged to this women's gang. And I was fascinated with them; there was a feeling of wildness and a kind of rawness that, as a good Catholic girl, I couldn't really own in some way. And so I used to study them and wonder about what it was that attracted me in them—even though I was also scared of them.

I wound up being moved from there, to a place where I wasn't in the same situation. I feel like I was really affected by that, though. I didn't grow up naive or protected, because I was right in the middle of quite a bit of violence. One of my dear friends was beaten up because I had talked to the boyfriend of one of these women, and that had been seen, and somehow they couldn't get to me so they beat up my friend.

PENNY: *From watching you work, you really seem to have a strong sense of your own power. I'm wondering where that comes from in you?*

COLLEEN: On the top of it I would say I don't know. But I feel like I've gotten more in contact with that through my practice of the art of aikido. My experience of it is that it comes from the earth, through the soles of my feet and up into my belly—and if I keep that connection, then I'm in contact with my power. And I almost couldn't really call it *my* power, because it's *our* power.

PENNY: *Go into that a little more—our power.*

COLLEEN: You're asking me some great questions. It's really making me think very deeply. I had a vision about Chaco Canyon in New Mexico, but it's really Chaco Canyon a long time ago when women had intimate knowledge and contact, and were channels of the natural forces of the earth. And I don't really understand it, but I feel that competition started to develop and that there was a way in which that relationship of women with nature got misused. This is something I've been shown in vision—I've only talked about this a few times—but it felt so right to me, that somehow that had happened way, way back. And then I think because of something that might have happened that was really devastating, [many] women shut down that contact with nature and the natural forces. Only indigenous peoples around the world have maintained that connection.

And I feel like now, I'm beginning to discover something I knew a long time ago, and aikido has helped me make contact with that—that we *are* the earth. And that power flows through us if we can be open channels to it. When I'm in my power, I somehow have the experience of this direct contact with the earth, deep into the earth, with the winds…The founder of aikido talked about this all the time; he said that this was the power that he used in aikido. He would call the spirits of the air, he would call the earth, and then he would be the channel for those energies. And that's why I revere him so much. I feel like he had contact with the Feminine in some way that is quite awesome.

PENNY: *From the aikido, Colleen, and from your experience as a political activist, or drawing on whatever other experiences you want to, could you give some examples of abuses of power, and healthy uses of power, that you see in this country today?*

COLLEEN: Do you mean, women's abuse of power? Cause when I think of abuse of power, I always think of men first [laughter] and I think that the reasons for that are pretty obvious. But lately I've been really delving into the abuses of power by women. It's the sins of omission, rather than the sins of commission—the places where we give our power away—which then allows others to have power over us.

I feel that one of the places we see that very much currently is in our government. Men and women have abdicated their responsibility for participation in our government, leaving it to our elected officials to take care of us. People are beginning to wake up and realize that that leads to a corrupt government.

I had a wonderful discussion here with a woman about a women's circle and we were talking about the quality of women—that even though women have been dominated and there has been abuse of power by men, that underneath it there is this underlying feeling of [women's] superiority nonetheless [laughter]. When she said this to me I laughed fully, because I thought, this is *so* true. So, in terms of abuse of power, that's what I would say—it's all around us, and it exists both in terms of those who grab the power and those who don't take the power when they really should.

And there's also something else...when I went to India I really experienced what I would call spirit power, or Shakti, feminine energy—that kind of power where things get done without effort. It doesn't take the kind of effort and ambition that we think of in this country. Yet these absolutely magical things can happen; synchronicities happen. You get led to the right place and it just sort of unfolds somehow. When I stepped into India that was my experience there; it was one of the most incredible experiences of my life actually.

It also ties very much into aikido, because aikido works with that—it's *soft* power, not 'power over.' And yet it is the strongest power, I believe, that really exists.

PENNY: *Can you lead a country using that kind of power?*

COLLEEN: I would say that it's the only way to live our lives. And I struggle with it all the time—because I feel it for awhile, I live in it, I lose it, and I have to find it again. But I feel like it's the only way to live our lives.

PENNY: *How do you find it for yourself?*

COLLEEN: For me it's come through the study of aikido, and it's come through meditation. I have been moving into a role as an activist—stepping out and then stepping back. I feel like I'm on the border of taking an activist role, particularly in this nuclear waste issue. But I'm not sure that I can keep this soft power, this 'doing without doing,' letting what you might call the Spirit or the Divine Mother or the Goddess work through me. I'm not sure that I can keep my compassion, my open heart, my groundedness. So I feel like that's my threshold right now; that's where I'm working—I can keep it in my studio; I can keep it in aikido; I'm working on having it in all my relationships with friends and intimates. And now I'm working with, can I extend that into the world?

PENNY: *This is a lot what I wanted to talk about. Because given all the work that needs to be done in the world, how can we do it better? Meaning more healthfully for us as human beings, as political activists, as people who clearly want to save the earth? I know that you're in the middle of this process yourself, but I'm just wondering if you can share your process more?*

COLLEEN: I've been part of a group called Concerned Citizens for Nuclear Safety. They've actually had a fair amount of press recently because of the events happening in New Mexico which affect the whole nation at this point. Because if that waste depository opens to take all this [nuclear] waste that we've generated through the military, then…it hasn't opened because of protest, which has clogged the works, so the waste is backing up in the Hanford plant in Washington, in the Idaho National Engineering Lab and in Colorado's Rocky Flats plant. Part of the reason that all of this has come out into the press is because of the waste not having a place to go. The Concerned Citizens for Nuclear Safety came together to work on this, and I was invited to join them after we had brought Joanna Macy to New Mexico. We wanted to visit the site together and determine whether we felt good about this place or bad about it. It's a real problem—we *do* need to do something about the waste.

One of the things that I think we have *got* to do—and I don't know that I can always do this but it's really important—is *to keep our hearts and minds open to the people that we think are doing it wrong*. Because one of the things that I'm finding is that these people have often gone into their lines of work because they have ideals. We may not agree with how they see doing it, but they're not all just in there for the money. They're not all just in there out of greed.

And Joanna and I had this wonderful conversation after visiting this Westinghouse plant: we were so affected by the dedication of the people we met there who feel like they're pioneers—that they're really doing something to stop the pollution from this waste going into our environment—that both of us were having this impulse to sign up! [laughs] Flying back on the plane both of us talked about how we got caught in that, and we realized that there were some real ideals there, as well as all of the other things. So somehow we have to keep our hearts open, even though we *really* disagree with the way they're doing it. And that's my challenge. I don't know if I can do that—to keep my heart open when I'm saying, '*No*, I really disagree, I *don't* think that stuff should go in the ground, and I will do whatever I can to prevent it from going into the ground.'

PENNY: *Speaking of challenges—what's been your greatest challenge?*

COLLEEN: As a personal challenge, I would say, overcoming my self-hatred. Being able to look at feelings of lack of worth, self-contempt. And I've tried to trace it—I don't know, it seems to be like a malaise of the soul. I have also connected it to being female, and I've worked with that a lot.

Also I would say just being able to look at the suffering on the earth, and really feel it, and open to it fully. I was afraid to do that. When I first started painting, I think I was trying to create a pure land, to create a world that was safe and beautiful that didn't have suffering in it. As I grew with my art, I went into a period of deep personal suffering, through an experience of being hypnotized and uncovering a tremendous amount of grief. Then that went into my paintings, and I worked with this grief and this deep sorrow through a period of some years...all my paintings became black, indigo, dark. Actually I'm just stepping out of that period now. But the challenge was to be able to really open to the suffering of the world and still want to be here anyway.

PENNY: *What had scared you from doing that?*

COLLEEN: I was afraid my heart would break—that I would lose my mind with grief.

PENNY: *But you haven't.*

COLLEEN: No, it's just made me bigger. It's like Deena Metzger was talking about this morning: the tender broken heart can contain the whole world. And that's what I've found. And I did really fear for my sanity for a period of time.

PENNY: *Whatever you've been doing, it's obviously had an impact. To have had the kind of self-hatred that you talked about—that I can certainly relate to, as a lot of other women can—and then to see you as I've seen you, in the role of teacher...you come across as someone who loves and accepts herself in a quiet and gentle kind of way. You're on to something, Colleen.*

COLLEEN: [laughs quietly] I just went on a vacation to Mexico that turned be more like an initiation. I went with a very dear friend, and both of us were somewhat stressed out, looking for fun and a good time. I had just been given a practice in which you visualize yourself as the Guru or the Teacher, so I started to visualize myself as this woman, who I've had contact with over the last year, named Ammicci. She's from India and is called Divine Mother. And I feel like this is healing me, to start to see myself as the Divine Mother; I visualize myself as her, and this feels like a really big step for me.

PENNY: *And you're working on some kind of book?*

COLLEEN: The book started as a newsletter that came out of the work we were doing some years ago—trying to create some instruction for people who wanted to visit sacred places and make pilgrimages. It turned into a research project on what was happening to the environment. We realized that going to sacred places was wonderful, but there is an awful lot of the world that's being destroyed, and we need to visit those places too—the places that are wounded. Now it's becoming a series of books; we're trying to create an initiation for people to help them open their hearts, to rebond with the earth, and out of that deep place be able to act, to help turn around what is happening and help us all to make change.

PENNY: *That sounds very empowering. I was just going to ask what direction you see us all moving in, what's the vision for the future? What are the next steps and how do we get there?*

COLLEEN: Joanna Macy has started talking about the Beings of the Three Times[2] in her work with the nuclear waste issue. She asks the Future Beings for their help in what we should do now, because it's their future that we're caretaking. I think one of the things that has happened to us is that we've lost the feeling that we're going to *have* a future. So for me, reaching into the future and affirming that there *is* going to be a future, and then asking for *guidance* from there, is really powerful to do.

PENNY: *Do you do that through meditation?*

COLLEEN: Yeah, we just sat down and said, 'Hey, out there [laughs], *Help!* you know, through our imagination. But also that brings up our caring, and it brings up our sense of responsibility, and that's real powerful—because out of that many many things can happen. From the Women's Alliance Camp this year, I have such a sense of women being able to somehow turn the tide, step in, pick up their vision, have the faith to do it, and *do* it. It's time, it's really time for that to happen.

PENNY: *One last question, Colleen. Who are your heroes, your heroines?*

COLLEEN: I really have a lot. The founder of aikido, Morihei Ueshiba. Ammicci. Pearl Shannon, who had a spiritualist church and had the courage to do the kind of work she did in spite of ostracism. The animals—I feel like they are such teachers to us, such witnesses to us. They give to us constantly. We take; we don't even realize how much we take.

My mind is reeling with other people whose names I don't even know, sisters and friends and brothers, who are keeping love in spite of terrible suffering or wrongdoing. Like Thich Nhat Hanh and Sister Phuong[3] from Vietnam who, in the midst of tremendous suffering, are still able to keep this open heart, this loving caringness, and who continue and bring this to other people. I wish that for myself.

PENNY: *Is there anything else you want to add about women and power?*

COLLEEN: I think I would just repeat what I've already said—it's really time. It's women's time. And as I'm saying that, I'm hearing the words of one of my aikido teachers, Bob Nadeau—he's also one of my heroes. I went into the dojo one day and he was running around the mat, saying 'It's coming up everywhere, can't you feel it? Can't you feel it? The *Feminine* is coming up *everywhere.*' He was saying 'Soak it up!' and he meant 'Feel it coming out of the ground—soak it up and let it come through you.' I really feel that's true.

N O T E S :

1. This action successfully protected the forests for the time being. The issue is not yet resolved, however, and is still tied up in the courts.

2. The knowledge that nuclear waste has to be stored for 240,000 years before it is no longer lethal has led Macy into an expanded view of time, and has compelled her to seek the advice of the 'Beings of the Future.'

3. Sister Phuong does work related to that of Thich Nhat Hanh and is a colleague of his.

For information on Thich Nhat Hanh, see notes following interview with Deena Metger. For Joanna Macy, see Fran Peavey.

Photos by Happy Hyder

Lakota Harden

MAY 1991

"What we've all come here to do is to learn that balance. We decide what the balance needs to be—the fear and the love, and the place for both. For each of us, it's trusting ourselves, and getting back to why we came here."

Bursting through my door clad in gym shorts and an American Indian Movement T-shirt, Lakota Harden holds each second of life just as it's being born: opening a peace rally with sacred blessing...romping along the estuary with her children at a local music festival...holding hundreds of conference attendees at rapt attention with her blend of creative insight and warm humor. Lakota's strength is solid but fills only her own space. Her wisdom is flushed with childlike glee, peeking through the folds of responsibility she wears. Vulnerability, self-knowledge, compassion, joy—these are her garments; these are the gifts she brings.

Lakota, or Tašina Ska Win, is from the Minnecoujou, Yankton, Lakota and Winnebago tribes and grew up on the Pine Ridge Reservation in South Dakota.

PENNY: *Lakota, when I saw you during the Gulf War, I was almost broken by feelings of powerlessness and grief. I felt drawn to you for answers, knowing you and your people have had to deal with these same feelings, because of the genocide practiced by the U.S. government on indigenous peoples in this country. At that time you reassured me. You said the earth would continue and would survive, and that if every day I had contact with children and with the earth, that would help me. That gave me a lot, and I wondered if you could talk more about that.*

LAKOTA: Well, you know, we've been through this before. We've been through a lot of what we're going through. There's such a difference between a universal way of thinking and the way that we're socialized to believe in the United States at this time. I call it the 'matchbox' way to live. We're forced to reduce ourselves and our vision to that of climbing into a matchbox, to be a certain way in the world. And there's several other ways to look at things, all kinds of perspectives. When we're looking from the matchbox, it looks like it's going to be crushed, and we're going to be crushed with it. But when we step outside of that, we realize there are many other lifetimes, and there are also many lifetimes that have happened on this planet itself.

When I was growing up, I remember hearing all the reverence for Mother Earth and how powerful she is. All she has to do is shake her elbow, and people and buildings and civilizations are crushed—if that's what she decides to do. She's giving us a lot of warning right now. Each time we do something, she does something in return to warn us: 'That's not good for the future generations.' She is much more powerful than we can imagine.

We were told in our traditions about this and I interpreted it in many different ways as I was growing up. When I was seven years old, my great-great-grandmother was ninety-six, and she used to tell me stories about the way to be in the world. I never realized how much that stuck with me until my adult life. A lot of it keeps coming back to me as time goes by. For example, the whole concept of this way of life being temporary. When I was in second grade and she said this was temporary, I thought, 'Oh good, I won't have to go to school much longer.' We hear things the way we need to in order to survive, and that information helped me survive a lot of the racism, prejudice and oppression I went through as a young person.

[So I had those teachings] along with the teachings of Catholicism which we were forced to learn in the Catholic boarding school system. Nuns and priests were very terrible people to me when I was growing up. Many of them were pedophiles and sadomasochists. People don't believe that nuns and priests are capable of doing the things they did to us.

PENNY: *Louise Erdrich[1] has written about that too.*

LAKOTA: There's also a book [about it] by Tim Gallego, who is the editor of *The Lakota Times,* called *The Aboriginal Sin.* Some of this still happens, especially molestation cases, by doctors or teachers who come to the reservations. Not always. Some of them are really sincere—

the do-gooders, you know. They want to 'save the Indian,' which is another form of racism. Then there are others who come to the reservations because they have malpractice suits against them and have one chance to get out of Dodge—so there are numerous stories of our people dying in hospitals and dying under a physician's supervision because they were given the wrong kind of care. Or because the health care available to us is so poor to begin with.

When we were little, as I said, a lot of us went to boarding school year after year; that was our home, and that was what life was about. I got through that by knowing there was more coming, that there was a reason. When I do oppression work, or I hear stories about some of the horrors that women, especially, or young people have gone through, I think, 'Yeah, I know what that's like; I've been through that too.'

But there's also a lot of things that *didn't* happen to me, where I was saved by the bell, or I would decide to turn around or move a little to the left. A lot of that came from my inside knowing, though not understanding. There were so many minute insignificant things that determined if I were to fall into ruin of some kind or to be liberated from an oppressive situation.

In Catholicism there's this heaven and hell, good or bad dichotomy, that just keeps us in the matchbox way of thinking and believing about ourselves. Luckily that was a good example of how *not* to be for me, and I constantly questioned, 'There's more to this...'

Within our own sweat lodge is the closest thing I can come to in actually going beyond this world and expanding. One of the first times I ever went in, I remember I didn't know what we were doing. Nobody said, 'Okay, this is a purification ceremony, we're going to return to the womb,' or anything. They just said to take off my clothes, and I took them off, and we went in. Me and my cousins were all little, and two of my cousins were whispering during the sweat cause they were trying not to think about the heat. But for me in that experience, I went in to the sweat lodge—this completely dark place—and it felt like the whole place expanded, like it was unlimited in space. That was what the darkness gave to me. I even felt behind me, trying to feel the back of the lodge, because of that feeling of being completely unlimited in where I was. It was scary at first sitting there naked in total darkness—yet that was the most incredible feeling, almost like I had completely left this realm. That always stayed with me and taught me a good way of looking at both ways: the matchbox world that we're in and how people think in that—I can understand it real well from the boarding school mentality, the colonization mentality and all the other consumerist mentalities—but I can also remember that other part, the darkness and the returning.

An example is, when the earthquake happened, my daughter was freaked out because she had never been through that experience before. First we ran outside and lay down on the ground. I had her close her eyes because her eyes were racing wildly. She kept saying, 'What's happening, Mom, what's happening?' I had never seen her that way and I knew that I needed to take care of her. So we lay down on the ground and I had her close her eyes. I said, 'Just go down, all the way down, deeper and deeper, deeper and deeper, keep going, keep going, and once you get down there—there She is. You see the Old Grandmother? How does she look?' And my daughter said, 'Well she's real fat, and she's got big breasts. She's very smiling and has a lot of wrinkles and she's saying she's not going to hurt me.' I said, 'That's right, she's not going to hurt us.' And that was it. We came back up, and she was fine after that.

My son, on the other hand, who during the earthquake was at his childcare, just rolled around giggling. All the other children were screaming and running, and he was rolling and thought it was fun. He was saying, 'Grandmother Earth is rolling over.' The teachers were real impressed with him in that one incident, because he was aware of that. So that's the kind of unlimited vision that we all have, if we use it.

What's good about what's happening with people nowadays is that we're learning what the matchbox looks like, the internalized oppression. I do workshops for Battered Women's Alternatives right now in Contra Costa County, and I'm the statewide coordinator. I mention that because it's really significant as far as the situation of my people and the barriers that were put up for us to hurdle.

I look at where a lot of my peers are now—the people I identify with the most—and they just seem to be on a dead-end treadmill. I mean, I was a woman on welfare, raising two children. But when I was going to school in Nebraska, I got involved with Ricky Sherover-Marcuse and her Unlearning Racism workshops, as well as New Bridges camp. And I realized *this* was the world my grandmother was talking about. The other world was temporary, where I was forced to be in this box and forced to live someone else's life. That was all the oppression: be a good girl, be a smart mother, be a strong woman, be the 'Native American,' be friendly—all of these things that were *reactions* to oppression.

You know, if somebody saw me in those days, they were immediately afraid. Even now, at least once a day, I'll surprise somebody in a store or walking down the street. They're just in their own world, and all of a sudden they see me, and there's that look of panic or fear, just for a second [laughs]. Then they compose themselves and say, 'Oh, hello,' or they smile or look away or go the other direction. Because I'm usually wearing some kind of beadwork or…I mean I can't hide my *Indianness*, you know? It's kind of obvious with me, there's no ambiguity about it. That's sometimes the reaction I get from people, and that's the culture we live in. Even at the Y, I go to take a shower, and on the shower curtain there's the Marx Brothers with an Indian. Last night at my son's school play, there were people dressed up like Indians. Sometimes I get really angry and have to decide at that moment what I want to do with it—if it's beneficial to rage and do something about it, or to just turn away—because those are some of the ways I've decided to survive at this point in my life.

But getting back to my involvement with New Bridges and *seeing*…my great-great-grandmother Agnes and I used to sleep together, because the fire would go out at night. We would be laying in bed and I was real chubby, so she would wrap herself around me because I was her bed-warmer. And she would talk about all of this stuff, and I would listen and listen. I couldn't believe this world of where she lived and what it must have been like; I wanted to go there. That vision always kept me going. And with New Bridges, I thought, 'This is the world that I was waiting for.' I keep Ricky with me all the time because of that. She's like my grandmother, come back.

I've also learned a hard lesson on how they leave. My grandmother died when I was eleven, and then Ricky died a few years ago. So there's a lot of lessons involved with how we need to continue on and *trust* our vision. It's great to have it validated with someone else. But the biggest test, I think, is to trust your own vision. Because that matchbox mentality taught us that someone else knows more.

It's the whole oppression of adultism: the teacher knows more, your parents know more, the cop on the corner knows more, the store clerk knows more. That as children we really *don't know*; that we're supposed to completely believe what they say and not necessarily trust what we think or feel. And we internalize that for the rest of our lives. It sets the groove where racism, sexism, ableism and all the other oppressions can lay. If there were no groove there for the other oppressions coming at us, [it would be easier to say] 'No, *that's* not right, *my* thinking is right. I belong here completely and deserve total respect.' But because we don't know what that feels like—and there's a groove there that says, 'You really don't know'—when racism occurs and somebody says, 'You don't belong here,' then it fits right into that groove, and you say, 'Maybe I don't.'

PENNY: *When you say, 'we' or 'I,' are you saying that as women, as women of color, as...?*

LAKOTA: I think that anyone who relates to this, that's who I'm talking about. I'm not sure if there are really any people who don't ever doubt themselves. You know? I mean everybody has an Achilles heel, where we had some kind of oppression affect us. We can be strong and powerful in many arenas in our lives, but there is always one place where we doubt ourselves, and that's what keeps us in line. Otherwise we would never accept this kind of government, we would never accept this way to be in the world with each other, we would never accept what is going on around us.

PENNY: *But that's what I mean: don't we want someone like George Bush to doubt himself? We don't want him to hold on to his vision. So how do I interpret your words in terms of who they apply to?*

LAKOTA: I don't think George Bush really has a vision. The problem with this oppression and the way that I believe it works, is that each time we suffer some kind of oppression or pain, we put up a shield to try to guard that spot where we've been hurt, to protect ourselves. Then we put up another one. It's like a bandage over a wound. The wound might not get healed, but the bandage or shield is still there. People then put up so many shields which keep getting reinforced, and pretty soon it's the *shield* behaving and not the person inside. People like George Bush and a lot of people that we see around us every day [are really] walking in their armor; it's obvious by the way that they present themselves in the world.

In the sweat lodge when we were kids, we always prayed for the President and for all the white people in the world: that they would get their hearts back, that they would get their bodies back. Those shields isolate and disconnect us from each other, from the earth, from the rest of the world—and that little light that's inside of us gets isolated. It doesn't recognize the lights inside other people or other beings around us. We need to hope and pray and give examples of ways for these people to be able to take some of the shields down and get their light back. That's the only way. Otherwise they'll destroy themselves and everyone else around them.

I spent a lot of years being very angry and carrying a lot of hate around. People could see it in the way I carried myself. You can watch a person walking down the street, and just by looking at them you know that there's a lot of pain and suffering going on, a lot of anger and rage. For women I think it's important for us to use that anger and use that rage; it's one of the most powerful things that we have. Unfortunately, the overall culture doesn't advocate for a place for women to be angry, to unleash that anger and power in a way which will actually heal us and the people around us, and eventually heal the world. So we all are finding these places on our own. But often this anger gets turned back on ourselves. I've seen so many powerful women who are out there using that power, but it ends up being used against them. I know that women in all areas are working on this. And we'll get there.

All the anger and rage can be used as a lesson to propel our own selves and who we are. But that's a real hard one. When I was on welfare and raising my babies and having to go to court to fight to keep my children—because of racism and because of classism—I would not have wanted to hear your New Age goody-goody philosophy about using my oppression to propel me through to the next point. I would have told you to get out of my face. But somehow I did use it, not knowing that's what I was doing, and I got to where I am now.

I've held out for that vision about having the world exactly how I want it: being able to be my full self and knowing that I am completely honorable and respectful, two things that were taken away from me when I was little...really believing in every cell of my body, not just in my brain or heart but in every cell, that I am worthwhile and completely brilliant, loving and worth loving, all those things that get taken or damaged. This is now the world I exist in, for the most part.

After I started giving New Bridges workshops [like Unlearning Racism] I was in school at UC Berkeley. I was doing New Bridges for free on the side, because I wanted to spread this and help these young people. Then I began teaching a course at The New College of California, called Society and Self, so I was actually getting paid for doing my New Bridges work. That was the first step, you know. Now, working at Battered Women's Alternatives, a lot of what I've gone through has paid off. From giving all those workshops I have developed some incredible allies.

You know, my boss, Allen Creighton—it always feels weird to say 'boss'—the person who officially supervises my position at Battered Women's Alternatives, is one of the best friends and allies in the world. He's a white male, heterosexual gentile [laughs]. He has worked through our alliance-building workshops and through his own personal life to be an effective ally to women, to people of color, to poor people, to young people and to anyone on the down-side of the imbalance of power in this country—and it's great! When I go into my workplace, he says, 'What's your best thinking here?' And I say, 'Well, I'm doing this and I intend to do this,' and he says, 'Great, how can I help?' It's incredible to have that kind of support in the workplace. And in terms of all the inter-agency paperwork and logistics and unaware racism he's my shield; he deals with that part so I don't have people badgering me to make sure these forms are in or those statistics are filled. He makes sure that that happens by allowing me to do it in my own way, and to be completely Indian, to be completely a mother, to be all these things in my workplace. That's an incredible gift that we all deserve to have. So here I am, from the time I was six to now being almost thirty-four, getting to have that in my life.

It's very hard work to maintain this. We struggle with the people within my program, because the other people are all white, and we have to look at their racism, and my internalized racism, and my rage, and their rage. We try to make room for all of it to be expressed and to be able to heal, which is difficult to do. To take this theory and put it in a practical setting, and actually *do* it, is hard work, very hard work.

And we all do it at our own pace. I did a workshop yesterday that I called the Workshop from Hell. With progressive people who are very conscious, very political, in an institution that is known for being very radical. And it was hard, because the shield there was, 'I'm politically correct so this is the way I'm going to do things, and don't you dare look behind the shield.' And we all need to look behind the shield. I'm constantly noticing inside myself if it's the internalized oppression speaking or reacting, or if it's really me in a powerful place. Because the two powers here are love and fear. We're either acting out of one or the other. So the symptoms of those reactions can always be traced down to fear or love. A lot of times I ask, 'What am I afraid of right now? Or what do I passionately *want* right now?' [laughs]

We were told a long time ago in all the different tribes about this time coming with Grandmother Earth. This was before or aside from the New-Agey stuff that's happening now; I don't have anything to do with that at this point. Just Indian people who were raised in and lived within the Indian societies would come together, and people would speak and talk. In Indian culture where I come from, people would say one sentence or one paragraph and everybody would hear it. It would be very important not to waste words and to give time to taking it in. And people just acknowledged it with their voice or by nodding their heads or by beating the drum. You had time to take it in and really listen. There was a lot of respect in the way people spoke to each other.

I remember when they said, 'The time of purification is coming, get ready.' As a child, I pictured these kind of *Grapes of Wrath*-type settings, of us walking through the dust and me holding my children, with no water or food and nobody in sight. We're in that barren wasteland now. When you look at what's happening to homeless children and families on the street, what's happening to the psyche of corporate executives locked up in their offices. That barren wasteland looks a lot of different ways. And that's hard for us to see, because we're taught that people with money have all these *things*. We *all* have a barrenness in us, and it looks different. Part of the tendency of the culture to romanticize being poor or being working class is because there is a camaraderie, a sense of self and a sense of power, that people have who are dealing with the basics.

John Trudell,[2] who was one of my mentors, wrote a poem that talks about when the police were arresting and brutalizing him after Wounded Knee, and they told him to go squat by the trash cans. They thought they were humiliating him, but that's where he got his power: by squatting and being close to the ground, getting connected and gathering his strength. That's what the poem is about. It doesn't matter how much money you have sometimes; it's not always about money. It really comes from within, and that's the lesson we're learning with this recession.

A brother of mine came out here recently from back home [South Dakota]. In Minneapolis and the Twin Cities areas, they're offering the tribes in South Dakota a dollar an acre to bury the waste there from the cities. And of course the reservation is poverty-stricken, with no jobs or income, so that looks real tempting. It's the same issue around mining in the Four Corners Region.[3] It angers me when environmentally-conscious, politically correct people say, 'How can they do that to their Mother?' They judge Indian people who are wanting to sell their land and say, 'Oh, they're supposed to be Native American, they're supposed to care about the earth.' Well, that's valid thinking and we all wish we had the privilege of having that thinking. But when you see your babies dying of malnutrition and poor health care, your people drinking alcohol and killing each other because the poverty is so bad, you want to do anything to get out of that. You're not thinking long-term; you're thinking survival.

My brother was telling me about the organizing they are doing on the reservation, educating Indian people that this is not a good thing to come and bury all this toxic waste from the cities on the reservation for a few bucks. The controversy on the reservation about that brought me back to where I come from, reminding me of who our people are and who I am inside. We were going across the bridge from the San Francisco Airport and my brother was looking around amazed. He said, 'Look, all these cars only have one person in them. In time there's going to be no more oil or gas, and all these people with these cars are going to have nowhere to go. They're going to come running to us on the reservation—so we can't bury toxic waste there.' You know, he's thinking in the seventh generation from now [laughs] and he says it's not going to be very far down the line. Everybody who's working their jobs right now and getting their degrees to get those cars—we need to be thinking about the other goals we should be having also.

And again, that kind of thinking gets us scared. The fear jumps up and we think, 'Oh my God, I better stockpile water and food.' And that would be a good thing. But we have to remember not to let the fear run amok, because it immobilizes us. If we can turn the fear into an ally, use it to motivate us to do something, that's powerful.

PENNY: *But how do you do that? How do you keep fear from immobilizing you?*

LAKOTA: That brings us back to what I had said to you during the Gulf War, and that is to really connect with the earth. How many of us do that? How many of us really go and sit and greet our Grandmother Earth, and spend time with her, and ask her what's our next step? Going back to the concept of time, in this culture it's A, B, C, D; 1, 2, 3, 4—it's in a linear fashion—and we never really go back to A. We're on C, but we're thinking about Z. It immobilizes us in that way. Whereas when we go down into the earth, when we sit in a sweat lodge, when we meditate in a grove of trees, when we spend time on the ocean, with our sisters, our families, with children...

I always go back to children because they're the ones returning—I've been told that over and over. There's this bird that comes back to South Dakota every spring, and it makes a noise which means in our language 'We've come back'; and they're all the returning people who have fallen, who have chosen to come back, who are in other planes looking at us and saying, 'You know, I'm with this person.' So there's a spirit, an entity looking at you who chooses to be with you in your lifetime, who watchs over you, who says, 'Penny really needs me right now and I want to go back.' Who will be born in this life to be with you or to teach you the things that you are seeking out. A lot of the children being born now are choosing to come at this time because of the knowledge they have and still remember.

Unfortunately, child abuse and molestation, along with the education system and television, all bombard the children to forget. We must constantly encourage them to remember that what they're thinking and feeling is exactly correct, and they should speak it. We must give them a voice so we can learn from them. I learn the most right now from my children. My son will say something that blows my mind almost to a subservient position, where I can't speak after he speaks. And my *daughter* is incredibly powerful. It's tough because they're in the school system, which is very hard. I've been going to meetings with teachers about my son's 'irrational way of behaving.' Part of me is saying, 'Akicita, you've got to do your homework, and you've got to learn to read.' And part of me is saying, 'Good for you, son! Hang in there, don't let 'em get you.' It's a constant balancing act.

And really, what we've all come here to do is to learn that balance. We decide what the balance needs to be—the fear and the love, and the place for both. For each of us, it's trusting ourselves and getting back to why *we* came here—who did we come to help when we chose to come back to this earth? What was our reason for coming back to this lifetime, what lesson were we supposed to learn? When we start getting back in touch with that, going down to the mother, going up to the universe, connecting with the animal that's in our life, or whoever's around us, whatever's around us, the wind that comes... every time the wind comes, even if I'm half asleep—and my building lets me know when the wind is here—I get up and go sit with the wind. Even if I don't think I'm feeling anything, I just take it in anyway. The same with the thunder beings, the rain, the fog. All of these beings are here for us, and we completely ignore them. We get in our matchbox, and we don't even know that they're there.

The answer that I have is that I have no answers. That you have your own answer. This guru mentality that we have, where one person says something profound and we all flock to them to give us something...that's a normal reaction, because we recognize the light in that person. Our light is jumping out and saying, 'Hey, there's something to be said there, listen to that!' It's not that they did something to us. It's because *our* light sparked and got brighter, and the shields went down a little bit more. We heard truth, and the truth recognized the truth. Instead of flocking to this medicine person or this wise person, we need to do it in a way that recognizes that *we* have that knowledge—*we* recognized it. We may have forgotten after forty years or however old we are, but the inspiration that we think came from that person, actually came from inside ourselves.

And again, the way to get in touch with that is to spend time with children—getting back to the child inside of ourselves, getting back with the essence of who we are. The dirt, the stones that we use, our crystals and sage, whatever we're drawn to, are tools to help us get back that light inside of ourselves. I shun the New Age mentality because there is so much confusion around it. People are real clear on their psychic and on their Tarot cards; they're real clear on what their tool is. That's not what I'm talking about when I say confusion. The confusion is giving the power to that thing instead of within ourselves.

When I told somebody I read Tarot cards, they looked at me kind of confused, like 'aren't you a Native American and don't you have a pipe?' And that's true. I do. That's my tool, that's something of mine that I use and share when I feel like it's beneficial. The Tarot cards are something that people in a linear context understand, that help me in *my* linear thinking [chuckles]—I live in this society too—to give me a tool, to say, 'the cards say this, now I should do this.' I didn't always read Tarot cards, but at this point in time this is a tool that is helping me. Because I've always thought, 'I don't know if what I say is right.' And when I read a deck of cards for somebody, all of a sudden I'll get all these images and I'll start recognizing what it's about and it just starts pouring out of my mouth. The person who's getting the reading is completely dazzled and thinking, 'That's right, that's right.' And it's not so much the cards, as it is the energy between the two of us. It's me focusing my energy on that person and on the images that come and trusting that what I'm doing is valid. It's not any kind of magical power that comes from somewhere else—it comes from within us. That's one tool I'm using to help me develop my own power, my own trusting of my light that's inside.

PENNY: *Lakota, you've mentioned a few times having problems with New Age spirituality… how do I ask this question? My involvement with what I'll call women's spirituality has put me in touch with traditions from your people that have been healing, that have provided connection for me. Traditions such as the Medicine Wheel, such as sweats. Is there a way that I, as a white woman, as a Jewish woman, can participate in traditions from your culture that will not rip it off?*

LAKOTA: That's always been the tough one, and I don't have any answers for it. Because everybody's on their own path. I speak for my people who are outraged, and I will constantly tell the story about how people suffered and died to keep these traditions intact with the utmost respect. You can't imagine what that looks like. You really can't imagine. When I go home, I see the situation my people are in. I know my history, *feel* my history in the cells of my body; I have the memories of being cut up, my body parts…I do have those kinds of memories. What it took for our people to hang onto these traditions, when they were persecuted *because* of these traditions…The cavalry really couldn't beat us *because* of our spirituality. The government recognized, 'they have something else that's more powerful than these guns or cannons, and that's their spirituality, so let's get that.' People were hanged, people were burned, people were ostracized, people were completely wiped out because of these traditions. And people held fast to them.

A grandmother that I have talks about her husband and their family—he was a Medicine Man. The Catholic missionaries came in and completely brainwashed and brutalized our people into accepting Christianity. Otherwise they would have died. So our own people turned against our Medicine People, who fought and hung in there anyway, who suffered incredible oppression. And their families are still suffering that same oppression, only to have their spirituality be on display and for sale and in catalogues. And to see Lynn Andrews[4] making a bundle, you know. It's unspeakable what that kind of exploitation and attack really feels like. That's where the pain and the anger and all of our retaliation comes from: 'How dare you? You've taken everything from us. You've cut off our legs, cut out our eyes, cut off our arms, and now you want to cut out our hearts too? That's all we have left—so here, take that too.' That's the feeling, that's where we're coming from when we're angry about that.

With that feeling and that anger I went back to my Medicine People. I asked the Spirits, 'What do I do with this?' They said, 'You have to forgive them, they're very ignorant'—and those were the words they used [laughs]—'about their exploitation of your people right now. They're fumbling, trying to find their way, and they'll fumble long enough until they find their own way. Then they will leave you alone. So be *patient*, my child.' Which is always my lesson, to be patient and to remember that eagle's vision, that eventually people will all find their own way.

When I was growing up as a child, we all prayed everyday that white people would 'get it,' that white people would learn about the earth and about the healing. Now that that looks like it's happening, it's a terrifying experience because of the *way* it's happening. I'm not saying that there aren't people out there who are sincere; everybody who's picked this up is searching and is sincere! People don't intend to offend or intend to be racist—I mean, a lot of people do, like the Ku Klux Klan, but that's their whole intention. For the most part, people in the New Age spirituality, and especially in women's spirituality, have all the best intentions. But we need to recognize the ground that we're treading on.

The thing I like best about the groups I take part in is when we all bring our own traditions and share them, in acknowledgement that they are our traditions. I went to the *Revolutionary Nutcracker Sweetie*[5] with a friend of mine who's been working on her racism. The production features many different traditions, and when the bunji-cord Raggedy-Ann type of dolls [representing dolls from Appalachia] were dancing, she looked at me and said, 'Now there's *my* tradition!' It was like, 'right on!'

It's so good to take pride and to go back and honor your own ancestors. I sometimes think how hard it must be to be an ancestor of somebody who's ashamed of their own self, to watch them try to be somebody else and divorce from themselves. Because that's a lot of what people are saying when they are taking on these other ways to be. 'I was a Native American in a past life.' Well, I was a *tree* in a past life! *This* life is why we're here, and when we remove ourselves from this life, we're removing ourselves from the real reason we're here.

As far as the women's circles, and using or acknowledging traditions, I'm not sure if I'll make it through this life where that doesn't bother me. I'm working on it. I've worked damn hard on it and will continue to work on it. There are times, in a safe place, where it feels alright. People learn from me and then somebody will respectfully present something in a circle they learned from me, or from another Native American person, and it feels alright. I'm not sure what makes that different than somebody having sweat lodges and saying, 'This is a Native American sweat lodge,' when it's not—it's a dozen white women getting together to pray and find their light inside. It's not a Native American sweat lodge. It has nothing to do with that.

One of the criticisms I've heard about our people is, 'they think they have cornered the market on spirituality' or 'they think they own it.' We need to look at the history of racism in this country and how racism has affected us. There is a way to bridge and pray together and be able to do that in a respectful way. I encourage women to seek out their own traditions. For example, I have educated myself about Jewish tradition, and I probably know more Hebrew than many Jews I know. I can take part in Shabbat or honor the Havdalah[6] with Jewish people, without trying to be a Jew. We can educate ourselves in honor of those traditions but not try to take them away.

Because we all have our own traditions, and we will get there. It's an honorable thing to want to return to the earth; and everybody had earth religion, not just Native American people. If you look far enough back in Gaelic tradition or Celtic, all of these different traditions that I've studied, they're exactly like ours. They're just using their own languages. It bothers me every time I hear a non-Lakota pray in Lakota. Why don't you find out what the word for Grandmother is in *your* language? Why don't you learn how to say 'all my relations' in your language? That would be the most powerful thing, because that's who you are in this lifetime. When I speak in my own language, it's the most powerful thing. I can sing the South African National Anthem in solidarity with South African people, but it's more powerful when they can sing it and it can be acknowledged. Whereas if I sing a Lakota song, that brings me power because that's who I am.

So there's something about really reclaiming all of who we are and being able to share that. Because if we're comfortable in who we are, then we are not threatening to somebody else and we're not threatened by somebody else. And that goes back to George Bush. He wouldn't have the need to destroy if he didn't feel [threatened]. That's why it's important that we all heal; it's why we say, if one of us is not free, then none of us are free. We need to really live that, because we're all related. Mitakuye Oyasin.

Wanbli (The Eagle)

Wanbli, teach us how to live,
Guard our sacred hoop of life forever.
Keep your wings outstretched in flight,
Protect us with each feather.
Your strength is mine in flight
Whenever you're around me.
This path is old but new to me
Like the sun, the moon, the sky
And creation
Created with perfection.
Flying is your freedom.
Searching for protection.
Sacred in my vision.
Wanbli, stormy winds will change

When I lift my pipe to the Four Directions.
Keep us in your sacred light
Remind us to be humble.
Your strength is mine in flight
Whenever you're around me.
This path is old but new to me
Like the sun, the moon, the sky
And creation.
                    —Margaret Zephier, one of Lakota's Grandmothers

---

NOTES:

1. Louise Erdrich [1954 –] is an award-winning, contemporary Native-American writer of the Turtle Mountain Chippewa tribe. Her books include *The Beet Queen* and *Love Medicine.*

2. John Trudell is from the Santee-Dakota tribe. He is a political activist, poet and actor. FBI agents burned down his house, killing his family, in an unsuccessful attempt to intimidate him and halt his activities.

3. Lakota is referring to the mining of uranium and coal in the region where Arizona, Utah, Colorado and New Mexico meet.

4. Lynn Andrews is a white woman who has written a series of best-selling books about Native spirituality that have angered many Native and non-Native people. She is often referred to by Native activists as a primary example of Anglo-European exploitation and appropriation. Although these Anglo-Europeans may be misinterpreting and misusing Native religions and cultures, their work is often more readily available to the mainstream public than the words and ideas of Native peoples themselves.

5. The *Nutcracker Sweetie* is an alternative version of *The Nutcracker Suite,* the classic holiday ballet written by the Russian composer Peter Ilich Tchaikovsky. Produced each December in the San Francisco Bay Area by The Dance Brigade, a women's dance/theater company, this parody of the original ballet is a highly satirical call for social change.

6. The Havdalah is the ritual done at the close of Shabbat, the Jewish Sabbath.

For information on the earthquake, see notes following interview with Naomi Newman. For Ricky Sherover-Marcuse, see Bernice Lee.

RESOURCE GROUPS

The following groups have been suggested as empowering to women by the women interviewed. They are listed here alphabetically, to provide other resources in the search for healthy uses of power; they are in no way intended as a 'master list' of such organizations.

Academy of Intuitive Studies
PO Box 1921
Mill Valley, CA 94941
415-381-1010
Teaches, trains and empowers individuals to recognize their own unique intuitive capabilities.

Common Agenda c/o AFSC
2160 Lake Street
San Francisco, CA 94121
415-752-7766
Works to build a national coalition focused on rearranging federal priorities—specifically to reduce the military budget by fifty percent, to channel money into social programs, and to develop a full-employment program.

IKWE Marketing Collective
Rt. 1, Box 286
Ponsford, MN 56575
218-573-3411
For native, certified-organic wild rice, hand-harvested by women.

Indigenous Women's Network
PO Box 174
Lake Elmo, Minnesota 55042
612-770-3861
A Continental and Pacific network of women actively involved in work in their communities "within the framework of the vision of our elders"—rebuilding families, communities and nations. Publishes *Indigenous Woman* magazine.

Kitchen Table: Women of Color Press
PO Box 908
Latham, New York 12110
518-434-2057
Founded in 1981, Kitchen Table publishes and distributes books by and about women of color from all racial/cultural heritages, sexualities and classes.

Middle East Children's Alliance
2140 Shattuck Ave, Rm. 207
Berkeley, CA 94704
510-548-0542
Provides humanitarian aid to children in Palestine and Iraq; sends peace delegations to the West Bank, Gaza and Israel; and networks for peace with justice for the Palestinian and Israeli peoples.

The Motherpeace Institute
PO Box 5544
Berkeley CA 94705
510-649-0883
Provides education and healing for women and the planet.

National Black Women's Health Project
1237 Ralph K. Abernathy Blvd, S.W.
Atlanta, GA 30310
1-800-ASK-BWHP
Provides wellness education and service through self-help groups, centers, information-sharing and advocacy for women of African descent and their families.

National Network of Women's Funds
1821 University Ave, Suite 409 N
St. Paul, MN 55104
612-641-0742
A network of 60 women's funds across the United States.

Palestinian Women's Research and Training Society/Women's Studies Center
PO Box 19591
East Jerusalem via Israel
Documents the Palestinian and Arab women's movements, provides logistical support and research for and about Palestinian women and their organizations, empowers Palestinian women and publishes *Sparks/Wamid*—a women's magazine in Arabic and English—about the above issues.

Rapproachment Center for Dialogue and Understanding
3 Avigail Street
Jerusalem, Israel 93551
Organizes dialogue groups of Israelis and Palistinians to meet "to understand each other's goals, needs and concerns; to overcome stereotypes, prejudices and fears."

Resourceful Women
3543 18th Street, Box 9F
San Francisco, CA 94110
415-431-5677
Serves as a resource center for women with wealth and provides financial education.

The Video Project
5332 College Ave
Oakland, CA 94611
510-655-9050
Distributes quality, low-cost videos for a safe and sustainable world.

Womanspeak
2462 Matilija Canyon
Ojai, CA 93023
805-646-9721
A rites-of-passage organization devoted to empowering women of all ages through spending time in the wilderness, both in a supportive community and alone.

Women Against Racism
130 N. Madison
Iowa City, Iowa 52242
319-335-1486
A multicultural group of women working to dismantle racism and other forms of oppression, at the personal as well as the institutional level.

Women in Resistance/The Weaving Project
1140 Guerrero St.
San Francisco, CA 94110
415-647-0556
Coordinated by Dine women and involving more than 78 weavers who represent the joint use area of Big Mountain, this project helps in the restoring of a traditional self-sufficient economy in the area.

Women's Alliance
PO Box 21454
Oakland, CA 94620
510-658-2949
An educational organization whose mission is to support women's empowerment as a foundation for personal and planetary healing. Believes that calling for the leadership, creativity and innate wisdom of women is essential to protect the future of the planet. Sponsors a week-long Summer Solstice Camp as well as workshops year-round.

The Women's Foundation
3543 18th Street, #9
San Francisco, CA 94110
415-431-1180
Empowers low-income women and girls by providing grants to non-profit organizations.

PRINT / FILM / CASSETTE RESOURCES

To provide additional access to the vision of some of the women interviewed in these pages, listed below is a sampling of their publications, video/film and cassette projects.

Rachel Bagby
1. *Daughters of Growing Things: Reweaving the World, the Emergence of Ecofeminism* (San Francisco, CA: Sierra Club Books, 1990)
2. *A Power of Numbers: Healing the Wounds* (Santa Cruz, CA: New Society Publishers, 1989)
3. "Building the Green Movement" (*Woman of Power* magazine, Somerville MA: Spring 1988)
4. "*Reach Beyond the Lines*" (Ladyslipper, Inc. PO Box 3124-R, Durham, NC 27715) music cassette tape.

Veronika Cohen
Veronika occasionally publishes articles in English in the [English language] magazine *Challenge*, written by and for Isreali peace activists. *Challenge*, PO Box 2760, Tel Aviv, Isreal 61026

Suha Hindiyeh
1. *Socio-economic Conditions of Female Wage-Labor: Gender and the Intifada* (Washington DC: Arab Women's Studies Association/University Press, 1992)
2. "Literacy in the Occupied Territories" (*Convergence* magazine. Toronto, Ontario: International Council for Adult Education, 1991)

Colleen Kelley
The Box—A Journey Home: an artistic collection of self-guiding teaching and healing tools to respond to the ecological crisis and the crisis of spirit (available from The Terma Company, 1807 2nd Street, #29, Santa Fe, NM 87501, 505-983-5589 June 1992)

Winona LaDuke
1. Short stories in: *Reinventing the Enemy's Language* [an anthology of Native women's writings], ed. Joy Harjo (University of Arizona Press, 1992)
2. Essays in: *A Gathering of Spirit, A Collection by North American Indian Women*, ed. Beth Brant (Ithaca NY: Firebrand Books)
3. "Native Americans and Energy Development II," ed. Joseph Jorgenson (Cambridge, MA: Anthropology Resource Center)
4. "Critical Issues in Native North America" (*International Working Group for Indigenous Affairs*, ed. Ward Churchill Copenhagen, Denmark: December 1988)
5. Publications in: *Akwesasne Notes, Business and Society Review, Cultural Survival Quarterly, Harvard Crimson, Indigenous Woman, Insurgent Soci-*

ologist, New America, Radcliffe Quarterly, Union of Radical Political Economics.

Deena Metzger

1. *Writing For Your Life: Creativity, Imagination and Healing* (San Francisco, CA: Harper, 1992)
2. *A Sabbath Among the Ruins* (Berkeley, CA: Parallax Press, 1992) poetry.
3. *The Other Hand*
4. *What Dinah Thought* (NY: Viking/Penguin, October 1989)
5. *Looking for the Faces of God* (Berkeley, CA: Parallax Press, 1989) poetry.
6. *The Woman Who Slept With Men To Take The War Out Of Them & Tree* (Los Angeles, CA: Peace Press, 1981; Berkeley, CA: Wingbow Press, 1983) drama/novel.

Papusa Molina

"Recognizing, Accepting and Celebrating Our Differences" *Making Face/Making Soul*, ed. Gloria Anzaldua (San Francisco, CA: Aunt Lute Books, 1990)

Naomi Newman

Snake Talk: Urgent Messages from the Mother (A Travelling Jewish Theater, PO Box 421985, San Francisco CA 94142) video and audio cassette.

Vicki Noble

1. *Down is Up With Aaron Eagle* (San Francisco, CA: Harper, 1993)
2. *The Snakepower Reader* (San Francisco, CA: Harper, 1992)
3. *Shakti Woman: Feeling Our Fire, Healing Our World, The New Female Shamanism* (San Francisco, CA: Harper, 1991)
4. *Snakepower: A Journal of Contemporary Female Shamanism* Vol. 1, Issues 1 & 2 (Published by Vicki Noble)
5. Motherpeace Tarot Cards (U.S. Games, Inc. 1983)
6. *Motherpeace: A Way to the Goddess* (Harper & Row, 1983)

Fran Peavey

1. *A Shallow Pool of Time: One Woman Grapples with the AIDS Epidemic* (New Society Publishers, 1991)
2. *Heart Politics* (New Society Publishers, 1986)

Barbara Smith

1. "A Press of Our Own: Kitchen Table, Women of Color Press," "Communications at the Crossroads: The Gender Gap Connnection." ed. Ramona R. Rush and Donna Allen (Norwood, N.J.: Ablex Publishing Corp. 1989)
2. Co-editor: *All the Women are White, All the Blacks are Men, But Some of Us Are Brave: Black Women's Studies* (Latham, NY: Kitchen Table: Women of Color Press)
3. Editor: *Home Girls: A Black Feminist Anthology* (Latham, NY: Kitchen Table: Women of Color Press)
4. Barbara Smith, Elly Bulkin and Minnie Bruce Pratt. *Yours in Struggle: Three*

Feminist Perspectives on Anti-Semitism and Racism (Long Haul Press, Box 592, Van Brunt Station, Brooklyn, NY 11215)

Vivienne Verdon-Roe

1. Produced/Directed the film *Women for America, For the World* (Oscar Winner, 1987)
2. Co-produced the film *In the Nuclear Shadow, What Can the Children Tell U?* (Oscar Nominee, 1984) The Video Project...

Many of the interviews included in this volume are available on audio tape from Pacifica Program Service. For ordering information, contact:

    Pacifica Program Service
    3729 Cahuenga Blvd. West
    North Hollywood, CA 91604
    1(818)506-1077 or
    1(8oo)735-0232

Photo by Irene Young

PENNY ROSENWASSER is a producer and broadcaster at Pacifica radio station in Berkeley, California. She is also Special Events Coordinator for the Middle East Children's Alliance and a community activist. A Washington, D.C. native, Rosenwasser has been organizing around a wide range of issues—women's and lesbian rights, international solidarity, peace and justice, labor struggles, anti-racism, AIDS research and education, health care, prison reform, childcare reform, safe energy—for over twenty years. In addition, she has coordinated and produced numerous festivals, tours and concerts as part of the second wave of the U.S. women's cultural movement.

She is also the author of the book *Voices From A 'Promised Land'* published by Curbstone Press.